PENGUIN BOOKS

THE FOURTH COAST

Mary Blocksma has been a librarian for ten years, a writer for eighteen. Of her seventeen children's books, one has been offered by the Junior Literary Guild, another is featured on PBS's *Reading Rainbow*, and five are now available in Spanish. Her first book for adults, *Reading the Numbers* (Viking Penguin, 1989), became a dual main selection of the Quality Paperback Book Club and was acclaimed by the American Library Association and *Scientific American* as one of the best science books of the year. Her second, *Naming Nature* (Penguin, 1992), has been offered by the Nature Book Society.

She lives within sight of Lake Michigan.

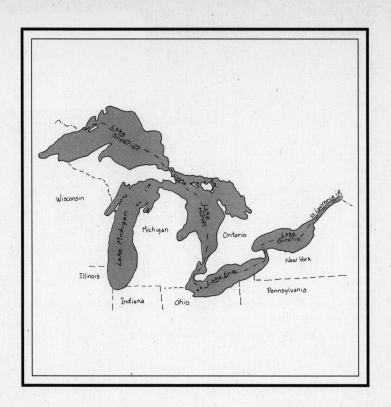

THE
FOURTH
COAST

Exploring the Great Lakes Coastline from the St. Lawrence Seaway to the Boundary Waters of Minnesota

MARY BLOCKSMA

PENGUIN BOOKS

PENGUIN BOOKS
Published by the Penguin Group
Penguin Books USA Inc., 375 Hudson Street,
New York, New York 10014, U.S.A.
Penguin Books Ltd, 27 Wrights Lane,
London W8 5TZ, England
Penguin Books Australia Ltd, Ringwood,
Victoria, Australia
Penguin Books Canada Ltd, 10 Alcorn Avenue,
Toronto, Ontario, Canada M4V 3B2
Penguin Books (N.Z.) Ltd, 182–190 Wairau Road,
Auckland 10, New Zealand

Penguin Books Ltd, Registered Offices:
Harmondsworth, Middlesex, England

First published in Penguin Books 1995

1 3 5 7 9 10 8 6 4 2

Grateful acknowledgment is made for permission to reprint an excerpt from
"Smelly Feet," words and music by Tom Savage, © 1975. Used with permission.

Maps by the author

LIBRARY OF CONGRESS CATALOGING-IN-PUBLICATION DATA
Blocksma, Mary.
The fourth coast: Exploring the Great Lakes coastline from the St. Lawrence
Seaway to the boundary waters of Minnesota / Mary Blocksma.
p.   cm.
ISBN 0 14 01.7881 3
1. Great Lakes Region—Description and travel.   2. Natural
history—Great Lakes Region.   I. Title.
F551.B63   1995
917.704'33—dc20   94-25713
                                                                    CIP

Printed in the United States of America
Set in Garamond #3
Designed by Katy Riegel

To my lake-loving dad,
Ralph Blocksma,
for his eightieth birthday:
with my thanks and love.

ACKNOWLEDGMENTS

THIS ADVENTURE WAS born before I was, when my dad, Ralph Blocksma, paddled, sailed, and fished the Great Lakes as a boy. Now a retired plastic surgeon, he and my mother, Ruth Blocksma, recently formed a *Fourth Coast* cheering section, accepting my calls, collecting my tapes mailed from remote POs, supplying emergency equipment, and getting my film developed. They even read the manuscript. For all this and much more, I thank them.

Thanks are also due to the many organizations and their dedicated staffs who fielded my calls, answered my questions, sent me materials, offered their maps, and supported my efforts. Among these are the Center for the Great Lakes, Chicago, Illinois; the Great Lakes Commission, Ann Arbor, Michigan; the Great Lakes Natural Resources Camp, Lake Ocquenoc, Michigan; the Institute for Great Lakes Research, Bowling Green University, Perrysburg, Ohio; the Michigan Department of Natural Resources, Lansing, Michigan; the Sea Grant Communications Office, Madison, Wisconsin, upon whose Great Lakes maps I based most of my drawings; the many chambers of commerce that contributed to my collection of materials, maps, and brochures; and always, the many public librarians—so often reliable guides to an area—who answered my questions and pointed me in interesting directions.

Most thanks belong, of course, to the many persons, both named and unnamed, who appear in this book, contributing their opinions, knowledge, stories, humor, love of and concern for Fourth Coast waters and shores. I ought to name them all here, but the list is so long, the individuals get lost. Better to encounter these good folks, along with me, where they belong: at home, work, or play, usually in a place they love. I also offer thanks and apologies to those whom I did not have room to include but who offered me hospitality, stories, expertise, and encouragement.

Thanks also to all the towns, motels, hotels, and campgrounds that accommodated, fed, and entertained me, and my sincere regret and apologies to those places that, due to the pace of my trip, uninviting weather, or my odd inclination, either were missed altogether or received short shrift. Trying to understand the Fourth Coast as a whole, I was not able to fairly or with any accuracy represent particular places. Some took it worse than others: Ashtabula, Ohio, for instance, can hardly be represented by its water treatment plant, and there's much more to see in Ashland, Wisconsin, than a belly flop contest.

And let me not forget to jump up and down about my Penguin editor, Mindy Werner; my art director, Kate Nichols; my agent, Gina Maccoby, for sticking with me through the years required to research, write, and produce such a book and, despite busy schedules, affording without exception great care for my work.

Finally, thanks to my dear friends who never let me give up. And to Daniel K. Kuhn and our now adult son, Dylan K. Kuhn: thanks for posting my itinerary on the refrigerator and caring where I'd got to.

CONTENTS

INTRODUCTION

A walk, following your intuitive promptings, down the
streets of a foreign city holds rewards far beyond a
planned tour of the tried and tested. . . . You cut a
path . . . that is yours alone, which brings you face to
face with surprises destined for you alone. When you
travel this way, you are free.
—Stephen Nachmanovitch, *Free Play*

HAVING GROWN UP on Lake Michigan, I always wondered
what it was like on the *other* Great Lakes, so one summer I
decided to find out. Via minivan, I poked along more than five thousand miles of northern coastline from New York to Minnesota, covering forty to fifty miles per day for ninety days, adventuring here
and there, exploring this spot and that, interviewing many persons I
found along the way. After a while, I became a little nervous that
what I was reporting might be taken as the wrong kind of "truth."
So let me try to define what kind of truth will, and won't, be found
here.

Land adjacent to any large body of water is replete with fish stories
and similar tales, and it's often hard to tell fact from fiction. I decided
to include some material I suspected to be apocryphal, believing that
there are different sorts of truths and that even a tall story reveals as
much (if perhaps only of the teller) as honest journalism. I verified
what I could, but many claims flowed from memories alone, and if
mine is any indication, memories sometimes remember wrong.

Then there's the matter of issues. I want this book to inspire
readers to treasure and care for the Great Lakes, but I didn't write it
to set anyone straight on any particular issue. Before I began this trip,
I had only the vaguest notion of the area's environmental, economic,
and other problems, so I tried to observe and learn about these, with-

holding judgment as best I could. I was not always able to maintain this detachment, and my biases, when they appear—and they do—will be obvious. Still, I tried to uncover as many points of view as I could, sometimes becoming ever more confused as I worked around the various sides, each passionately held.

So although some of the "facts" that follow may be incomplete or even untrue, they are sincerely believed to be true by the persons who shared them with me. Sometimes I interviewed experts, but often I listened to self-appointed experts who offered an emotional, personal truth the professional experts would overlook. I advise readers to consider the source and decide for themselves what to believe. To the intensely interested, I suggest the great American public and academic library system. It is the best in the world and it is free. I used it often in the writing of this book and thank every last librarian who helped me.

The most important truth I wish to convey about the United States side of the Great Lakes, however, is a sensuous one—a sense of being there in the summer of 1990. Although some things may have changed since then, most haven't. I want to share how it feels to camp beneath a heron flyway on the St. Lawrence River; fish with a famous charter on Lake Ontario; sing around a Lake Erie campfire; watch freighters on the St. Clair River; observe the discovery of the first zebra mussel found by a diving outfit on Lake Huron; hike the Indiana Dunes on Lake Michigan; sail a tall ship; parasail at sunset; hunt for agates and ancient pines on Lake Superior; climb lighthouses; ferry to nine islands; tour four archipelagos; gather wild snacks; and travel and camp as a single woman for weeks and months alone.

I took this opportunity to test Joseph Campbell's advice about following one's bliss. Although I stuck to my only rule—take the road closest to the shore—my selection of whom I talked to and where I stopped was based mostly on gut feeling. I made no frustrating, impossible attempt to fairly represent any particular town, state, or area; the number (or absence) of pages devoted to one place or another is based solely on whatever or whoever irresistibly engaged me. It worked: I seemed to know intuitively, effortlessly, just whom to approach. In the process, however, some big cities are skipped altogether while a place I'd never heard of might receive comparatively in-depth attention. Now and then I take a day off to visit friends, which explains occasionally skipped days.

Although this is not a guidebook, it is a sort of guide to adventure. One could easily take a similar trip by following similar rules: keep the water to your right (or left) and stop when you feel inclined to. For those who would like to explore some of the places I describe, I have drawn rough maps, for which I do not claim absolute accuracy but include to help orient the reader as to the whereabouts of one place in relation to another; an itinerary listing all my stops and their general locations; and a Guide to Guides, to help those who seek more exact information, such as specifics concerning food and lodging.

Finally, my Fourth Coast trip was more than a writer's research; for reasons I didn't understand then, I felt compelled to make it. In the beginning, I was worried: Could I stand being alone so much? Could I live for three months without visiting my therapist? Would my vehicle and my body make it to the end without major breakdowns? Would anyone talk to me? Could I maintain my enthusiasm? The answers were yes, yes, yes, yes, yes. I even found the place I now call home.

Mary Blocksma
Beaver Island, Michigan

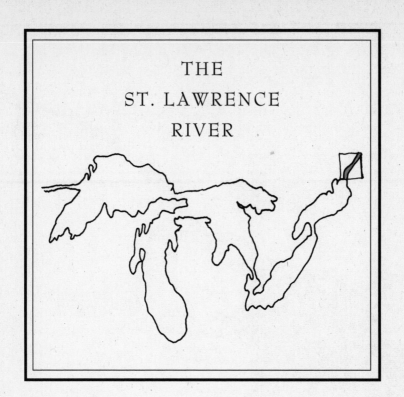

THE
ST. LAWRENCE
RIVER

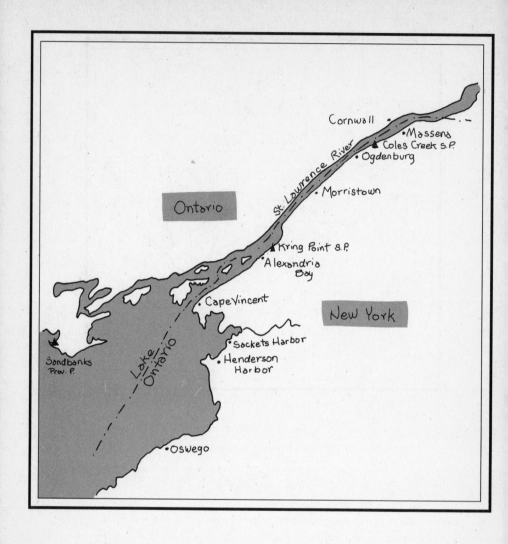

The St. Lawrence River

MAY 18

MY TRIP AROUND the Fourth Coast, the United States side of
the Great Lakes, begins at Massena, New York, where I'm presently
waiting for a ship to come through the Eisenhower Lock. East of here,
the St. Lawrence River flows through Canada to the Atlantic, but to
the west, my intended direction of travel, it forms the New York–
Canadian border. I chose this starting place a year ago at a used-book
sale, when a map of the Great Lakes fell into my lap from a back issue
of *National Geographic*. Across the two-by-three-foot spread, five Great
Lakes arched around oddly shaped states like blue fish at play, but
they appeared to be connected. I was just beginning to realize that
the St. Lawrence River and the Great Lakes formed a northern coastline when I noticed that another line hugged nearly the entire shore,
a red thread clinging unbroken to the United States side of every
Great Lake from Massena, New York, to Grand Portage, Minnesota,
a distance of perhaps five thousand miles. Tracing the coast by car
became an obsession.

Well, here I am. I figure that at fifty miles a day, my journey
could take three months, plus a little breakdown time, but I worry
that I started too early: this May weather has me shivering. Stubborn
drizzle prickles what looks like an acre of water lying at platform level
in the giant sunken tub outside the lock's huge viewing windows.

I lift half a Styrofoam cupful of ripe coffee to my mouth, recon-
sider, put it back on the small table, and resume typing silently at
an electronic keyboard. For all the hype, this place isn't much of a

3

brass band. The lock's gray observation building is fronted by a large, nearly empty parking lot. Nearby, an enormous power dam parts the gray river like a wide-tooth comb. Gray roads curl here and there through expansive shaved lawns over which mom-and-pop Canadian geese hustle troops of obedient goslings. Apart from the birds, it feels dismally official, governmental, and damp.

Yesterday, I drove for twelve hours across Michigan and Canada and camped at Sandbanks Provincial Park on Lake Ontario. It was my first night in the van, and although the twin-sized mattress was comfortable, the rain beat on the roof all night and I was nervous about camping alone. This morning, a park shower, controlled by a navel-level electric eye, didn't turn on until I stepped in, fully clothed, to figure it out. An hour later, in a fresh set of clothes, I buzzed up the busy highway on the Canadian side of the St. Lawrence River, crossed the toll bridge at Cornwall to Massena, New York, and ended up here around noon, where it's as lively as a Friday-night funeral. I feel as if I'd been deposited by an all-night Greyhound bus. Hard to imagine Queen Elizabeth standing here, but she did once, along with President Eisenhower, the day the lock opened in 1959. By 1963, a million people a year were showing up to watch the ships go through.

The scheduled vessel is an hour late, and I long for a nap or Lindbergh's famous flight food, a ham sandwich, which, if I had one, might cure the slump I seem to be in. But wait . . . here comes the *Catherine Desgagnes*! She slips through the upper, open gates, heading toward the Atlantic, looming so near I have to go outside to see the top of the mast, which towers about four stories high. Sleek, black-hulled and white-decked, the 383-foot bulk cargo carrier fits easily into the vast "pool" designed to accommodate ships almost twice its size. The upper gates close behind it, unseen valves open at the bottom of the lower, eastern gates, and twenty-two million gallons of water begin pouring out of the lock (I've been reading the info sheets). The *Catherine Desgagnes* visibly descends. In ten minutes she sinks forty-four feet and vanishes into the pit, the peak of the mast barely clearing the top. The ship is so low, I have to lean over the chain-link fence to see the deck.

The whole business has been accomplished by gravity. A vessel is lifted without pumps, too: The lower, downstream gates open, the ship floats in the lock, the gates close, and the filling valve under the upper gate opens. Water is forced into the lock by the weight of the water outside, just as water is forced out of the lock by the weight of the water inside. It takes no longer to raise a vessel than to lower it.

The Eisenhower Lock is just one of seven such locks that make up the St. Lawrence Seaway system—the 190-mile section of the St. Lawrence River between Montreal and Lake Ontario—which, in turn, is part of a larger system of Great Lakes locks built to ease the 600-foot ascent from Montreal to Minnesota. Thanks to the locks, the strong currents created by so impressive a slope are today fairly well controlled by the Great Lakes / St. Lawrence Seaway system, administered jointly by Canada and the United States. The St. Lawrence River and the Great Lakes now rise (going west) like a giant, uneven staircase. A ship coming in from the Atlantic Ocean headed, say, for Duluth at the far end of Lake Superior will be lifted a total of 226 feet by the seven locks along the St. Lawrence Seaway, 326 feet by the eight locks along the 26-mile-long Welland Canal (the Niagara Falls bypass on the Canadian side), and 24 feet by one of the four Sault Ste. Marie locks at the entrance of Lake Superior.

I could hardly have found a better beginning for my Fourth Coast book. As I drive down the St. Lawrence River, I tune in a Canadian radio station, sing along with a piano sonata, sort out a long conversation in French. The Royal Canadian Mint announces that it now costs one and a half cents to manufacture a penny. I fall in love with Canadian radio.

THERE'S NOTHING LIKE a great meal to feed one's optimism, so here I am, washing down a plateload of seafood Newburg with a nice, cold "Genny" (Genesee beer) at the Chase Mills Inn. Sounds upscale, no? I thought so, too, which is why it took me so long to find the place, driving by the peeling, white frame building twice before I realized that the Rooms sign was supposed to be enough. No one else seems to have had any trouble finding it. The restaurant, although remote and small, is jammed, famed for its food and ambiance. Droopy strings of rainbow Christmas lights radiate from a center ceiling hub. Elegant entrees are chalked on a blackboard. My waitress, a jolly, white-haired woman whose attire includes a straw hat, jogging shoes, and a front-and-back red-and-white apron, offers me the time-out table in a small room off to one side so I can type in peace.

I was sent here by the friendly rangers at the Coles Creek State Park, who, after a brief tussle with their new machine—New York state parks now computerize their camping reservations—found me a twelve-dollar view of the St. Lawrence River I'd pay dearly for if it came with HBO and a private bath. Birches, newly leafing maples, and soggy grass surround my parking place. Long boats hum past, headed for the locks. Herons cruise overhead. Canadian geese crowd the shore.

MAY 19

I'M DRIVING DOWN the same section of the St. Lawrence River that I drove up yesterday on the other side, but while the Canadians have provided their travelers with a scenic but hectic superhighway, over here on the New York side the two-lane road sometimes takes on a meandering, down-home feeling. Aside from the few towns, wetlands dominate, crowding the road. Goldfinches burst from bushes like fireworks. Great blue herons float over with regularity.

In Ogdensburg, a jail jars me out of this back-road intimacy: the government of New York apparently has chosen to provide some of its inmates with a better view than most of us can afford. I drive up to the barbed-wire fence that encloses the old, ornate red-brick building, then change my mind. I doubt my tape recorder will be welcomed, and I probably won't find much to eat there anyway.

Because what I'm really looking for is breakfast, or by this time lunch, but I can't find a restaurant on the water. Finally, having driven a third of New York's nearly hundred miles of St. Lawrence River, I park on the hill in front of Joe's Grub, a three-table deli in tiny Morristown. There, from a Styrofoam container and using a plastic spoon, I devour steaming goulash made by Joe himself, which hits the spot on this dank day, while Joe explains the great number of herons—they nest on a nearby island—and a couple of locals discuss family and business problems. I'm tempted to tape all this, but I have the feeling that the place will go silent, if not vacant, if I pull my mini-recorder from my jeans' pocket, and I've decided not to tape people without their knowledge.

Today's drive shot down some assumptions: what I never expected to see on waterfront property—penal facilities—has appeared, and what I fully expected to be annoyed by—a lot of development—hasn't. The St. Lawrence River is a wonderful area: state parks appear nearly every twenty miles; the country feels remote but gentle; the wetlands thrive with plants, birds, and other wildlife. So where are all the motels, restaurants, boutiques, billboards, condos, ice cream parlors, shirt shops, and fast-food joints?

ALEXANDRIA BAY, that's where. Here reigns the spirit of play, a tourist's fantasy, a teenager's dream, a hotel/motel/condo–filled delight. Want to go fishing? Charter a boat. Hot to shop? Boutiques overflow. Hungry? Line up with the rest of the happy "kids." The season has just begun, and everyone seems jazzed about it. Early vacationers already crowd the restaurants, one of which floats. Condos stack up high around the harbor.

At least two boat companies offer tours of the glamorous Thousand Islands, which pepper the river here. I buy a ticket at Uncle Sam's Boat Tours for tomorrow morning from a tall, balding man who resembles an amusement park barker. When I despair about the weather, he drawls, "Seen six islands, seen 'em all. Don't worry about it."

I am too tired to enjoy this excitement. I backtrack a few miles north to Kring Point State Park, a convoluted campground at the end of a deeply fluted peninsula, where I select a lovely site for the night, once again on the river. The park is crammed with a surprisingly quiet group of campers, a horde of mosquitoes, and almost as many birds. While I eat my supper—a cheese-and-jam sandwich on a stale hamburger bun, instant chicken noodle soup, and a plastic container of applesauce (just about anything tastes great outside)—I am visited by four robins, a blackbird, a heron, several goldfinches, and three kinds of swallows. Later, sidestepping puddles on roads looping through the campsites, I capture in my binoculars a fiery Baltimore oriole, a prancing killdeer, a white-crowned sparrow, a chipping sparrow, more herons, a gang of grackles, and a phoebe's (or is it a pewee's?) nest under the eaves of a recreational building. At my damp wooden picnic table, scarf wrapped twice around my neck, I now type furiously in a brief surcease of rain, waving the bugs away and watching freighters float through the sunset. Nearby, a small pole-toting boy knocks on a trailer door, announcing, "Mom, I've got good news and bad news. The good news is, I love you. The bad news is, I broke my line."

MAY 20

I WAKE UP at five-thirty to rain. Go back to sleep, wake up at eight-thirty: no change. Wake up at ten: still raining. Give up, get dressed, breakfast on granola, and head for Alexandria Bay. Waiting for the next boat tour, I take refuge in a tiny coffee shop next to Uncle Sam's Boat Tours. A big fellow in a yellow slicker two seats down the Formica counter belts out a fish story: "First cast, the pike hit— but he broke the line! Second cast, I hooked him and the whole rod went *slummmmmmm,* like that, and I couldn't believe it! I thought I was in heaven!"

TOOT TOOT! We're off! I'm sitting next to a window in a ballroomlike enclosure, which, I note gratefully, is heated. Turquoise chairs line long church-supper tables that jut from the side windows. A pink-and-blue carpet sweeps up to a bar. I notice an attractive man seated alone across the room, but he is soon joined by an equally attractive woman. As the three-story paddleboat chugs out into the river, the captain begins a live commentary over the loudspeakers. I learn the following:

Although the town is called Alexandria Bay, there is no local bay by that name. . . . Five 5-million-dollar estates perch on various St. Lawrence River islands. . . . The river is 130 to 320 feet deep to accommodate the lakers, freighters, and salties that regularly traverse it. . . . In winter, the St. Lawrence River may freeze solidly enough to stop navigation, becoming a highway for cars and trucks. . . . Leach fields are impossible on the mostly granite islands, so sewage is picked up by a "honey barge" for a "modest yet substantial" fee. . . . During the "golden era" between 1880 and 1925, a hundred millionaires

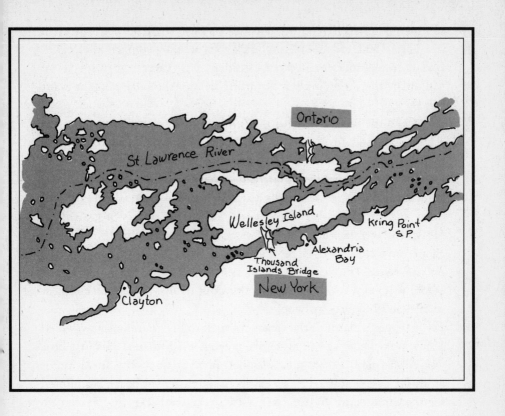

The Thousand Islands

summered here. Fifteen enormous hotels have since burned or rotted. . . . The "Thousand Island" archipelago is actually comprised of 1,793 islands, three-quarters of them Canadian. . . . Over eighty species of fish swim the river, pike and muskie being especially popular sport fish.

When the windows fog up, I climb to the top level, knock on the pilot's door, and am invited in by a middle-aged man in a blue trucker's cap with the Uncle Sam's logo on it. From here I can see everything while Captain Ken Hartman, standing at the wheel, skillfully maneuvers the three-hundred-passenger boat past one island after another and entertains me with "river rat" stories. He is proud to call himself a river rat, he says, and resents it when wealthy weekenders adopt the term. "A river rat was born, lives, works, and hopes to die on the river. You learn to swim before you walk. You get a boat before you get a car. This is no rinky-dink river—if you don't respect it, it'll swallow you up whole."

Hartman's claim to the title goes back to his grandmother, "who'd fish in a bucket if she thought she'd catch a fish there." His first boat was a "sharpie," a triangular, flat-bottomed affair with a small motor on it. He first captained a "six-pack" (a six-passenger boat), has piloted for the same company for twenty-two years and likes it. He can go home every night to his wife and three daughters, carve decoys (he's halfway through a Canada goose) and work on his country house (he's shingling). Winter jobs for river rats, he says, include guiding, fishing, trapping, and hunting.

The captain interrupts himself to point out the castle we are approaching; it is owned by the Thousand Islands Bridge Authority, which has renovated it. We stop there briefly to let off and take on passengers, then continue. Ghostly islands, often lot-sized, occupied by a single house, glide by in the mist. A few trees wave in the air. Most of the islands are neither densely forested nor populated. It's "duck soup" out there, passing pilots complain on the radio. After a while, past thwacking window wipers, the islands all start looking the same, just like the man said.

I turn back to the captain. "Do you hunt?"

"Oh, not much anymore. Too busy at the boat line now. I did a lot of trapping as a kid, and I always wore Bear Paw snowshoes. To this day, I'm called Bear Paw." Nicknames are common here, he says. Nearly everyone has one.

Does the river crowd enjoy any special celebrations?

"Every Labor Day weekend, when things quiet down a little, there is the Riverman's Picnic, a family affair held on one of the islands. We go fishing and deep-fry the catch on a wood stove, along with any of last winter's venison left in the freezer, and serve it with salt potatoes. For dessert we make French toast from a special, traditional recipe." Hartman's face lights up just thinking about it.

Update: Much later, when I call to check some details, a nearly breathless Captain Hartman tells me that as we speak, the wooden boathouse that stored—among other old wooden boats—the first Uncle Sam's tour boat is burning down in flames so hot they are melting the fire-truck loudspeakers. "Boats are stored for the winter with full gas tanks," the captain explains. "If you leave the tank empty, you get frost and condensation in there." There'd been as much as two hundred gallons of gas in some of the tanks. And I thought that devastating fires along the lake shore had been a threat largely past.

THROUGH THE GLASS of a toaster-size aquarium outside the nature center on Wellesley Island, I watch a cecropia emerge from its small cocoon and slowly expand into a huge brown moth. Inside, stuffed waterfowl, hawks, owls, and other creatures look alive but aren't. I am given a long list of local bird and wildflower species but see few of them as I hurry along the short trail loops, hoping to beat the next cloudburst. Wellesley Island, probably the largest of the Thousand Islands, is attached to both Canada and the United States by the two sections of the Thousand Islands Bridge. I had hoped to walk the bridge—in sparkling sunshine, the islands would be a glorious sight—but the rain pelts on. I explore some shops in Alexandria Bay, then retreat to the campground to read, rest, and spend another night.

MAY 21

CAPE VINCENT seems a sleepy place compared with Alexandria Bay; I had expected something livelier. After all, this is where all the Great Lakes—the largest freshwater system in the world, with a watershed (the area encompassing all the streams and rivers that drain into the lakes) of nearly 300,000 square miles and a surface area of 94,000 square miles—pour into the second longest river in North America. The only action I see, though, on or off shore, is at a local cafe. I go in and happen to sit next to the treasurer of the chamber of commerce, who rushes out immediately to fetch me a pile of brochures, leaving me to watch "Family Feud" on a black-and-white TV through a haze of smoke.

One of the pamphlets directs me to the Cape Vincent Fisheries Station Aquarium, which I find along the river in the basement of a several-storied, ivy-covered brick building. It is an unassuming place with a feeling of having been in business awhile. Along both sides of a chilly corridor, brown-, gray-, and green-hued fish, examples of Great Lakes species, hang, barely moving, behind dimly lit glass. The fish all look alike to me; I could probably identify them better filleted.

Upstairs, I find some affable people who work for the New York State Department of Environmental Conservation and seem to know their way around fishery and conservation programs affecting the Great Lakes in general and Lake Ontario in particular. Gerard Le Tendre, supervising aquatic biologist (which means he runs New York's Lake Ontario fishery program), tells me that among their activities are keeping the public informed and assessing the fish stocks, which include smelt and alewives.

Alewives? Along Lake Michigan, these small fish used to wash up on the beach by the millions, rot there, stink, and draw flies. I thought that the salmon had been introduced to get rid of them. "Salmon eat alewives and we love salmon, so we like alewives here," explains the amused researcher. "Our problem was cladophora (accent on the *oph*), an alga. Used to be all along the Ontario shore—very unpleasant. During a storm, the long, slimy strands break off and pile up, sometimes ten, twelve feet thick. If there is an alewife die-off at the same time, the stench can become overpowering. But when the United States and Canada signed the 1972 Water Quality Agreement, New

York stopped using phosphates in soap, and the impact on Lake Ontario has been tremendous. Now we rarely have a problem with cladophora and the PCB levels in fish are going down as well."

Speaking of PCBs, I say to Le Tendre, a recent report prepared by the National Wildlife Federation called "Lake Michigan Sport Fish: Should You Eat Your Catch?" has made me very nervous about eating Great Lakes fish. It appears that alarming levels of carcinogens such as PCBs (polychlorinated biphenyl, found in transformer coolant, hydraulic fluid, and industrial lubricants) and pesticides (such as DDT, dieldrin, and chlordane), even though most of these are no longer in use, are stored in the fatty tissues of many Great Lakes fish, especially the larger sport fish, like lake trout and chinook salmon. The contaminant levels appear to drop in smaller-sized fish of all species, and in those properly cleaned (see p. 26), but PCBs stay in the human body, passed along at birth to a woman's children. There is evidence that the learning abilities of children who regularly consume these fish can be affected. The report cautions against the consumption of any Great Lakes fish by children, who seem to be more sensitive to these chemicals, or by women who are pregnant or plan to become so.

It's my impression that this report has not been welcomed by fishing enthusiasts or Great Lakes communities. The Great Lakes tourist and fishing industries depend heavily on Great Lakes fish. Many authorities resist endorsing a view that could spell economic disaster. It's a sensitive issue nobody likes to talk about. Most claim that the National Wildlife Federation has exaggerated the threat to health, that the levels of pollutants in fish are going down. So I ask Le Tendre, "Are Great Lakes fish safe to eat?"

"New York State takes a conservative view, publishing safety standards in the fishing regulations, and there are persons, such as pregnant women, who shouldn't eat Great Lakes fish," he says. "Still, you have to keep this in perspective. It's probably more dangerous to smoke a cigarette or drive to your fishing spot than it is to eat your catch." Lake trout and salmon are sport fish and can't be fished commercially in the United States, he says. Those served in restaurants are from Canada. "The one commercial fishery on our side of Lake Ontario sells yellow perch and bullheads, which have never been proven a health hazard."

We are joined by William A. Pearce, "Father of Lake Ontario," who headed up the salmon program and whose honorary doctorate represents a lifetime of dedicated work in the interest of the Great Lakes. Dr. Pearce launches into an articulate, positive analysis of progress on Great Lakes pollution. "Nowhere in the world has a country been as open about the contaminant problem as we have about the Great Lakes," he begins. "In New York, it was addressed directly and not hidden. The Great Lakes are now used as an example to the world for how to address these problems. Not that we've licked 'em, but we're dealing with them. We have set a precedent, a pattern.

"I've seen tremendous progress. These doomsday people drive me up the wall. True, it's frustrating in our system of government to get anyone interested in a problem, but once the mechanism starts to grind, despite an admittedly tremendous amount of duplication and overkill, out of it comes a solid core of dedicated professional people who make the thing work. There's been a partnership not only between the United States and Canada—done with a handshake and a smile—but between research and management."

On that hopeful note, I ride three miles west through settling fog to greet Lake Ontario.

LAKE
ONTARIO

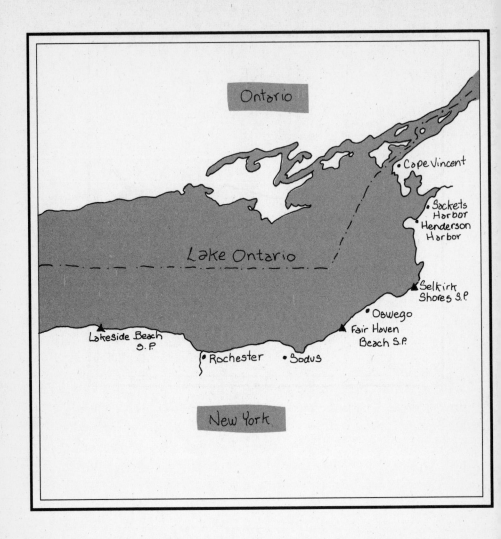

Lake Ontario

I T'S A LONELY DRIVE from Cape Vincent to Tibbetts Point, where Lake Ontario meets the St. Lawrence River. No one is here; the American Youth Hostel, housed in the keeper's quarters, does not begin its season until June. Like all Fourth Coast lighthouses, the Tibbetts Point Lighthouse has been automated, and the light, once fueled with whale oil, is now electric, this one visible on clearer days fourteen miles over the lake. A radio beacon has replaced the foghorn. Nearby, a little road hugs a shore that soon narrows into a water-flanked ridge. I park there and emerge. On my right, Lake Ontario tosses large and restless; on my left, countless terns swoop like small, sleek gulls through a swirling mist above a flat, dark backwater, hover, plunge, and flutter off, emitting high-pitched screams. Two tern species—inky black terns, white underwings and forked tails looking painted, unreal; and white, black-capped common terns, whose tangerine bills provide accents of color—mingle like a moving Escher. Slowly the swarm thins as the birds become aware of my figure in the mist, and the silences between their cries expand, merge, until all I can hear is the lake breathing.

AFTER FOUR WET DAYS AND NIGHTS, I crave a long, hot shower, a warm, dry room. I follow the scalloped shore and then lose it in dairy country, driving past black-and-white cows and bright white gulls feeding together on shining, green pastures. The gray, snaky road is sleek with rain. I'm trying to stay by the water as much as I can, the one rule I travel by, which sometimes requires the exploration of small roads not on maps, and right now I have no idea where I am. I'm not lost, really—there's no such thing as "lost" on a trip like this. I'm just turning right when it seems appropriate, a method of lakeside navigation that sometimes works and sometimes doesn't. I stop often to get my bearings.

THE SNUG HARBOR BAR is situated somewhere on a marshy inlet. Inside, transparent green, brown, and white bottles are lined up on a sill behind the bar, and behind those, where one would usually find a mirror, a stretch of windows affords a view of bird feeders and the marsh beyond. The place is packed—it must be happy hour— but I can't imagine where all these people have come from. From a stool at the bar, I sip a beer and watch birds fly into the feeder, terns dive in the drink, gulls soar. Suddenly a chunk of grass and cattails the size of a rowboat floats by. It must have broken away from the shore somehow, but it is a decidedly odd sight.

"Sell ya an island!" offers one barfly.

"New piece a real estate!"

"Wonder what the taxes are on that one?"

A heron lands like a small plane about fifty feet away. "Somebody shoot one a them, they'd drop like a tonna bricks," says the man next to me.

"They're massive," agrees the man next to him.

"Ever see one a them loons?" asks the first man.

Man Two laughs a loon laugh.

No one knows of a motel.

TWO OLD BARGES, with peeling white paint and dark red trim, angle up on a deserted beach as if recently crashed. Inside, white upholstered parlor chairs are pushed up to white tablecloths in a large room. Waves break against the far windows. I warm up with hot coffee while the only patron tells me over his plate of meat and potatoes that several years ago a tug was towing livestock across Lake Ontario in these barges when a storm hit, the lines broke, and the transport washed up here. Seemed too much trouble to move them, so *voilà*, a restaurant. What? A motel? Not around here.

HENDERSON HARBOR, a tiny village perched on a bay, stylish buildings interspersed with bait shops and boathouses, feels like a ghost town in the gloomy damp. It's getting late. I walk into an elegant old frame inn, shout about; no one is there. No one is on the streets, either. A newer, expensive-looking restaurant up the street is closed. Still, I hear music, so I walk around to the back. A man appears, wielding a broom. Sure, we're closed. No problem, come on in. Have some coffee. What am I looking for? A modest motel on the water? Got the perfect place. He makes a call, can't rouse anyone, and says he'll try again later.

Tony Cocuzzoli's wife, Ann Marie, appears, and while we wait, Tony describes a nearby island where a petroleum company entertains its executives. "Miss Texas came by helicopter. They bring in trailerloads of ice coolers, fly in live turkeys and pheasants. You can land stark naked and they'll outfit you from head to toe for hunting and fishing. This is executive camping. You just go over there and shoot things." Area natives, the Cocuzzolis confide, find this hilarious.

As for the quiet town, I have just missed the annual Rod and Reel Derby,* the biggest event of the year—all-out fishing, partying, street dances, thousands of people—so now everyone's recuperating. There's also a good wind, so the bartenders, surfers every one, are probably out "shredding."

Tony calls again. At last—a room.

MAY 22

A LOON IS fishing just past the clunking docks outside my window at the Sunset Motel, where I sit typing at a small table. This place is perfect. I am not just on the water; I can hear it lapping underneath the floor, in a boat "garage." No phone, no TV, but there's a hot shower and a warm room fragrant with lilacs that Jack and Phyllis, the owners, just dropped off. Outside, gulls sail past, swallows swoop, terns dive, and a northern shoveler, a mallardlike duck with a huge bill, just paddled in.

I have plugged in my automatic coffeepot to heat water for tea

* Now called the Pole and Winder Derby.

and instant soup. "The Victoria Day Show," a funky Canadian radio program, is cracking me up. "Victoria Day" describes her taste in music as the sort of thing you might hear trailing from an old Chevrolet. She reads a poem about radishes from a book called *The Garden That Got Away* and sings along, off-key, with a group called the Rumaniacs.

My tape recorder has stopped working, so I'm waiting for an express-mail replacement from my father, who has taken an active, envious interest in this adventure. He has loved the Lakes since childhood, introduced by YMCA-sponsored camps and canoe trips. I seem to have inherited his fondness, if not for boats, at least for offbeat Great Lakes places. This is one of them.

LAST NIGHT, dining at Verilli's, touted as the best restaurant with a view of Lake Ontario, a claim I find no reason to dispute, I was introduced to a couple by Jack and Phyllis, who thought we'd have something in common. I was, after all, a writer, and the husband was on the board of a large New York publishing company. He and his wife lived here all winter, he said, and the snow was worse here than anywhere else, feet and feet of it. His wife, hearing of my project, told me that I absolutely must write about the local history. Had I been to Sackets Harbor? The renovation being done there was marvelous —old barracks, battlefields, and cemeteries. The Union Hotel, the finest Federal building in northern New York, was there. The first shots of the War of 1812 were heard there. It is a National Historic District.

I was embarrassed. Actually, I did pass through Sackets Harbor yesterday, observing the many restored brick buildings, plaques, historical this-and-that. It felt like some place in New England—Newburyport or Boston—a costly combination of tasteful new and well-preserved old. I watched well-scrubbed families file off yachts into a warehouse-turned-chic-restaurant. I found one of my books in the tiny library housed over the sanctuary of an old brick church. Enough. I was just an exhausted traveler looking for a lakeside motel. Not finding one, I got in my car and drove on.

The problem arises: how inclusive can I be on a trip of five thousand miles? Important places are going to be overlooked, victims of bad timing, bad weather, or, most likely, my own moods and interests. I've put whimsy in the driver's seat; and, with apologies to all those good people and places I'll miss, I think I'll leave her there.

I'VE BACKTRACKED, returning briefly to Cape Vincent to hitch a ride on a small Seaway pilot boat, which is ferrying Captain Richard J. Menkes, who happens to be the president of the St. Lawrence Seaway Pilots Association, out past the breakwater to the 579.5-foot *Olympic Dignity*. These foreign "salties" often take on special pilots to navigate the Lakes or the Seaway—Captain Menkes will pilot the Greek freighter downriver to Massena, where the ship may then take on another Seaway pilot to Montreal. The captain resembles an airline pilot—graying at the temples, courteous, with an air of authority. I arrived on time, but, he notes, just. He asks for my business card, which I do not have. I start feeling like a stowaway.

The trip is short—in minutes Captain Menkes is climbing the ladder up the side of the ship. Heads of sailors pop up along the top, high, high above us, like birds on a wall. A woman! Foreign exclamations! More heads. Arms appear and wave at me. A rope snakes suddenly through the air and a bucket labeled U.S. MAIL drops into the boat, is filled and pulled back up. A dashing, graying man hurries down the ladder and declares, as his boots hit the deck: "I'm the best-lookin' pilot of 'em all! And the crew, they made me an honorary Greek citizen."

He is Captain Richard Tetzlaff, and he has just brought the ship across Lake Ontario. Scheduled shortly to board another, he's anxious to get going. The pilots change every fifty to a hundred miles on the Seaway, he tells me. This particular ship is carrying steel, a cargo so heavy that most of the hold is empty. She is owned by the Onassis company in Monte Carlo, registered out of Monrovia. We pull away from the looming black hull, waving at the sailors, who shout down at us in Greek.

MAY 23

SHOUTS WAKE ME at seven-thirty. I part the motel curtains and peer out: a tall, blue-jeaned sportsman on the dock is pulling in a fighting fish while another man holds out a net. Wow. I plug in the coffeepot, jump into my clothes, and stumble into—hallelujah!—sunshine! The anglers, Jeff Erdly and Doug Nieman, businessmen from Virginia, are soon freeing a big muskie from a triple-barbed hook. Jeff shows me the attached lure, a three-inch white-and-yellow plastic fish full of BBs called a "rattle trap." "He" rattles alluringly as "he" slithers through the water, Jeff claims fondly. Amused by this anthropomorphizing of fishing equipment, I try not to laugh. "The thing I like best about the rattle trap, though," continues Jeff as the lovely lure sails back to the lake at the end of a graceful cast, "is that he stays pretty near the surface and won't tangle in the weeds." Jeff counts to three and starts reeling it in. Damn—"he" gets caught in the weeds. Jeff laughs and cuts the line. "Hate to do this—probably cost Doug five bucks."

No matter, Doug says; he has a few lures left. He shows me a treasure chest that opens out into layers of ice-tray-like compartments neatly crammed with red, blue, yellow, and green lures of many sizes—an inch to maybe six inches—sinkers, hooks, bobbers, little silvery light-catchers, thin spools of transparent line, little bottles and packets. "My insurance agent couldn't believe how much this thing is worth!" beams Doug. Obviously, his agent hasn't seen it.

I run back into the room to get my camera, and when I come out Doug has already hooked a big one. Can't keep a photographer waiting, says Doug. He has hooked a fish as long as my arm, but not through the mouth—through a nearly inch-thick piece of rope. It's a pike with a head like an alligator—a carnivorous mouth lined with sharp teeth, and eyes that appear to be sizing me up for dressed weight. The rope is tied through the mouth and gill. Doug cuts it, avoiding the teeth, puts the pike back in the lake, and pulls the fish by the tail, forcing water through its gills. The pike revives. Suddenly, a swish, and it's gone.

"He probably hasn't eaten in a long time," guesses Doug.

We theorize about the rope. Jeff thinks someone might have

caught the pike out of season and tied it up to "catch" for last week-end's Derby, but then it got away. On the other hand, at 28 inches, it wasn't all that big for a northern pike. (A friend told me once he caught a 44-inch pike that fed twelve people, "and there were left-overs." The Michigan record is 51.5 inches.) If the pike had been a lake trout, Jeff tells me, it would have been a "slot fish," a fish in its prime breeding size. If you catch a slot fish, you have to throw it back. Sports people honor this, he says, because "it keeps the fishing good."

Well, the fishing is certainly good here. The birdwatching, too: I spot a family of oldsquaw scoters—a type of diving duck—out on the bay and a huge flock of soaring black ducks. The two men give me a couple of casting lessons before retiring to their quarters. When they emerge from their rooms in smart suits and ties, I hardly rec-ognize them.

CORRECTION: My "black ducks" were cormorants. I have just learned this from Bill Saife III, son of the creator and host of "Rod and Reel," a widely distributed PBS sports program. The older Bill Saife is filming in Alaska, but Bill Saife III, a dark-bearded man I guess to be in his twenties, host of his own television program, "Cabin Country," is stretched out on the motel dock in a deck chair, soaking up the rays, while I sit cross-legged on the planks at my electronic typewriter.

"The cormorant is a federally protected bird," says Saife, "but we have too many of them. They nest on Little Galloup, an island so tightly packed with birds it looks alive. Downwind, it smells like a slaughterhouse." Fishermen don't appreciate the cormorant's efficient fishing abilities. When the fisheries release a new group of fish, unless they do it by helicopter in deeper water, a bunch of cormorants can finish off 60 percent of them in no time. "I've filmed seven or eight thousand cormorants on a sandbar, gorging on young fish," says Saife.

In addition to doing their popular television shows, Saife and his dad run a five-boat fishing charter business out of Henderson Harbor. "The show was first," Saife says, "but we got so many calls, we started the business." Now they charter out boat and guide for four hundred dollars a day. Saife's a fishing guide all summer, a duck-hunting guide until Christmas. He gets a couple of weeks off in January before starting the winter trade and sport show circuits.

He does take time for play: in the summer, he surfboards, Lake Ontario–style, "knee-boarding" on a small oblong board with a Velcroed strap. "You just crank yourself right into that board, so when you leave the surface of the water, the board comes with you. You do 360s, spin around—it's a lot of fun. We have these sessions we call 'ride or die,' when there's a foot and a half of chop in the harbor but everybody wants to go anyway. That's when we hit the wild stuff."

I ask him if shooting ducks doesn't threaten their numbers, but Saife insists that duck hunters are often dedicated environmentalists. "And we're in for a big change for ducks," he says. "Right now in the eastern flyway there are approximately forty-four million ducks, but we're trying to increase this to a hundred million by the year 2000." The plan is called Waterfowl 2000: the U.S. Army Corps of Engineers, Saife says, will develop a good plot of wetlands as duck habitat if the owners will agree to leave it that way, undisturbed, for at least ten years. Before he leaves, Saife offers me a fee-free (I pay gas) fishing expedition if I'm willing to be there by six.

MAY 24

AFTER A CLEAN, clear dawn, over water like a satin quilt—fifty-one degrees, air somewhat lower—I head out of Henderson Bay on a powerful boat that would comfortably hold six, but this morning carries only me and Captain Jerry Read, a good-natured college student also known as Mouse. Saife himself is guiding a group of four men who, it turns out, did not want a woman onboard. They think it's bad luck, Mouse tells me apologetically. Not to worry, I assure him. I am happy.

Jerry and I leave first, lowering the aerials to pass under a low bridge out to the lake. Bill's boat, in radio contact, is a few minutes behind us. We're only going out about five miles, shouts Jerry over the roar of the huge motor. "We'll be fishing for lake and brown trout today. Later in summer we go so far out, you can't see anything but water—maybe fifteen, twenty miles. Salmon fishing starts in June, gets really good in August." He tells me he's lived in Henderson Harbor all his life.

Jerry slows the boat to a crawl. I steer while he rigs four sturdy fishing rods in the two substantial-looking black holders braced on the back of the boat. (There are more of these on the sides of the boat to accommodate a larger crowd.) Soon our lines trail off the back. "The real secret to this kind of fishing is knowing the water," Jerry tells me. "See that line between the light- and darker-colored water? That's where the warm water butts up against the cool water, and that's where we usually find some fish." We head in that direction.

It isn't necessary to pay close attention—each line is attached to the big orange weight and a release mechanism of a down-rigger, a device that causes the fishing pole, usually bent, to snap up if a fish hits. It isn't ten minutes before I hear one go. Jerry rushes to the back to help, and after a short struggle I have caught a silvery, white-spotted lake trout. It isn't terribly large, but too big for a one-person meal, so I ask Jerry to throw it back. "We encourage catch-and-release," says Jerry as he does so, but he warns against handling the fish too much—the slime on their bodies helps them breathe and resist parasites.

Snap, there goes another pole. It is beautiful out here, this glassy, emerald water, sapphire sky, silvery fish whipping out of the foam. This one is a Seneca Lake trout, Jerry says. It comes from the oldest strain of stock fish in the lake. He can tell this from the clipped upper fin. Maybe twenty inches long, the fish is all muscle. It has the taut energy, the grace, of a dancer. "Let it go," I say.

About now, Bill radios in. Are we getting any bites? Jerry reports our catch. "Oh. Don't seem to be getting much here," says Bill. I smile. I can hear those guys now: "Beginner's luck," I hope they are saying. "Damn woman." Oh yes, I chortle in my secret heart. The witch is on the water, boys—watch out!

Back goes the line. I excuse myself to use the "head." To flush it I turn a switch, pump some water in, and switch the pipe closed again. Back in the cabin, Jerry tells me that there are three "lady" charter captains in the harbor. We are looking at blips on the electronic fish finder when another pole goes. Hey, I'm getting good at this. I pull in a little brown trout, round black ink spots on the top half, a few red ones along the golden middle. We head back—it's about ten o'clock and this one's just right for breakfast.

Back at the Quonset-hut headquarters, I pay $27 for the gas we used (my God, we were only gone a couple of hours!), which, added to my $15 New York nonresident fishing license, totals my breakfast at $42. Actually, this is an incredible bargain: the usual expense includes a guide fee—$400 a day—which I have not been charged, and all that elaborate fishing equipment, which I did not buy, and, of course, the beer that often flows, which I did not bring. I ask Jerry if this very expensive fish is safe to eat, and he says, "It's all in how you clean it. The contaminants are mainly in the skin and fat, so if you get rid of those, you get rid of most of the bad stuff." Jerry takes my fish to a big cleaning room and hands it to a young man who casually whacks up my supple catch with an electric knife. He dumps most of the fish—head, tail, skin, fins, guts, and bones—through a hole in the floor—splash! "The snappers swim in at night and clean up," he says, handing me two thin fillets.

Outside the motel, I balance my mushroom-shaped propane stove at the end of the dock and fry my fish in the upside-down lid of my water bucket. While it's sizzling, Phyllis comes by and tells me about a "60 Minutes" team that came here about seven years ago. "They tested the fish, they tested the water, and they couldn't find a story, so they left and they never came back." She also tells me about a ninety-four-year-old woman who skinny-dips daily in chilly Lake Ontario, adding, "I think she'd be pleased if you'd mention her in your book."

I slip the hot brown trout fillets on a green plastic plate, sprinkle them with salt, butter a hamburger bun, and (water lapping at the pilings, sun shimmering on blue water) dig in.

WHILE MURRAY OR MERRILL, who knows which one of the identical Scott twins, is fixing my car door and dash lights, I wander into the tiny white two-pump service station and gape at the mountain of cartons, plastic jugs, and cans there. I would never have driven my precious van past the junk strewn up the driveway if Bill Saife hadn't suggested it. "We call them Harbor Control," Saife said of the twins. "They're real nice guys and they know what they're doing. You go in there and say, 'I need such-and-such spark plugs, such-and-such size, such-and-such brand,' and one of 'em'll reach in that heap and, I promise, he'll come up with exactly what you need."

According to Saife, the Scott twins—one is president of the chamber of commerce—have been pushing the phrase he says his dad coined for the area: the Golden Crescent. I myself find this stretch of coastline, which runs from the St. Lawrence River to Oswego and includes four distinct bays, more like a complicated puzzle piece, but Saife claimed that it's "the longest stretch of continuous sandy beach on fresh water in the world." Well, this may be the first bit of Great Lakes exaggeration (some coastal natives use another word) that I encounter, but I get the idea—the beaches are great here, surely some of the best on Lake Ontario's often stony shores.

Van's ready. No charge, says Merrill, or Murray: "just took a little squirta oil, and as for the dash lights, you just hafta turn this little knob to the left and they'll come right on." Didn't crack a smile.

FROM HENDERSON HARBOR, I drive through rich green wetlands mirrored here and there in muskrat ponds, stroll pleasant country roads over picturesque rolling hills, nearly colliding with a deer bursting from a leafy backyard, tossing her head and bounding off. I explore a sweet, quiet finger road, seeking the shore. But I can't seem to escape Oswego's nuclear power plant, which pops up like a waisted wart on one vista after another.

Once in Oswego (population 20,000), I snarl at the city traffic. I call my friend John Knapp from a fancy service station, a place I once would have preferred to the Scott brothers'. But now, as men rush in and out, diagnose car problems, ring up purchases, talk on the phone, I think, already nostalgic, of the garlic mustard blooming between the junk at Scott's Mobil station.

John drives me past a row of utilitarian buildings with a watery view, the State University of New York at Oswego ("the only university on Lake Ontario," he claims), then to the Fort Ontario State Historic Site, a star-shaped fort built in 1755, now restored, and a popular attraction here. I can't get interested in military installations, not even important ones, but people around here seem crazy for almost any kind of history. On my way here, I even noticed a plaque identifying a house as the childhood home of the founder of Avon Products.

John warned me that the shoreline I observed at the SUNY campus would probably be the last I'd see until I reached Rochester. He would have been right if I'd followed the attractive Seaway Trail signs—a white footprint and wave on a vertical green rectangle—which, I am discovering, tend to direct one along main drags and developed tourist spots. I often turn off on smaller roads, hungry for a glimpse of water, which is how I ended up at the L-shaped counter in a marina coffee shop in Fair Haven.

Brown plastic chairs sit empty at tables scattered over a large, painted tan floor. White plastic tablecloths. It's still early in the season, and only one other customer—a charter-boat captain living all summer on her thirty-foot Sea Ray—shares the counter with me. Perhaps in her late twenties, she wears jeans and a black jacket with CHINOOK HARBOR printed on the back in bold white letters. She chats with the waitress, but neither woman will talk to me until I drop Bill Saife's name. "That's a really nice family," says the captain. "Not stuck up, even though they have that TV show."

Back on the road to Rochester, I entrust myself to Seaway signs, rarely seeing the water. On my favorite Canadian radio station someone reads a story concerning a young woman who loses her lover to cancer. Oh my, how I cry as I drive through the sunny green day, over the hills on some small road, as the poor woman weeps in her best friend's arms. Not to worry: I am soon cheered by a song called "Bud the Spud," performed by Stompin' Tom Ingle, about "a great big load of the best potatoes ever growed, and they're from Prince Edward Island."

Just outside a tiny place called Sodus, I stop at a roadside stand advertising itself as LANCASTER HELLUVA GOOD CHEESE STAND.

"Aged in Sodus," adds the graying proprietor.

"Have you bought cheese here before?" I ask an older couple selecting some "sharp."

"Oh, thousands of times," they both say.

I pay for some cheese and a loaf of home-baked bread. I'm tempted by the rhubarb pie, but I'll never eat it all. This is the first roadside stand I've seen. The proprietor says that there aren't many left—"too big a hassle dealing with the New York Board of Health."

I AM RIDING a white rabbit, possibly a hare (I am becoming aware of such distinctions), up and down, up and down, to the honky-tonk music of a huge turn-of-the-century carousel, round and round, again and again, past a first-rate view of the lake. I had the pick of three tiers of horses, lions, tigers, ostriches, and other animals leaping along the revolving platform on tall brass poles. It sure beats what I just drove through.

I was fine until I emerged from the long, lovely drive through Rochester's woodsy lakeside Eastman Park (Eastman Kodak is an oft-seen name here), an impressive approach to the city with beaches and picnic areas. When the Seaway signs directed me onto a superhighway, however, I turned toward the lake on a city street and was soon swallowed by massive road construction. But it was worth frying at traffic lights, dodging bulldozers and lethal-looking rollers, to end up here at the century-old Seabreeze Park, where a wide, sandy beach accepts the season's first sunbathers, a shady boardwalk is crowded with strollers, an amusement park is thrilling screaming kids of all ages, and the carousel whirls and whirls in its own high, windowed enclosure.

As the oompahs slow and I dismount, the operator, a cheerful gray-haired man, offers to take my picture with my own camera. I pose astride a white, pink-saddled, blue-reined horse. "You could put that in a magazine," he says, beaming, so I tell him I am a writer, beaming back when he responds, "I *thought* you were somebody special." I stroll the ample, sandy beach and scare up thousands of gulls that crowd the shore. They wait until I'm on them and then suddenly the air is full of them, white feathers against blue sky, like ticker tape in reverse.

EVERY DAY there is this nagging anxiety: where will I sleep tonight, and when do I start looking? Reservations would kill spontaneity, but by the time I feel like stopping, I'm exhausted and may have to spend several hours finding something agreeable. I wasn't worried today, though, because I checked my New York map and counted four state parks along the forty-mile stretch of lakeside superhighway west of Rochester.

Well, so much for planning: I forgot that it's Memorial Day weekend. The first park had no camping facilities; the second one was full;

the third had no camping facilities. As I turned with a heavy sigh from the last, Lakeside Beach State Park, which was full, too, the ranger called, "Wait! We have a cancellation!" I took it, site unseen. Fortunately, there aren't any awful sites in this well-groomed park, but I escape the early-evening heat in a little restaurant across a small road from the lake. Breeze Inn fits right into its unpretentious, cottage-crammed neighborhood, just the sort of place to shuffle into with sandy flip-flops. People talk to each other in places like this, and I have been joined by a local resident who's feeling sad about the death of a wild rabbit that she's been nursing for a week.

Once, she tells me, a loon injured itself trying to land on the road and she took it to the vet college at Cornell University in Ithaca. "Loons and diving ducks have to land and take off on water," the woman explains. "Last winter an oldsquaw got trapped out on the ice—he must have popped up through a blowhole—and after a few days I had to go out and get him. He wasn't injured; he just couldn't take off on ice. We let him go in the river, the only open water, but he spent the whole winter down there. We'd come down to check on him and he'd eat right out of our hands."

MAY 26

A MELODIOUS RED-EYED VIREO began a rich, nonstop wake-up call high in a maple about fifteen minutes ago. It was only 6:30, but I actually have an itinerary today—Niagara Falls on a holiday weekend—so I'm up. I've been to the washroom and back and now carefully balance a two-cup pail of water for coffee and instant oatmeal on my one-burner stove. The sole early riser, I'm trying not to clank things, but the bird racket is louder than kids in a gym and the vireo's still singing. A frenzy of robins feeds manically in the mown grass: step-step-step, peck . . . step-step-step, peck . . . step-step-step, peck . . .

I'm beginning to love this camping out. At night I tidy up the cardboard boxes containing the kitchen, the office, the laundry, socks and underwear, stuffed in the narrow spaces left around the foam mattress. Serving as curtains are T-shirts and sweatshirts hanging over the dark-tinted side windows. My towel, hung to dry between the front seats, blocks the view through the windshield. I stretch out on a blue-flowered sheet under piles of quilts and read (last night, *The Beans of Egypt, Maine*, by Carolyn Chute), the beam from a red plastic torch splashing circles of wavery light on the pages. Paul Horn's flute fills the van like a balloon, and soon I am sleeping like a child.

I camp lean: at night, except for my van, my campsite is bare. In the morning, I spread a plastic cloth on a dewy picnic table, boil water, eat, pack up, and drive away. But most people come for days, sometimes weeks, setting up house outdoors. Campsites overflow with outdoor furniture, equipment, clothes, toys, food. It's incredible what people bring out here. Last night, a noise so loud I thought it was an RV's generator turned out to be a pump inflating a small air mattress. One family even brought the cat.

THE
NIAGARA
RIVER

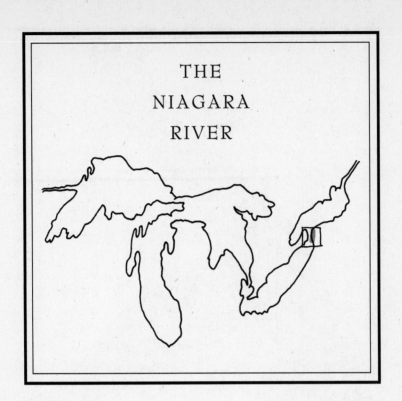

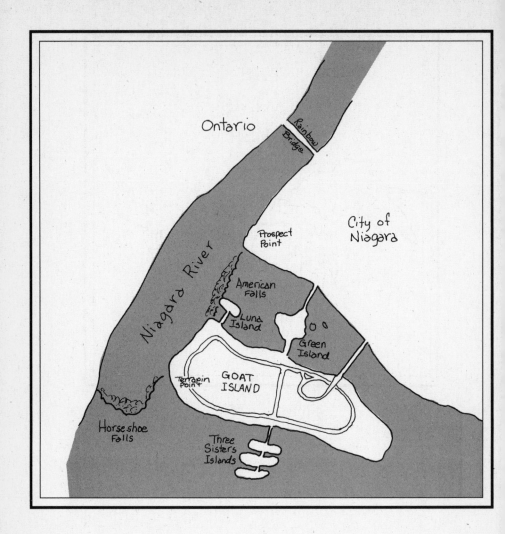

Niagara Falls

FROM LAKESIDE BEACH STATE PARK, I take Highway 18, which on the map appears to skirt the shore, but doesn't until I'm nearly upon the Niagara River. It's a beautiful drive, though, flowering dogwood and magenta crab apple trees glorifying rural roadsides, lilacs and horse chestnut trees filling town yards with massive, upright clusters, and Baltimore orioles flashing through moderate, deciduous woods. By 9:30 A.M., I have secured a huge corner site at Four-Mile Creek State Park, only fifteen miles or so from the falls.

The ranger, a seventeen-year park veteran, proposes the following one-day Niagara Falls itinerary: Park free at Prospect Point (thanks to my camping permit). Go first to the Interpretive Center movie, then do the *Maid of the Mist* boat ride, and, finally, walk around Goat Island, viewing the Canadian, or Horseshoe, Falls from Terrapin Point. "They were bombing the stones there for a while, but they're all done now," she confides. If I have time, take in the observation tower or the Cave of the Winds.

I ignore the quick route—the Robert Moses Parkway—wending instead through trim, lovely Youngstown and Lewistown on a two-lane highway. It is a good choice: beautiful homes and breathtaking views appear along both sides of the grassy bluffs that rise high above the Niagara River gorge. I pass a turreted, red-roofed stone convent, a picturesque stone monastery. Across the river, huge white castles poke out of rich green. The landscape feels European until, nearing Niagara Falls, I get on the Robert Moses Parkway, where the Niagara River is so far down—350 feet!—it looks like dropped string. I nearly go off the road ogling the Niagara Power Project, the largest electric power plant in North America, I read later, supplying 14 percent of New York's electrical demands.

Despite the holiday, there's very little traffic. At just after ten, I park at Prospect Point. On my way to the Interpretive Center, located amid masses of precisely planted pink tulips, I pass Japanese couples posing against the river, Indian women in brilliant gold-hemmed saris following clusters of meticulously dressed children. Inside, I watch an exhilarating movie, much of it photographed from a plane or helicopter, on a screen that surrounds me. Flying over Niagara Falls fueled only by a bowl of oatmeal sends me to the kiosks for an egg salad sandwich, which I eat on a park bench along the foaming river, seated next to a couple from Japan, who ask me, pointing and smiling, to take their picture with their fully automatic camera.

Then it's down the crowded glass elevator, the spectacular view gasped at and remarked upon in Japanese, Hindi, German, Spanish, Danish, Arabic, and Brooklynese, to *Maid of the Mist*, where I don a yellow-lined blue slicker and, after a short wait, step onto a boat so jammed that I am in physical contact with at least three passengers at all times. Whoa! We *need* these raincoats! In no time, the boat turns slowly in the middle of Horseshoe Falls and we all get wet, especially a young man from Brooklyn, one of a foursome, who takes off his slicker and stands in the spray, his sleeveless red jersey soaked, his tattoo glistening. I laugh and he hands me a neon-pink-and-green plastic camera: Take our picture! I do, and I take one with my camera, too, of the four of them laughing, dripping, arms around each other. They are having more fun than anybody else.

Trying to describe the falls, I collapse into statistics. Eighty million gallons of water per second (over two billion gallons an hour) spill over the 1,500-foot-wide American brink and the 2,500-foot Canadian Horseshoe, falling over 170 feet into water equally deep and spray almost as high. (This is only half the water that used to fall here; now half is diverted to hydroelectric plants.) Ninety percent of the water pours over Horseshoe Falls, where our boat spins slowly and gulls fly eerily in the mist and we are swallowed in a roar so loud it drowns out the helicopters hovering overhead. I try to imagine what it was like here when no dams or locks controlled the power, when water all the way from Lake Superior thundered through unchecked, and there was only nature here, no booths or sidewalks, highways or helicopters, only someone—myself, perhaps—standing at the edge, astounded.

Back on land, I hike the bridge to Goat Island, which divides the American Falls from the Canadian Horseshoe Falls, turn right on a paved road and soon discover Luna Island perched practically on the brink of the American Falls, accessible by a small bridge. There, under a sign tacked up on a tree (FALLS HISTORIAN ON DUTY TO ANSWER YOUR QUESTIONS), a man wearing white shoes and trousers, a green windbreaker, and a Panama hat sits in a chrome yellow director's chair. My conversation with Paul Gromosiak, high-school teacher and author of several books on Niagara Falls, is frequently interrupted by tourists inquiring:

"How high are the falls?" ("The American Falls are one hundred and eighty feet high.")

"How fast is the current?" ("Maximum speed here: sixteen miles per hour.")

"How many suicides?" ("During July and August, one or two a week.")

Only one question—concerning a four-gallon orange barrel stuck on the brink of the American Falls—annoys him: "What's that barrel doing there?" "It's garbage; it's temporarily stuck," replies the author impatiently, and then, to me, "If one more person asks me that . . ." Gulp. I'd almost asked him that myself. Do I dare ask how many people have gone over in one? ("A dozen. All survived except three.")

Gromosiak is passionate about Niagara Falls. He grew up here, works here, writes here. An outspoken environmentalist, he feels that his complaints about the hype, development, and threats to nature here are not always appreciated by park authorities.

Continuing my loop around Goat Island, I view Horseshoe Falls from above, at Terrapin Point. At the bottom of the cliff, a long zigzag line of dripping yellow slickers waiting for the Cave of the Winds reminds me of a James Bond film finale until the Brooklyn foursome glance up, see me, and wave. On the more famous, Canadian side, crowds stroll wide sidewalks lined with restaurants, shops, and formal gardens.

Rain threatens. I'm about to dash for the van when—"Now children, we don't want to miss Three Sisters Islands. They're the best part!" It's a teacher addressing a group of New York schoolchildren.

I like the way she looks, hiking easily in high heels, filling out a bright, tight dress, and the way she walks, with a sort of secret joy. I follow her and she is right. Three Sisters Islands lie like stepping-stones off a part of Goat Island hidden from all the falls. Here the kids leap over shallows, chase each other from island to island, skip stones, climb rocks. This place feels secret, intimate, far from the craning crowds and chirping cash registers. I dawdle, dangle my shoes over a rock. On my way out, I pass a wedding in a leafy nook, women bright as Gypsies in royal blue and scarlet, the men reminding me of the Cape Vincent Holsteins loafing on spring green.

GETTING LOST often provides an opportunity for serendipity, but I don't recommend getting lost in the city of Niagara Falls. Maybe I'm just tired, but the signs for the Robert Moses Parkway appear to be a private local joke. I go around and around far too many city blocks until, passing the Prospect Point parking lot for the third time, I stop for directions. The parking-lot attendant wordlessly hands me a shred of paper about as big—and as helpful—as advice from a fortune cookie:

> *Left out of lot, right at corner, left at 2nd light,*
> *right at 3rd light, quick left at 4th light.*

Well, I manage the first four maneuvers, despite late-afternoon holiday traffic jams, but there's no left of any kind at the fourth light. I circle again. Finally, I make an illegal left where there *isn't* a light, honking my way through a jealous lineup of cars and onto the highway.

I stop for a beer, then return to the state park, but to get to my site I have to squeeze past an enormous RV. It's the most amazing RV I have ever seen: an elegant, gleaming tan RV, a queen of RVs, a veritable RV limousine. Just as I am wondering out loud why the owners didn't just buy a Spanish villa, I back into it. I get out, crank at the owner for hogging the road, and storm off. After a long walk, I go over and knock. "I'm sorry," I say to the thin, irritated man who comes to the door. "It was all my fault. Can I reimburse you for any expense I've caused you?"

The man looks at me and replies abruptly that it's all right; it's just a small dent. "It's your attitude I didn't like."

"I know. I was awful."

"Yes, you were."

Suddenly, his wife appears. "Dear, she's trying to apologize," she soothes. We part in peace, if not in friendship, and I have decided that in future, if I want a cold one, I will bring it to my campsite. No more beer until I'm safely tucked in.

At sunset, after a delicious nap, I discover a swamp alive with small boys hooting along the shore and enormous carp thrashing in the shallows. The entire lagoon is roiling with monstrous jumping fish, scaly backs skimming the surface, loud splashing, underwater mud trails.

"They're spawning," explains one of two middle-aged sisters I find fishing for rock bass. "Some are as big as her." She points to her Pekinese.

I watch a fawn feed on a small island, silhouetted against a rosy sky. When I return to my campsite, a huge boat trailered behind a powerful four-wheel-drive vehicle looms above my van from the next site. It's big as a charter boat, and its name is *Salmonella*.

MAY 27

BETWEEN NIAGARA FALLS AND BUFFALO, I am jolted by the stench of industry as I approach Grand Island, a paisley-shaped land mass in the Niagara River. I'm suddenly aware that this is the first heavy industry that I've seen: if anything remotely resembling this blighted landscape—miles and miles of big round gasoline containers, storage tanks, smokestacks, and complex-looking facilities— appears on the St. Lawrence Seaway or Lake Ontario, I missed it. I cross the three-part Grand Island Bridge and exit to a mild *glim bim,* a Pennsylvania Dutch term for that unattractive stretch of highway where car dealerships, fast-food joints, motels, and malls cling to the road between red lights. This one includes small manufacturers of this and that, a KOA, and Fantasy Island (one hundred rides!). But in Beaver Island State Park, I find 952 acres of rolling hills, trees, ponds and lakes, expansive lawns, picnic tables, lovely shade trees, a golf course—so meticulously kept, it feels like a billionaire's estate. I park and climb a hill to take a picture, fitting three mallard-studded ponds into one frame. A road takes me along the water, trees dripping with moss on one side; across the river, an industrial skyline.

Dumped back in smoke city by another enormous bridge, I take a two-lane road, go by one factory after another, smokestacks, massive, deserted brick buildings, broken windows. I don't seem to be in the best part of town. I get back on the interstate and whiz over **Buffalo**. On my left, a cinematic skyline swings thrillingly close; on my right, a freighter heads for the scalloped Peace Bridge to Canada, and I gaze down at Lake Erie.

LAKE
ERIE

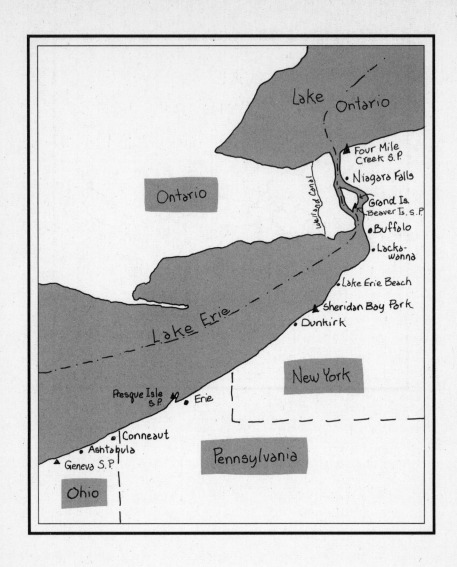

Eastern Lake Erie

N O S O O N E R do I glimpse Lake Erie than I lose it, blocked from my intended shore route, detoured inland to fight commercial districts, industry, and stop-and-go traffic. In Lackawanna I take refuge in a tropical paradise run by the Buffalo and Erie County Botanical Garden Society, a sort of glass Taj Mahal, topped by a cupola and situated, of all places, next to a golf course. I wander from room to huge room, breathing in the humid fragrance of bougainvillea, geraniums, begonias, lantana, bracing for the crash of a golfer's disastrous slice. Nothing disturbs the moist silence, however, except a squirrel, running from room to room. There's a pond crimson with koi; a waterfall; ferns; a house-high Norfolk Island pine; banana trees; spiky three-armed cacti and other oddly limbed plants; bromeliads; orchids.

Refreshed, I head lakeward (at least I hope I am heading lakeward), eyes peeled for occasional green Seaway signs sprouting like grass in a junkyard. I pass railroad cars, smokestacks, enormous power poles, a grim *glim bim,* big locks, iron bars. P-U. I close the windows, turn on the air conditioner, stop breathing.

At Lake Erie, the views gentle into suburbs, one after another, same scene, different names, nice, stable, year-round houses. I just start to relax when DETOUR!—one bridge, possibly five, are out. I go around and around and around.

Finally, back on Route 5, I stop at a pretty marina and talk with a retired Bethlehem Steel worker, now parking-lot attendant, who emerges from a recycled Fotomat booth. We're twenty-two miles from Buffalo, which is visible on clear days, he tells me in a pleasant, low voice. He points out the steel mill where he worked for thirty-eight years. "That's coming down this year," he says. "Used to be twenty-three thousand workers there; now there's maybe around twelve hundred. Coal companies are still operating, some of the old mills, but that's about all."

I walk out on a breakwater built recently from angular rocks big as dryers, washing machines, refrigerators, lying like a long line of bulldozed appliances but forming overall a graceful, embracing arm into the lake. Upon this stuff, which is called riprap, little groups of people sit uncomfortably here and there, fishing. The water is the color of indigo jeans, the sky, faded workshirt blue. Dazzling white sailboats and yachts float like resting gulls in the marina.

Although Lake Erie is the smallest Great Lake and plagued by industrial, navigational, municipal, and recreational pollutants, its extremely shallow waters are the warmest and biologically very productive, supporting the largest sport fishing industry of any Great Lake. It almost lost this distinction when pollution damaged spawning areas, commercial fishing reduced fish populations, and immigrants like rainbow smelt, alewives, white perch, and sea lampreys began pushing out native blue pike, muskellunge, whitefish, lake herring, and sturgeon. By the 1960s, Lake Erie became known around the world as a giant cesspool, victim of exploitation, abuse, and neglect.

According to recent reports, Lake Erie, although not nearly rescued, is doing a turnaround: a cleanup effort by all states and provinces concerned has been aided by the shallow lake's fast flush rate. The lake has been stocked with coho and the larger chinook salmon. Native fish are making a comeback, especially walleyes. Along its Ohio shore, marinas average almost one per mile. But the blue pike are gone for good.

Note: Most people call the angular rocks supporting many Great Lake piers and shores riprap, but there seemed to be some disagreement as to what the word means. Engineer Tom O'Bryan at an office of the U.S. Army Corps of Engineers explained it to me over the phone. Riprap, he said, is a protective layer or covering of quarry stones (usually limestone) of widely varying weights (from one hundred to one thousand pounds) piled along certain shorelines, jetties, breakwaters, piers, and embankments to prevent these structures, natural or otherwise, from washing away. Laid down loose, like an elephantine grade of gravel, riprap helps prevent erosion or scouring (see below). Stones bigger than riprap, used on some breakwaters, are usually referred to as armor stone.

It helps to understand the difference between a jetty and a pier, continued O'Bryan. There are very few piers on the Great Lakes. What are commonly called the "Holland pier" and the "Grand Haven pier" are not piers at all; they're jetties. A pier, more often found on ocean coasts supporting fish markets or amusement parks, resembles a huge dock—a person can swim or walk under it. A jetty is solid, often framed with fifty-foot steel pilings driven twenty-five feet below the lake bed and protected from scouring—water action at that underwater point where the piling meets the ground—with riprap. A breakwater is similar to a jetty but reaches beyond it to protect a harbor or shoreline from strong currents and waves. Usually one end of a breakwater touches the shoreline, but not always.*

I also learn that the United States Department of Defense is responsible for keeping shipping routes traversable, which explains why I keep seeing such a variety of boats from the U.S. Army Corps of Engineers.

SOMEWHERE AROUND Evans, at one of the small resorts sprinkled along the beaches among modest cottages, I am repelled by jokes told by a self-proclaimed racist into my tape recorder. I become conscious, suddenly, that almost everyone I have seen so far along the shore is white—except, of course, on reservations. Soon, at the Cattaraugus Indian Reservation, I learn that gambling is legal on Indian reservations. I guess everybody knows this but me: there is brisk business under the long, horizontal sign SENECA HAWK CATTARAUGUS TRUCK STOP COFFEE SHOP: PIZZA, SUBS, WINGS. Inside, I gamble on a handful of quarter games, pointing to tickets in cookie jars.

"How do you get these things open?"

"You just kinda bend them," says the woman behind the counter, kindly.

Bend, peel, tear. Bye-bye, cash.

Down the road, I walk out another pier, more riprap, where some

---

* Anything I refer to as a "pier" is actually a jetty unless stated otherwise.

people are angling for what a man calls "junk fish." I ask what junk fish are. "Sheephead." I still don't understand. "Carp," he explains finally. He says he hasn't caught anything, "but it's all for the fun, right?"

I stop at a popular place called Sunset Beach, where for a small fee one can use the changing rooms and enjoy a large, fairly sandy beach. The parking lot's packed. Kids run in and out. Swimmers shriek in the surf. Pale sunbathers redden on beach towels. It's a summer day out here.

Back on the road, still east of Dunkirk, where the beaches seem hard-packed and pebbly, I see ahead of me scalloped stone cliffs sprouting trees like hair. On my left, vineyards appear: real country-side at last.

By 4:30 I've snagged the last site in the Sheridan Bay Park, a small campground packed tighter than a love-in, eight bucks a night, tended by a retired couple who say they know everyone here. In the middle, boys play basketball; a smoky fire is already being poked and coddled by Leo Lichtenberger, a balding, tough-looking New Yorker who has been coming here for years—"first in, last out"—and shares the tiny blue trailer next to me with his longtime friend Mary McKeown. They offer me coffee, which we drink sitting at a picnic table covered with checked plastic.

I head for the shower, and when I return, Leo tells me that last year at this time the place was so deep in muck that when you went to take a shower, you needed another shower after the trip back. I crawl in the van for a long nap, while the smoke wisps into my windows, then watch a sunset down on the beach, a more-dirt-than-sand beach, but pleasant. The sunset proves lengthy and glorious, black silhouettes of trees against a pink-and-orange sky. As darkness arrives, Leo pulls out his guitar and we dodge smoke around the bright, snapping fire while Leo begins his nightly serenade: "Green, Green Grass of Home," "Up a Lazy River," "Home on the Range," he sings, as shadowy figures drift in and out, sometimes sticking a dollar bill in his guitar. A fingernail moon slides slick and sharp over the trees. "Old Hiram's Goat," sings Leo. We kick back by the fire, faces lit by coals now and by the Christmas lights that loop around the trailer.

Oh, isn't it grand to yield to the sleepies, slide open the van's side door, climb in, slide it shut, slip into long johns, and snuggle under quilts? Have I ever in my life felt this content?

"Yes, sir, that's my baby, that's my baby now . . ."

MAY 28

AT DUNKIRK, another little beach town, I find my way around the power plant to the U.S. Coast Guard Dunkirk (Point Gratiot) Lighthouse, where adults in brilliant regalia—black suits, red capes, and plumed hats—bustle over lush green lawns. Many flags wave. It's Memorial Day, and the elaborate preparations, Commander Beverly Busenlehner of the Disabled American Veterans informs me, are for a veterans' ceremony performed by the Order of Elks. I walk around the white-trimmed, square brick lighthouse with its square brick tower on the bright lawn scattered with cannons, anchors, and benches facing the sea. Way, way down a perpendicular bluff, the water is so clear and calm I can see stones on the bottom.

Back on the road, I note that beaches are often hard-packed dirt and pebbles. I pass some scruffy woods, more cliffs, ponds, parks, a busy little marina with a beach of clay and shale, vineyards, signs (WE PAMPER THE CAMPER . . . WORMS . . . MAPLE SUGAR), and finally, near a bright red barn, I cross the Pennsylvania line. At a winery, in a cavelike tasting room, I sample sherrylike cherry wine and purchase a bottle of peach.

All this I have accomplished before breakfast, because in two hours of driving I can't find a restaurant on the water. Soon, immaculate homes and landscaping turn into *glim bim;* then, in the city of **Erie**, I encounter a foul-smelling mix of fun and factories. Boat ramps are flanked with piles of coal and smokestacks. A state museum appears.

The United States Brig *Niagara*—the ship that served as Commodore Oliver Hazard Perry's relief flagship when American forces won the Battle of Lake Erie in 1813—lies in pieces behind a hunter's orange plastic fence in a sprawl of sheds, masts, ropes, and lumber. As I enter the area, I am met by four spit-shined 1812 sailors wearing white pants and blue-black tops with red trim. "They're a local group—schoolteachers, students, a fireman," explains a woman behind an indoor counter. "They do living history. My son is the one without the hat; he's a midshipman. They start out as a powder monkey—kids eight, nine, ten years old used to run powder during battle."

How do kids get interested in a group like this?

"Some are children of sailors; some saw us through school programs or are neighbors of other powder monkeys," says one of the uniformed men. "They grow up into other roles, just like a real powder monkey would."

There are other hints of authenticity. Wandering the shipyard, I come upon a huge man with a big gray beard, the very picture of an old-time sailor. Large tattoos run from shoulder to wrist on both arms, and he is winding a thin rope around a thicker one, producing coils thick as rattlesnakes.

"Is that like the original rope?" I inquire.

John Nickerson glances at me before answering. (Should I have said "line"?) "Yeah. Even bigger. These are what they call stays, what holds the mast up. They don't move, obviously. This here—the thinner line—is called serving. Lemme think about this . . . that's the last stage before it's tarred, but this end's gotta be all served up."

"There's steel cable in the middle."

"Right. And then it's wrapped with this line here. This is polypropylene. But before we do that this whole line is taped with black friction tape." He hands me a piece. "See how sticky that is? It's sticky on both sides. We use baby powder to make it slippery. You gotta put the powder on so it'll turn. We have a machine to keep the steel turning, but the rest is all done by hand, pretty much dog-boring routine. . . . Then it'll all be taken over there and tarred. Uh, it's a never-ending process. Once you get 'em up on the ship and all that, especially if you got a lot of heavy sun, you just start at one end and do the whole ship, and by the time you get to the other end, you turn around and do it again. You gotta keep 'em tarred."

"Do you get paid for this?" I ask.

"You better believe it. I'm not gonna kill myself for nothin'. I do this for a living. But I love it. I wouldn't trade it for anything."

We are joined by Tom Jares, probably in his late twenties, the official tour guide.

"I think I'll give you the tour that we give anyone who visits here," begins Jares. "Why don't we start with the rigging work? Everything that's being worked on here is part of the standing rigging, which is the stationary part of the lines that supports the masts and yards. It doesn't move. Now, traditionally hemp would have been used, but hemp stretches, which means you have to constantly readjust it. It also rots eventually.

"What we do here is start out with three-quarter-inch steel cable, wrap three spans of polypropylene around it, and then protect it with the traditional worming, parceling and serving. The whole ship is being constructed using authentic methods but newer materials, which are a lot more durable. We're trying to construct it so that if it's maintained properly it won't have to be done again. This ship has gone through four rebuildings. In the forties, after the second rebuilding, they put the ship in a concrete cradle at the foot of State Street. It sat on land for the better part of forty years before they took it apart in 1987.

"What we're looking at here"—lying at our feet—"are the trunk of the mast—the lowest part—and the top mast. The top gallant is constructed from these small ones over here.

"Now, the rigging that's already attached here is part of the shrouds, which are the lines that support the mast fore and aft, or from side to side. Okay? And these will form part of the ratline, which is the rope ladder that you need to climb up into the mast and get out on the yards"—the horizontal poles at the bottom of the sails—"and set the sails."

"It's an incredibly long mast!"

"Well, it'll be a hundred twenty feet off the deck."

The sails, which include a topsail, a top gallant, and a royal, will slide up and down on the mast. For a sail to be set, it has to be lifted up, so that the sail has room to unfurl. So the sailors will climb up the ratlines and then out the foot ropes that hang underneath. They uncoil the gasket—the line that ties the sail to the yard. "Lines that are connected to the corners, the middles, and the sides of the sail are hauled down on deck and the sail is unfurled," Jares explains. "It literally falls down. To furl the sail, you simply reverse the process. All this has to be done at tremendous heights, close to a hundred feet off the deck."

"You're not actually going to sail this ship!"

"Oh yes. This is a real working tall ship."

"Do you have women on the crew?"

"Of course! Historically there is documentation for women serving as seamen on ships of war in the early nineteenth century, usually disguised as men."

I am impressed. "You sure seem to know what you're talking about!"

"Well, I've been involved with the ship for six years now, and I've been interested in sailing vessels virtually all my life, so I very naturally took to this project. I've been here since the beginning, for every plank and beam, so it's kind of like a child to me—I've seen it literally grow up. If you get a chance, come when it's finished. We'll be doing historical presentations, gun drills—the ship will have real, working guns—so we'll be able to re-create the everyday life of the sailor."

NOT YET HAVING eaten today, I find a sunny outside table at the Buoy, a restaurant at the end of the Erie Public Docks, and sit down to a juicy shrimp salad. I am waiting for the next departure of *Little Toot*, a perky red, white, and black tour boat tied up next door at the dock.

At one o'clock, *Little Toot*, capacity fifty, captained by Tony Rugare, chugs into the harbor formed by Presque Isle (French for "almost an island" but pronounced "Presk Aisle"), a long peninsula to the west shaped on a map like a floppy fly swatter with a lot of holes in it. A prime example of a "flying sand spit," Presque Isle was and is formed by sand carried by wind or water up the western edge and around the tip. A hundred years ago, ships could sail in and out of this harbor—Oliver Perry's ships hid from the British in Presque Isle's Misery Bay—but when sand off Presque Isle threatened the entrance, a channel was dug.

As we enter this channel, now lined on each side with rusty-looking metal slabs that resemble recycled railroad cars set end to end, Rugare turns on a taped tour. "The channel is dredged yearly by the U.S. Army Corps of Engineers so that very large oceangoing vessels can come and go from the bay," the tape informs us. We pass a huge billboard that reminds us of the U.S. Coast Guard motto: "Always Prepared." Rugare's been doing this tour for forty years, he tells me. "I love it. I like people. You have to first like people. I just talked to two people Saturday from South Africa. Every year we meet people from Germany, Sweden, Russia, all over the world. I don't know how they get here, but they do."

As we leave the harbor to cruise Presque Isle from the lake side —"seven miles of bathing beaches"—Rugare tells me that *Little Toot* is his "base" boat. "We've had different boats, but we like this boat —it's cute, easy to operate, very inexpensive to run, and it handles beautifully. Sometimes we go out in three-, four-footers. Then we surf in! We do! We just ride the waves all the way in. People love it. We tell 'em, close their eyes and make believe they're in Waikiki."

When the ride is over, I drive to Presque Isle, passing two big water slides, cottages, hot-dog stands, ice cream places, a condo. I turn onto the potholed boulevard that stretches along the first half of the peninsula's length, a spit so narrow I can see water on both sides. Even this early in the season, traffic is thick. The many parking lots are jammed, especially the marina's, packed solid with pickups, powerful vehicles, and empty boat trailers.

At the state park office, a ranger confesses that the sandy beaches I see here are not entirely a gift of Mother Nature—the shoreline on the western (lake) side is eroding so fast that a "beach nourishment" program is required to keep beaches, roads, and facilities from vanishing during winter storms. "We dump tons of sand on the western beaches every year," she tells me. "If the dunes build up early enough, they help protect the shoreline through the harsh winters." (See note, p. 52.)

Back in my van, I feel guilty that I'm restless in this three-thousand-acre playground, which has been named a National Natural Landmark by the National Park Service. On the map, Presque Isle looks like paradise—a seven-mile-long peninsula lined with beaches, dappled with ponds, and providing habitats, says one guidebook, for 318 species of birds and more than 500 kinds of flowering plants and ferns. But up close and right now, I am overwhelmed with cars, people, boats, and roads. And I am irritated to near-madness by two huge speakers wedged in the trunk of a parked car, mercilessly pounding a capacious beachful of people with shrieking, bass-amplified rock music. I take to the beach, moving from towel to towel with my tape recorder. I tell people I'm doing a survey and ask if the music bothers them. This is what they say:

"Not really. It's not our kind of music, though."

"Lotta people left because of the noise. But nobody says anything."

"We brought our own music, but we can't hear it."

"I hate it."

"Kids! What can ya do?"

"It's kinda loud."

"Wish they'd leave."

"How come these guys get to dominate the beach?" I crankily ask the tan, attractive lifeguard, who calmly explains that a park this big can accommodate everyone. "When you have fifteen beaches, people get to know where to go," he tells me. "This is a tourist beach. It's one of the biggest, area-wise. If people are unhappy here, I can direct them to other, quieter beaches where people come out and read books. Across the road, where those cars are, is where the wind surfers go. At Beach One, you get a lot of families, because that's the first beach they see and the kids can't wait."

Note: During the two years since I made my visit, at least 560,000 tons of sand have been dumped on Presque Isle's beaches, an equivalent of 33,000 truckloads (one ton of sand equals about one cubic yard). Sand nourishment is probably one of the least destructive methods of maintaining the shoreline, but it's also expensive—about $4 million in this case—and awkward: that many trucks can't be used in tourist-thick summer, so most of the the sand was mined from the bottom of Lake Erie by a vessel called a hopper dredge, which transported the sand to Presque Isle, anchored offshore, and, mixing the sand with water, squirted it onto the beach through an enormous tube. The sand replenishment program has since been replaced ("Well, everyone *hopes* more sand won't be needed," a park naturalist sighs over the telephone) by fifty-five 50-foot breakwaters costing nearly $20 million that form a broken line about 200 feet from the western shore. The breakwaters diminish the power of the crashing waves with long piles of gigantic boulders weighing three to seven tons each.*

---

* The figures in this note come from Derosher Dock and Dredge, Inc., Cheboygan, Michigan, which did the both the sand nourishment and the breakwater work.

MAY 29

LAST NIGHT I pulled into a private campground after dark, slept to the banjo banter of bullfrogs, and pulled out early in pouring rain. A long drive down gravel roads through dripping tunnels of green ends in Conneaut, just over the Ohio line, where I find myself in a magically lovely town park. A creek meanders through undulating lawns canopied by spreading trees and scattered with picnic tables, a pavilion, a playground, mossy nooks. It's large, too, for such a small town, but no one else is here: the sudden appearance of a gnome or a flying cat wouldn't really surprise me. There's even a spacious, if gravelly, beach. Something's drawing me to Conneaut—the lushness, perhaps. It feels different from anywhere else I have been.

I drive along the lakeshore, dense with houses, looking for overnight quarters, but find no motels, no bed-and-breakfast places, only a little cottage declaring itself FOR RENT. I inquire next door and seconds later I am sipping coffee at a kitchen table, admiring the lake view and talking with Margaret "Bunny" Thayer, who fills me in on Township Park.

"When my children were young, we went there every single summer day and stayed for four or five hours," Thayer says. "It's got a mile of beach and it's still free. This town has always given away everything—every time we have any kind of tax levy for Township Park, it passes. On weekends, we get people from Pittsburgh and all over the place. I've suggested we charge a dollar a car, because they sometimes crowd out the townspeople. We are economically depressed, but everything we have that's good here we've always given away."

Maybe that's what I've felt about this place. There's something large-spirited here. I ask, "Do you like living on the lakeshore?"

"I'm addicted to it. My father was in real estate before me, and he used to say, 'Okay, Bunny, if you got to sell a place on the lake, all you got to say is, 'Here's your million-dollar view, a panorama that changes every day.' He was right. I can just sit and stare at the lake all day. People laugh when I say that my favorite time of year is winter. When I lived uptown, I never came down to the lake in winter, but here, I'm in love with the drama. Sometimes the water even freezes in mid-wave. When the lake is frozen, there's no sound; I feel like I'm on the edge of outer space."

I'm sold. I ask if there's an inexpensive house for sale on the lakeshore. Soon we are on our way in a massive four-wheel-drive vehicle that makes my van feel like a toy to inspect a charming $39,000 house one foot from a crumbling embankment. Looking down the precipice, I can see where brush and logs have been thrown and small trees planted to try to hold things, but the slender beach at the bottom looks to me a mere snack for a Lake Erie storm: waves will gnaw at the bottom and, well, the rest is gravity. I'm reminded of other narrow Lake Erie beaches I've been seeing, some resembling a war zone, armored with discarded tires, sandbags, riprap, logs, concrete in many shapes and arrangements, railroad ties, and other unattractive attempts to keep the eroding shore from gobbling up homes, industry, recreational facilities, and other structures built disrespectfully close to Mother Nature.

Why the expensive, frustrating effort to poke, prod, and girdle Mother? To developers, she threatens erosion, caused—in addition to the effects of wind, water levels, unstable shore materials, human stupidity and greed—by waves: when a wave hits the shore at even a slight angle—waves rarely hit straight on—sand particles are pushed in one direction, resulting in littoral drift, or a river of sand along the shore, and a constantly shifting shoreline. If there is no beach to buffer the waves, or if the waves are particularly large and forceful, they may begin undercutting the bluff, which, particularly if it consists of sand or clay, is likely to fall (collapse), slump (huge chunks of the bank slide downward), or flow with debris (plants, rocks, and other material slip downward), most or all of which eventually ends up on somebody else's beach.

This capricious property shift can drive landowners crazy, but it's meddling that got us into this mess. Early in the 1800s, jetties were built perpendicular to the shore at the mouth of inland shipping routes to keep sand from clogging the entrance, or even to force the river to change course, wreaking even more havoc. As lakeshore property became valued, jetties were followed by a profusion of seawalls (built of lumber, stone, or concrete and often backfilled with anything available—logs, tires, riprap, even old cars), groins (structures of wood, stone, or concrete built, like mini-jetties, perpendicular to the shore), and breakwaters. By 1973, there were 3,600 of these battlements on Ohio's Lake Erie alone.

Unfortunately, most of these structures interfere with the littoral drift, and even the experts have not understood the full implications of what even one such interference can do to a neighboring shoreline. A jetty blocks the river of sand, which collects on one side to make a great big beach while the beach on the other side, where the littoral drift begins again but without the normal replenishment, may quickly disappear. Groins may stabilize one family's beach while effectively destroying the neighbor's. Interrupting the natural flow of sand, then, causes more erosion, which brings me to the ludicrous but logical and scientifically supported conclusion that the main cause of erosion on the Great Lakes today is not the natural fury of the lake but the battle to control it.

"Thanks," I tell Bunny, "but no thanks."

ENTERING KILPI HALL, Conneaut's three-story, eggshell-white-with-eggshell-blue-trim community center, a tastefully renovated ex–Finnish meeting hall, I feel as if I've walked into a feel-good movie. (Indeed, I soon learn that Universal Studios has filmed here!) Director Joan Newcomb gives me a gracious tour, from the red-and-yellow basement Tulip Room to a main-floor auditorium of tongue-in-groove wainscoting and hardwood floors, where one can attend plays, concerts, and a holiday Madrigal Feast with serving "wenches," singers, wassail, a bear head on the wall, and a pig on a platter; to an upstairs dance studio with mirrors, a marbled floor resembling the inside covers of an old book, and barred windows, "thanks to a story about a little Finnish girl who fell out once." Music-student cacophony drifts from a new addition. A Finnish band will soon perform from a new outdoor bandstand.

Funded culture in an "economically depressed" town of just 14,000? I am impressed. I make a tiny confession to my tape recorder, though: my favorite part was the gift from U.S. Steel—a fire escape, once on wheels, that used to be pushed up to ore boats to let off the crew.

ON MY WAY TO Ashtabula, I am tempted to frustrate an unnecessarily rude tailgater by slightly slowing down, but I often pull over for folks who don't share my here-in-the-moment pace. Their hearts are already where they're going, and until their bodies get there they feel incomplete. I can see the angst in their passing faces and I understand. I've always loved the road, especially freeways. How fast can I get there? I'd wonder. How far can I go in twelve hours? Now, having a long-term goal but no immediate destination, I dawdle: over 45 mph, I miss things.

It's gray and grim on Lake Erie today, whitecaps all the way out. I pass a sprawling power plant with four stacks, then green, then Ashtabula and the Ashtabula Water Pollution Control Plant. Checking that out seems a good rainy-day thing to do.

"There's plenty to write about here!" says a man wearing big rubber boots and resembling an old salt. We're standing in the tiled front hallway of the one-story office building. People are running around punching time clocks. "It's very exciting," the man continues. "Waste water treatment is a lot more than what meets the eye. A lotta money tied up. Clean water, that's our job. The Water Works cleans lake water as it comes in and we clean it when it goes out."

The secretary is on the phone. While I wait, I poke my head in a lab off one hallway that looks like a mad scientist's—lots of beakers filled with colored liquids. I stand around ogling charts and buttons and lights. The secretary hangs up, carefully compares the name on my driver's license with that on my last book, and sighs. "You're going to have to get permission for this from our superintendent," she tells me. "He isn't here."

"I told her this was big money here," the older man chimes in. "Fifty-million-dollar operation. You're talkin' big money here."

"Well, maybe you can talk with our pretreatment person. He handles all the waste water."

"Waste water comes in here and goes through settling, aeration, chemical additions, and detention," begins Gary E. Shaffer, a big man in a small office who doesn't seem to mind at all explaining things to me. "We remove ninety-nine percent of the pollutants and discharges."

"Has this treatment improved over the last few years?"

"No. Last year they sort of lost the plant."

"Excuse me?"

"Right. There's biological activity that goes on, and if you don't treat the organisms right, you lose them. That's what happened down there in the aeration tanks where the biological activity is. See, the raw waste comes in and settles out in the preparatory tanks. Then it goes into your aeration tanks. Okay. That is like food coming into these bugs—they're eating the waste that comes in. You add just so much air to 'em, and they mix and stay in the tank for about six to eight hours detention time, okay?"

"You've got *bugs* in there?"

"Sure. Microorganisms. I call 'em bugs. So then it goes out to the final tank, where it settles out. As it does, the bugs will settle to the bottom, the sludge, and then you bring them back. It's a cycle, comes right around. There're some that die off. And when they die off, whatcha do with that sludge, that stuff we treat—we add polymers to it and we thicken it up. Then we squeeze the water out, press it out, and we get a mud form, like a cake, we call it." They haul a daily truckload ("about ten, fifteen wet tons") of that stuff to a dump site about a hundred miles away.

In a light rain, we wander among tanks of different shapes and sizes, open and enclosed, connected by large pipes and sprawling over the grounds along the lake, while Shaffer tells me what does what. While I never fully understand what happened here, I'm impressed by the vulnerability of an important part of the pollution control program: that someone made an expensive mistake, "bugs" not easily replaced had been killed, and the place did not function properly for almost nine months.

MAY 30

SOMEWHERE NEAR Perry, Ohio, I'm tooling down a delightful shoreline road to the tune of a cello concerto, soaking in morning sunshine, enjoying the sweet country air and the sparkle of dew and lake, when what pops into the emerald treeline but a two-towered nuclear power plant. Nearly in its shadow, I turn into a place called All People's Trail, park the van, and am heading up the garden path

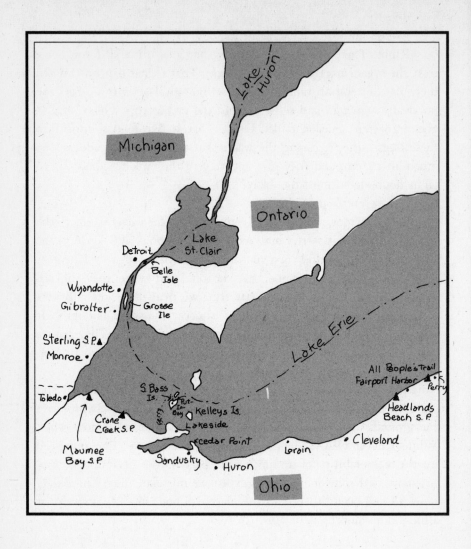

Western Lake Erie

when—YIKES!—my fingers, on their automatic pocket check, close on nothing but change: I have locked my keys in the car.

Rod Sharpnack, the groundskeeper, who is riding a large, roaring mower, turns off the motor, reaches for a radio, and presto, a ranger is "on his way." Rod stops for lunch, forking up tuna straight from the can while he tells me he went to Northland College, near Lake Superior's Apostle Islands, and describes some places on my itinerary—I must promise not to specify, lest tourists and developers ruin them—where eagles are "a dime a dozen" and pheasants proliferate.

"Maybe things are changing for the better," I suggest.

Rod gives me a sour look. "Take the blue pike," he says. "I mean, I've never seen a blue pike. I've never even heard of anybody catching one. But Lake Erie used to have a big industry in blue pike, there were so many of them. But yes, the lake's clearing up. Five years ago, you'd have been pretty hard-pressed to catch a walleye right out here, but now this is a real hot spot for walleye."

"Is that because of the nuclear power plant?"

"Oh, the warm water from the plant does attract them, but the lake's cleaner, too."

We talk about boats. Rod tells me that boat slips are available nearby, but "you'll pay twelve, fifteen hundred a year. Some people keep their boat on a trailer and for five bucks they can put it in the water, but a trailer isn't cheap either, and of course, you need something to pull it with."

"There's no cheap way to go boating," I wager.

"Yes there is. Make sure all your friends have boats."

Rod starts the mower and I read the bulletin board near the park entrance, drawn to a spooky poster instructing me on what to do in the event of a nuclear emergency. I shiver. And then the rangers arrive, not one but two of them, in separate vehicles, and who is to say which of them is more gallant? "Locked your keys in, didja?" grins one. To my feminist chagrin but great relief, they have the van open in minutes.

I begin exploring the park along an unobstructed walkway, easily traversable by wheelchair, rolling smoothly before me like pulled taffy. All People's Trail is a comfortable stroll past huge mowed lawns, tended gardens, woods, hedges, rounded concrete sculptures of uncertain shapes (a cross between mushroom and mammal?), labeled trees (pin oak, bur oak, Norway maple, red maple), benches overlooking a sandy beach, and, best of all, birds (finches, warblers, sparrows, woodpeckers, robins), a choir of jubilant soloists somehow harmonious.

FAIRPORT HARBOR, a prim little port, showcases a beautiful lighthouse-turned-museum, which shares its landscape with industry. Heading on foot toward the pier, I pass gravel piles riddled with holes from which little brown bank swallows zip in and out, swirling noisily around my head. Further along, at a boat ramp, I find Joe Mackey, who in winter "teaches and traps" and in summer tends the bait shop. He's a Finn, he says, and the gravel belongs to the cement plant. Freighters bring gravel in and take out salt. "We have enormous salt deposits here."

After a recommendable hamburger at the Village Ice Cream Emporium ("We pat them by hand, that's why," explains the waitress), I drive on to discover, next door to Headlands Beach State Park and securely enclosed by a sturdy fence, a Morton salt operation. At a guardhouse, where I am handed a thick packet and sent smartly on my way, I regret the impulsive nature of my traveling: given time for prearrangements, I might at this moment be riding an elevator two thousand feet underground to explore the salt mines deep under Lake Erie: offshore, sublake caverns three and a half miles out! I scan the water, looking for derricks like the oil pumps off Santa Barbara, but the view is unobstructed. Imagine! Trucks and miners are out there right now, bustling far under the lake, surrounded by white walls of solid salt.

HEADLANDS BEACH STATE PARK, a sumptuous stretch of sandy shoreline, provides enough parking for nearly a tenth of the population of nearby Cleveland. I drive past lot after empty mini-mall-sized lot. After about the twentieth, I spy a building with official-looking trucks in front. Inside I meet ranger Jim Fishbach and naturalist Bill Hudson, who, I soon conclude, would make a good sitcom called "Fish and Hud." With easy grace, they turn their day on a dime and usher me into the front seat of a green four-wheel-

drive vehicle so big that if a police car were a county jail, this would
be a penitentiary.

Fishbach drives. He carries a gun and wears a silver-and-blue
badge and an official red patch on his green shirt. He is a law en-
forcement officer and takes care of the recreational side of the park.
When I ask about the flashing light panel on top and the metal screen
between front and back seats, Fishbach points out that when you get
a hundred thousand people here on one weekend, which has happened,
although the average is forty thousand, sometimes you need that stuff.
When I admit my recent key episode, he says, "Once twelve people
lost their keys here in one day. Happens all the time."

Bill Hudson, smiling under a corduroy Browns cap, is a naturalist,
wildlife biologist, and artist who manages the neighboring substantial
Mentor Marsh Nature Preserve. "Ohio is the only state that at present
doesn't have a coastal zone management plan that sets priorities and
coordinates the agencies that affect the shorelines," he tells me. "Ohio
has resisted this for a long time, because condo and club owners and
such are afraid that a coordinated plan would restrict their activities."

I shrug. "It probably would."

"Plans will take effect, probably next year, however, and things
will change," continues Hudson. "The problem is, as with most plans,
its environmental aims—to save wetlands, promote natural shorelines,
and protect critical areas—often conflict with its recreational inten-
tions—to improve parks and access to the lake." It occurs to me that
Hudson and Fishbach represent these opposing aims.

We stop near the park entrance and pile out facing the lake, the
public beach on our left, a natural, sandy area called Headlands Dunes
State Nature Preserve (set aside in 1972) on our right. "Lake Erie is
sand-poor compared to the other Great Lakes, so a lot of our beaches
are narrow," says Hudson. "But here we have enough sand to grow
dunes. The angle of the shoreline has a lot to do with where sand
accumulates. The breakwater out there does, too.* Sand dune habitats
are so rare along Lake Erie that this is a real gem."

I search the expanse of barely rolling sand and scattered plants for
something more than a swell. "These are dunes?"

---

* The jetties, first built in 1827 to protect the Grand River channel just east of Headlands Beach,
demonstrate the way jetties encourage large beaches on one side by blocking the flow of sand.

"Absolutely," Hudson answers. "You see this?" He points to a knee-high pile of sand. "This wasn't here before now. You know, when we began this project, we tried to keep people out. But then we realized that if dune plants, even the rare ones, couldn't take abuse, they wouldn't be here. A storm can come in here and change the whole face of the beach overnight. Plants get sandblasted all winter, are buried in sand and grow right back up through it. It's partly their ability to do this that helps build the dunes—the plants act like a snow fence. This is also a really popular birdwatching spot," he adds, pointing out some offshore mergansers.

A man approaches us, points out a skimpy swimsuit on the beach, and asks if it's legal. Fishbach tells him it is. Then to me: "Where do you draw the line for indecent exposure on bathing suits? It used to be a kind of discretionary thing; now you have to have at least one inch of material on your derriere." He shrugs. "You can basically expose as much gluteus maximus as you want."

As we pass another expanse of sand nearer the swimming area, Hudson says, "Ironically, there's more beach pea"—a rare plant—"here than you'll find on our preserve. The reason is rabbits and people. Down on the dunes, the rabbits feel comfortable and eat all the beach pea they want. Here, they're bothered by all the people, so they leave it alone."

We're approaching an 800-acre marsh, an ancient riverbed, explains Hudson, left behind when the Grand River changed its course and found another outlet to Lake Erie. We park, get out, and gaze out over what I call "the largest expanse of pampas grass I've ever seen."

"It's giant reed grass—*Phragmites australis*—which gets seventeen feet high," says Hudson. "It's beautiful, but here it's destructive. This marsh used to have areas of cattails, arrowhead, and tree-canopy-covered open water, with many different water depths and a far more varied plant life. Then a property owner contracted to dispose of some salt fill. Although he took precautions, rainwater leached down through the fill and carried salt into the marsh. Even the very small change in the water chemistry gave advantage to the giant reed grass. In just over ten years, it's swept through the whole marsh. Now we have almost a monoculture here."

"*Phragmites* is so thick you either have to hack through it, crawl under it, or jump on a pile and roll to the other side," adds Fishbach.

Back in the truck, we turn onto Corduroy Road, which Fishbach says began as a floating road: loggers, to keep from sinking in deep muck, drove their trucks across logs laid side by side across the marsh. I find the road bumpy enough to deserve the name as it is, but it affords us a new view of the marsh—acres of golden grass that even this early in summer looks high and dry. "Couldn't this stuff catch fire?"

"Marshes burn," shrugs Hudson. "That's the natural ecology of a marsh; that's how it regenerates itself. It doesn't hurt the marsh grasses at all—they've got millions of years of evolution behind them."

"A kid started a fire here once during a very dry period," says Fishbach. "Stories claim the flames were thirty feet high and moving thirty miles an hour. I believe it; I've seen marsh fires before."

"So what do you do?"

Hudson: "What you do about a marsh fire is stand at the edge and watch it burn. Sometimes you can stop it when it first starts, but it's impenetrable out there. The fire's got way too much fuel and it's not going to stop and it won't hurt the marsh."

"What about homes around here?"

"As soon as a marsh fire hits the woods, the flames usually die out. Did you notice how much cooler it got when we stepped into the trees? These leaves are letting off water vapor all the time. And you've got green grass here. So the humidity in a woods is much higher than in a marsh. It's very scary if you live on the edge of a marsh—you're sure that the fire's going to come right up to your backyard. But it won't."

"He says with confidence!" laughs Fishbach, as we pull up at the maintenance building. "But please mention that we don't want to promote fire in the marsh."

I promise, adding how much I've enjoyed the company of "two such articulate guys."

"I'd prefer you said 'good-looking guys,'" responds Fishbach. "And make sure to say 'hardworking' and 'working together.'"

"Fishbach is right," says Hudson. "Although we both work for the Department of Natural Resources, we work for different divisions with different missions. But we work together every day."

I drive off hoping that the agencies they represent can work together half as well.

MAY 31

It's 7:00 A.M. in Cleveland and I have just emerged from a steaming shower, bare feet sinking into soft rose carpeting, after a luxurious night on the twelfth floor of the Sheraton Hotel. I open the curtains and look down on freighters floating on a blue, blue lake; a Greek-columned government building turned Midas gold by dawn; jets rising heavily over the water; a large port crowded with cranes, buildings, and boats. It's quite a switch from the night before last, when I drove around for an hour trying to ditch a man who followed me out of a restaurant, then followed my van. I passed a fearful night in the stately but (this early in summer) nearly deserted Geneva State Park.

I hit the sidewalks of Cleveland feeling fine. It's morning rush hour, so I stride along, too, but I soon find a lovely, quiet sidewalk along the lake where paddleboats, glossy as new cars, congregate like ducks. When I try to rent one, the owner tells me he has to wash them first—many people attending the weekend's National Rib Festival ate their well-sauced meals offshore, he says, rendering hopelessly sticky both the "tubies"—big rubber doughnuts with a roof and room for two—and the paddleboats.

From the lakeshore, the skyline gleams with glass. Everything that isn't really old seems really new. I've never been to Cleveland before and don't know what it was like, say, ten years ago, but it feels to me as if a pair of wealthy newlyweds bought the place, then roared in, hired a whole lot of decorators, and now it's about half-done. They haven't touched the Cleveland–Cuyahoga County Port Authority, though, an easy walk from the tubies. Completely fenced, it's more intimidating than Morton salt, but I'm welcomed into a closet-sized guardhouse anyway and offered the only chair. Trucks go by about every two minutes, bringing in fill for Dock 20, the guard tells me. "Yesterday a hundred and twenty-five trucks came through here."

The phone rings and I'm sent to a small office in a warehouselike building to meet Eric Hirsimaki, the chief engineer in charge of "facilities and maintenance," who agrees, with only slight reluctance, to drop everything and to show me around the 110-acre Port Authority of Cleveland, almost half a million square feet of covered storage, he tells me, with berthing for ten ships. We head toward a dark freighter called *Island Gem*, my middle-aged guide in a daffodil-yellow windbreaker, a color I would have guessed too bright for his tastes until I see it everywhere—seamen in yellow coveralls, tough-looking yellow vehicles of odd shapes and sizes.

Two ships are in today. "Are there usually more?" I ask.

"It varies." Hirsimaki speaks in a loud but clear voice over the roar of cranes and trucks. "Three or four is a busy day. Generally ships bring in steel cargo that goes to various local companies for appliances, automobiles, things like that. About ninety percent of our business is imported steel—last year we unloaded a quarter-million tons." A black crane attached to a caboose-red cab towers over the *Island Gem*. "Generally we use our gear to unload the ship rather than the ship's gear," says Hirsimaki, explaining why the row of four white "swivels," or cranes, centered along the deck of this "self-unloader" are not in use.

"How long does it take?"

"A couple of hours or several days, depending on how much cargo they bring in. Some will unload a whole cargo, up to twenty-five thousand tons, or maybe they'll just unload a couple hundred tons, then go to Toledo or Detroit or Chicago and unload some more. From there, the empty ship might go up to Duluth and load grain and then go to Europe or Africa or somewhere. Last year we got ships from forty-three countries. It's quite an international mix—a boat flying a Greek flag might be registered in Panama, have a Filipino crew, be captained by a Greek, and be carrying steel from Germany. In recent years a lot of these ships use crews from Southeast Asia, because they're cheaper.

"See this mark on the side of the ship?" Hirsimaki points to a vertical white ruler painted on the hull at the water line. "That's called a Plimsoll mark, named after Samuel Plimsoll, who devised it in 1860 to prevent overloading a ship. The '10 M' means there should be ten meters of water between this line and the keel [the bottom of the ship]. The 'LS' is probably 'load line summer,' and 'LW,' 'load line winter'—the load line changes according to where you are and the time of year. In winter the weather is rougher so you ride lighter."

We turn and walk toward the other side of the port, crunching under our feet large, delicate, winged insects. They are alive but motionless. Hirsimaki says they are called Canadian soldiers, the regional name for mayflies. "Sometimes they get so thick you can't even walk through here." ("They live long enough to copulate and lay eggs and then they die," Bill Hudson told me yesterday. "I don't think they even have mouth parts.")

We pass railroad flatcars called gondola cars. "We use them to carry steel billets," Hirsimaki shouts above roaring machines. At Dock 24, a giant yellow crane—a Buckeye Booster—has unloaded the steel slabs ("Each one weighs eleven metric tons") from a bullet-nosed yellow ship called the *Titan Scan*. "The Buckeye Booster puts 'em on the dock, and then a Mambo—that big blue forklift over there—will pick them up and stack them. Then they'll be loaded onto a gondola car, which will take them to steel mills for rolling."

All the machinery seems monstrous. "I've never seen a truck this big on the road!" I exclaim over one particularly massive vehicle.

"Oh, we've got bigger trucks. We've got pieces so big—say, a hundred and fifty tons—that we have to build the truck around the piece. Takes two lanes of an interstate highway to move the truck. Only do that a couple times a year. We can handle any type of cargo, but heavy lift is one thing that we're very good at, partly because Cleveland has one of the larger-capacity cranes on the Great Lakes. Do you know what a Hewlett unloader is?"

"No."

"We don't have one here, but if you look over there behind the white Coast Guard station, you can see a black object. That's called a Hewlett. It's the last dock like that on the Great Lakes. Except for one in New Jersey, Hewletts were used only on the Great Lakes. They're a Great Lakes phenomenon. They were developed in 1898 by George Hewlett, and they were used to unload iron ore for seventy-five, eighty years. Now they're pretty well gone." Hirsimaki appears to be the world authority on Hewlett unloaders and has published a number of articles on the subject.*

Something very large and heavy is dangling from the huge yellow crane. *Titan Scan* is loading a project cargo, says Hirsimaki. "That's

---

* The Hewletts are now inactive.

very heavy cargo. The *Titan Scan* is called a ro-ro ship—meaning 'roll on / roll off'—because she's got a stern ramp. She's also got a bow thruster, a propeller in a tunnel that goes laterally through the bow and allows the ship to move sideways, often eliminating the need of a tug." The bulbous bow and the sides are a wet-paint, slicker yellow. I think it the most beautiful yellow I have ever seen.

"The men unloading the ship belong to the International Long-shoremen's Association, which is the union down here." Hirsimaki has picked up his wonderful lecture. He's on a roll. When he started this tour, I could tell he was a little annoyed—he's tired of doing tours, and someone had just been hired so he wouldn't have to, but she is too new to know much yet. Anyway, by now we're both enjoying this. "And when there's a ship in, they'll be called in to work," continues the affable engineer. "They work by gangs—thirteen men to a gang, one gang per crane. How many gangs work on a given shift depends on how much cargo and things like that. But you can have a couple hundred men working down here sometimes. There's not enough union members for that, so sometimes they use day labor, sort of first come, first serve, anyone off the street, to do the menial work. But the union members have been at it for years. They're pros."

FOR FORTY-FIVE MINUTES I drive west of Cleveland without running out of swank—mile after mile of magnificent houses, some of them palaces—in stark contrast to yesterday's drive through the east side, where I endured one dingy suburb after another, heavy traffic, and tiny beaches. Now, at Bay Village, I stop to stroll the wide, sandy beach at the Huntington Reservation, one of Cleveland's eleven "Metroparks."

Across the road, an employee at the Metropark's nature center describes the only animal rehabilitation center in the county. "We handle about four or five hundred animals every year," he tells me. "We put broken bones in a sling and release the animals in three or four weeks. Orphans we release in the spring. Those you see here are awaiting release or can no longer survive in the wild."

We walk past the cages: the red-tailed hawk has a permanent gun injury; the raccoons are orphans from four different litters; the skunks were someone's pet and, now de-scented, have no protection; the foxes were taken from the den as pups and raised unsuccessfully as pets; the turkey vultures flew into high-tension wires, sustaining permanent wing damage; the great horned owl, raised in captivity, has had one of its wingbones cruelly removed; the snowy owl came from the airport: "A snowy owl sometimes ends up there because it looks like its home terrain."

I STOP IN the town of Huron, just east of Lake Erie's most famous playground, an area that includes two peninsulas, several popular island escapes, and a number of play-oriented towns. I rent a damp, chilly cottage that teeters on the edge of an eroding bluff at a place called the Wild Waves Motel. Several of these tiny cottages face a motel complex across a graciously treed lawn. Missing is an old hotel, recently torn down after the bank sloughed out from under it. In a very dark saloon next to the road, the motel owner's daughter tends bar. Peering through the gloom at my map, she directs me to Put-in-Bay, shouting the names of highways and crossroads over country music blasting from a jukebox. Young workingmen along the bar, one with a red bandanna around his forehead, ply me with drinks, candy bars bought from a charity, flattery (it really is very dark in here), and advice. One runs a charter fishing boat but can't work right now "cause the fish are spawning." A dredger is off work for the same reason. "These big dredges, they really tear up the bottom, you know?" he says. "You got four foota water? When I get done, you got twelve foota water. But you gotta protect the fish eggs. They sit on the bottom and they hafta sit so long, undisturbed, so until June fifteenth I'm sittin' still."

They discuss which of the largest islands—South Bass or Kelleys —I should visit. Both places offer tourist accommodations, historical monuments, caves, restaurants, boating, and other summer pleasures, but although Kelleys is claimed to be bigger and quieter, the consensus is South Bass: "You go to Put-in-Bay, you'll never want to leave."

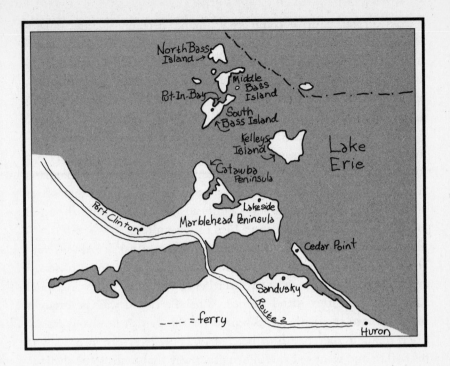

Lake Erie's Archipelago

JUNE 1

CONCERNED ABOUT weekend crowds, I get up early, but take time for coffee, sitting out on the front stoop of my little cottage. Clouds of Canadian soldiers fly like grotesque mosquitoes behind my glasses, fall into my cup, and float there. I fish them out, wave them away. A deer freezes twenty feet away, then crashes down the bluff toward the lake. A couple of rabbits stare, sun shining through diaphanous ears.

Warned that Friday ferry lines can be impossible, I tear past Sandusky on Highway 2, crossing Sandusky Bay on what appears to be a raised dike, water on both sides almost as high as the road. Things get marshy, green, and wild: a heron stabs through plate-glass water; an osprey flies over, clutching a large fish. At the end of Catawba Island, a ferry takes my van and me to South Bass Island.

On arrival, I drive completely around deciduously green, laid-back South Bass Island, looking for the state park. I pass a small airport, Put-in-Bay (pure beach town with a touch of class), a 352-foot Doric column honoring (natch) Commodore Perry, narrow beaches, stone beaches, breakwalls, cliffs, the airport again. I stop for directions.

"You're fresh off the boat, aren'tcha?" says Steve Donovan, handing me a map of the island. A youngish man, he flies over every day to run the airport on South Bass while his wife handles the mainland airport. He tells me about "green water snakes, which sun themselves on top of the water and swallow bullhead whole." I've never heard of green water snakes, and suspect him of leg-pulling.

"Did you go to Perry's cave yet?" Donovan asks. "Always nice and cool down there. During the War of 1812, Perry stored prisoners and ammunition there fifty-two feet below the surface. The Battle of Lake Erie made this island famous. What Perry did was, he brought his boats into this harbor and waited for the British fleet to come in. They thought they had him bottled up, but Perry dropped a lot of his ballast and went out through another way that tends to be shallow. The British followed him, went aground, and Perry turned cannons on them and fired."

I follow Donovan's directions to the state park, where I unroll a yam-colored tent on a lakeside bluff, fit twenty-one aluminum tubes into a frame, and stretch the tent tightly over it, the flap facing the water. I feel like a woodswoman, flawlessly pitching a tent that hasn't been out of the bag in years. Sunlight, filtering through the trees, now dances with leafy shadows across the smoothly staked fly. Inside, I loll around all afternoon, reading and sleeping. There's a whiff of fish on the breeze and a scent of something sweet. Leaves, surf, bugs, distant voices, and boat motors blend into a sensuous summer music that, drifting through a tent screen into this square private space, feels languorously lovely.

At night, I find Put-in-Bay alive with people happily doing not much of anything. I stroll its several blocks of shops and restaurants, then through a central park, where families and couples picnic at tables under trees. Slick, antique MG convertibles, here for an island perimeter race, buzz around like Matchbox cars. "We celebrate New Year's Day on the second weekend in September," a resident tells me.

"Everyone puts lights on their boats and everything. There's gambling in the street, and coins are issued stamped with the place, date, and year."

JUNE 2

THIS LAKE ERIE archipelago, the Marblehead Peninsula, and the towns around the bay add up to one wingding of a summer playground. At the end of a peninsula so narrow that the middle is sliced into one-house lots, I find one of the oldest and, my carnival-crazy friends assure me, most wonderful, exciting, and family-oriented amusement parks in America: Cedar Point. At 9:30 in the morning, tour buses are already linked like an Amtrak train down the road, cars are pouring into a parking lot big enough to declare independence, and lines grow at the gates. There's much to be enjoyed here, including swimming beaches, picnic areas, a marina, water slides, and other attractions; but the thing Cedar Point is famous for is thrills. I've heard of a Michigan man who loves the rides so much, he bought a plane and learned to fly it for the sole purpose of coming here.

Me, I'm a wimp. Scary rides scare me, and some of the very scariest, according to Carter Blocksma—my over-forty, ridin'-fool, coaster-wise brother—are here. "Cedar Point has more roller coasters than just about anywhere," he told me recently, "and they are incredible. One's called the Magnum XL2000, which is supposed to be the fastest and tallest roller coaster in the country. Another one, called Gemini, has two identical roller coasters racing on parallel tracks—the whole concept is to see which one gets there first. You go up a huge first hill and it goes *clickity-clickity-clickity,* and the initial drop literally takes you out of your seat—you have to hang on to the bar. Gemini was for a long time the biggest one in the Midwest. Then they also have something called the Blue Streak, which is a wooden roller coaster, and it's very important because the wooden roller coasters give you the bouncy effect that the rail-and-tube roller coasters don't. Then there's another one, called the Corkscrew, which turns you upside down about three times. There are others which I can't remember, but they are all a lot of fun."

For him, maybe; but my idea of a good time is the wave pool in

Sandusky, which I visit instead. Here, thanks to a machine that cranks up some pretty big waves, I body-surf in the comfortable confines of a swimming pool with a view of Lake Erie. It doesn't cost much, and after an hour of play I get on with my day.

I like Sandusky—it's down-home, close to the water, and who couldn't love a town with a city park department that springs for a wave pool? But it feels like a working town, too. At the New Shoreline Fishery I find six people in a dark shoe box of a room cheerfully and swiftly cleaning fish with thin, sharp knives. "You can't get the feel with an electric knife," explains Liz Segaard, the owner's daughter, who herself cut fish for ten years. Her dad is out fishing right now— he brings in yellow perch, white perch, white bass, catfish, bullheads, carp, and mullet. Fish are cleaned here, the ground-up guts going right into the sewer. Whole fish are shipped out in sixty-pound boxes to New York and Pennsylvania, or by plane to Texas and California in containers as heavy as eight hundred pounds.

From booths at an outdoor farmers' market down the street, I assemble a breakfast of hot coffee, jam-sweet strawberries, and homemade raisin-zucchini bread, which I consume on the spot, my gaze resting on the taut line between a pale sky and water smooth as a sheet.

CAN YOU BELIEVE a town where, from the last Saturday in June until Labor Day, you have to pay to get in? A ticket to a town? It's true, though—even the residents have to purchase a summer pass to get home in Lakeside, a strange, otherworldly community on the Lake Erie side of the Marblehead Peninsula. More than a hundred years old, Lakeside was founded by Methodists as a sort of spiritual resort, a wholesome family vacation spot where today some six hundred people live all year. I drive through the arching gate and feel as if I've gone through a time warp, as I encounter block after block of charming, immaculately kept old frame houses painted pink and yellow, beige and white, some dense with gingerbread. I leave the van next to brilliant flower beds and busy shuffleboards in a little park and walk to a huge Victorian hotel, where I let myself into a wide, unoccupied veranda filled with white wicker furniture and big flowered cushions. Outside, a breeze ruffles the tops of big shade trees. A church bell sounds. I wander past ice cream shops, a pizza place with red-checked curtains, a gleaming white replica of an old pavilion. Families fish off a wide cement pier.

"It's a Christian resort area, that's what's important to me," one fishing woman tells me. "It's been a part of my life for sixty years. I came here with my parents when I was very young. It's a great place to bring up children, because there are so many activities for them— free swimming lessons, tennis, bikes, boats, baseball, basketball, miniature golf."

Ship horns blow chords; gulls cry. I approach a man who looks administrative. Bingo! Don Wales is director of operations. "The Lakeside Association is a nonprofit organization that operates the hotels and businesses and a three-thousand-seat auditorium where there is programming for seventy consecutive summer nights," he tells me. "We charge a gate fee of seven dollars per person [up to eight dollars by 1994] plus a dollar for the car, but after that, recreation and entertainment is free. We have thirty-six hundred feet on Lake Erie, good swimming, an extensive sailing program, tennis on old English hard clay courts. Next week we host the West Ohio Methodist Conference, which brings about five thousand people to our grounds. We rent out rooms, cottages, hotels. Then we have the East Ohio conference. Our gate-fee season starts after that."

EXTENSIVE WETLANDS at the west side of Lake Erie block me from the shore. At last I have discovered some Lake Erie wilds— thousands of acres of wetlands smack on the track of migratory flyways, alive with wings, singing, snakes, flowers, and water-loving plants.

Along the road to Crane Creek State Park, an area flanked on one side by the Magee Marsh Wildlife Area (hunting in season) and on the other by the Ottawa National Wildlife Refuge (no hunting), I observe egrets, herons, and flocks of ducks, and brake for families of Canadian geese crossing the puddled road. Inside a lovely beam-and-glass building, I discover nine huge glass cases crammed with beautifully mounted birds, from an astonishing assortment of tiny warblers and songbirds to hawks, owls, eagles, ducks, and other waterbirds.

"This area is one of the richest places in the Midwest for birds," a ranger tells me. "We've had over three hundred species sighted here—as many as a hundred in one day! Ducks come in from the middle to the end of March, songbirds in May—our biggest day is Mother's Day weekend, when all the Audubon people come here." I mention that Audubon shot many of his subjects so they would hold still for him, but the ranger assures me that these birds were all found dead or injured beyond recovery.

It was probably the decoy display and gun collection that inspired that comment. I suddenly realize that western Lake Erie is not just a great place to sight waterbirds, it's also a great place to shoot them. Hunters and fishermen are among the eccentric few who have not in the past treated wetlands as wastelands and can probably be thanked for the small percentage that have not been drained and filled. It's the destruction and pollution of habitat, not hunting, that accounts for the decline in waterfowl populations, hunters often insist. Many acres of these remaining wetlands were once owned and kept at considerable effort and expense by hunters' clubs, for the purpose of raising, attracting, and killing "game" fish, "game" birds, and "game" animals. The "gaming" priority is still a big one—clear from the name of this building, which, although housing the Crane Creek Wildlife Experiment Station ("Ohio's center for the study of wetlands wildlife"), is called the Sportsmen Migratory Bird Center.

Hunters, whose donations and license fees finance the rehabilitation of many waterfowl-attracting areas, often have no time for "bleeding hearts," who are in turn appalled at those who take pleasure from taking life. So it seems odd to me that such a place caters to birdwatchers, even providing for them a beautiful beachside boardwalk over the wetlands, which, during a brief respite from the rain, I explore, feeling as if I were walking through treetops. Tiny wings flit everywhere, dripping and bedraggled—flycatchers, warblers, sparrows. When the rain resumes, I dash for the van, parked overlooking the mile-long beach where sometimes twenty thousand people play. Today I see only two, a girl and a boy, swimming and kissing in the rain.

IN CONTRAST to the rich wildlife areas, the nearby Maumee State Park camping area resembles a suburban mall parking lot—flat out in the open, no sheltering trees, no view of the lake. The campground is just the beginning, the ranger assures me, showing me a map that makes the place look like a plush resort. There are big plans for a major recreational area.

"End of April, beginning of May, when the walleyes spawn on the Maumee River, thousands of fishermen come here," he tells me. "You can't believe—these guys line the river, in all kinds of weather. Sometimes they fight when their lines get tangled up, or they get picked up by a ranger—you aren't allowed to snag a fish [hook its body with an unbaited hook], you can only catch him by the mouth. If you snag one, they can take your car and take you to jail and all kinds of things, so it's kind of a unique place. People come all the way from Texas to go fishing here."

"Do you fish?"

"Not really. I don't have time, and Lake Erie is a dangerous lake. Storms blow up real fast. You get these big rolling waves, twenty, thirty feet high. Or ten-footers close together. Guys go out in these little boats and some of them die out there. I had a friend got caught in a storm and never made it back. I took a safe-boating course and learned enough to sell my boat." Speaking of storms, he tells me, there's a tornado warning out tonight—about twenty funnels have been sighted in Illinois and Indiana, and the storm is heading this way.

The sky looks okay now, so I drive through a lot of country to a lakeshore restaurant he recommends called Sonny's Bay Shore Supper Club, where Sonny Berry himself tends bar, treating me to a sidecar, then a brandy alexander made with ice cream, claiming, "There's very little alcohol in that one—it's for a short person." Then, as he washes glasses, he says, "This area was a swamp years ago. Wasn't really that much to it. Then they drained the swamp and they cut down the trees and stuff."

"Was that an improvement?"

"Not really. But it is what they call progress. Civilization. It had to happen. No way could we live like they did a hundred years ago. We got two atomic energy plants now—one right across the lake at Monroe, another up the road. Some people come back, they'd never recognize the area."

The restaurant is very crowded, although it seems to me located a healthy drive from any town. Sonny talks while he works. "This place used to be a dance hall. During Prohibition, when the mob ran booze across the lake from Canada, that"—he points a dish towel at a table against the wall—"is where all the gangsters sat. If we took our paneling down, you could see bullet holes."

Back at the park, amid scattered RVs, I watch the storm, my view unblocked by anything taller than a trailer. Lightning, horizontal and vertical, shatters the sky; thunder crashes; rain drums on the roof; the wind tears through the park like a train come alive, screaming and rocking the van. My battery-run radio reports damage here, damage there. I move the van to a site next to the concrete washrooms, the only available shelter, then sit in the back, upright, tense as a cat in a boat, listening to storm warnings and terrible music until three o'clock in the morning.

JUNE 4

TOLEDO is a boat town. I discover this from Mike Schabeck, whom I have stopped to ask directions and who—how lucky can I get?—is the marina coordinator for the city of Toledo. "We've got eight yacht clubs and probably thirty to forty marinas on the Maumee and Ottawa rivers," he tells me. "There are thousands of boaters here within a few square miles." Schabeck's also a member of a private, nonprofit group called the United States Power Squadron, which "teaches safe boating and boating education to thousands. There's probably seventy thousand people involved nationwide. Classes are six weeks long, and most marinas know where to find us."

Up the road a piece, I find two unrelated yacht clubs side by side, an odd proximity, so I turn into a forked driveway and bear right, beginning with the more elegant Toledo Yacht Club. The place is very quiet: the parking places reserved for the Commodore, Vice-Commodore, Rear Commodore, and Past Commodore are empty. Inside, I'm swallowed by a luxurious hush of deep blue carpeting, high ceilings, gilt frames, white tablecloths. A tastefully dressed woman approaches to politely investigate my conspicuous presence here. "That was donated by President Taft," she tells me, pointing to the very large President's Cup in a trophy case. "It's for the annual Mills Race, which, as a matter of fact, will take place this Thursday. It's a sailboat race, started by Merrill Mills—the boats race from the harbor light to Put-in-Bay."

My inquiry about membership fees is met with appalled resistance, but I do learn that membership would involve an initiation fee and/or a social membership fee, a monthly fee, and a requirement to spend at least thirty-five dollars a month in the dining room. Should I be so blessed as to have acquired a place to put my boat ("This usually involves a two-to-three-year wait"), I will be charged an additional slip fee, which all by itself, for a thirty-by-twelve-foot vessel, could add something like $750 a season.

"But what's nice about belonging to any yacht club is that most of them are affiliated," she explains. "So if you belong here, you can go down to the Maumee River Yacht Club and use their facilities. You can use any club that's affiliated with yours. There's the AYC, which is the Associated Yacht Clubs; the DRYA, which is the Detroit River Yachting Association; the ILYA, the Interlake Yachting Association; the list goes on. Some people choose their clubs by their affiliates. For instance, if you live in Toledo but you do a lot of business in Detroit, you might want to join a club that has an affiliate in Detroit."

Next, I drive over to the Bay View Yacht Club and enter a large room with a vinyl floor, some tables, and a bar—something like a supper club off-hours. "So what's the difference between your club and the club next door?" I ask a couple of guys sitting at the bar.

"We're solvent and they're not!" The wisecracker is Wade Scanberry, who, after I introduce myself, explains that this is a working club. "Over there, you pay *x* dues. Here you also pay dues, but you can work off part of your dues at so much per hour doing stuff for the club."

"Yeah. Like he's a carpenter; I'm an electrician. We each do our particular trade," explains the other man.

"How much does it cost to be a member here?"

"Four hundred? Four-fifty?" guesses Scanberry. "But you can work off two hundred of that. You have to work twenty hours a season— you can take tickets, do wiring, or whatever. Anything less than twenty hours, you're fined ten dollars an hour."

"Do you have to wait long for a boat slip?"

"Forever. Seven, eight years—more. It takes years to get on the waiting list—we keep it to fifty—and then more years to get a membership—our last new member came in three years ago—and then more years to get a dock. We have 275 members and 162 docks. All docks are bid on a seniority basis. Me, I have a thirty-foot dock and a twenty-one-foot boat. Costs me about fifty-eight dollars for the whole season, and that includes the fifteen-dollar electrical fee. You can see why people want to get in here. We can be reasonable because if something goes wrong with the docks, we go fix it ourselves. We got our own pile driver, we got out own lift, we got the latest of everything."

Outside on the docks, Scanberry introduces me to the Associated Yacht Clubs' historian, Bill Glass, whom we find on his knees shining the deck of a lovely little sixty-six-year-old sailboat. "I love to watch men scrub floors," I tease, guessing that no sailboat would ever have a "floor." An old salt with a sense of humor, Glass welcomes me into the tiny, wood-paneled cabin. With his white hair and handlebar mustache, he could pass for Mark Twain. I am not surprised to hear that Glass has been voted Old Man of the River, which makes him an honorary member of every yacht club in town. Heck, he's even the honorary chairman of next door's Mills Race.

I TURN NORTH into Michigan, where more wetlands block the shore. Then, at Sterling State Park, Michigan's only Lake Erie state park, I park near a narrow gravel beach flanked by a coal-burning power plant on one side and a nuclear power plant on the other. The view is so uninspiring that I eat my lunch in the driver's seat, not bothering to get out, until two things change my mind: first, a guidebook propped on the steering wheel informs me that this nearly thousand-acre park has an excellent wetlands trail; and second, I see two killdeer mating at the edge of the parking lot. Wow!

I set off in a cloud of gnats, clutching a trail map, binoculars around my neck, bird book in my back pocket. Soon I encounter an educational display, which declares that "a wetland is not just a wetland." I learn about five kinds of wetlands (see note, p. 79) and some things I didn't know about the American lotus, the adopted symbol of Lake Erie wetlands revitalization: it has seeds that can take ten years to germinate, leaves that grow to three feet, and flowers, served up at summer's end, as big as dinner plates.

Along the two-mile-or-more trail, I am entertained by a Baltimore oriole's liquid song, a woodchuck dashing across my path, a muskrat slipping into the lagoon. I am dive-bombed by a blackbird. Cotton from cottonwood trees drifts through the air. It's just turning into a nice little hike when I pass under sizzling power lines coming from the power plant. I climb a wildlife observation tower and find myself directly under fourteen power lines, slung between a series of towers straight out of *Star Wars*. Electricity crackles and spits, buzzing deep in my guts. Surely, I think, an observer, standing at some distance, can see my bones. Below me, all manner of birds flit; spawning carp slap the lagoon; pale lavender fleabane blooms; and a bluebird shares a tree with a yellow warbler.

Back on the trail, I cut through woods along a dirty-looking channel under arching branches. Mosquitoes whine, dine on the softest part of my neck. Birds sing against a far-off hum of factories, jets, power lines, and trains. A chipping sparrow, chestnut head nodding, hops importantly in front of me. I observe a blue heron, an egret, a long-haired young man aiming an arrow into the lagoon. *Zing!* He pulls in a huge carp, yanks out the arrow, slings the carp into the grass, aims again with a powerful-looking weapon strung with lines and pulleys.

"What do you do with the fish?" I ask him.

"Throw 'em over there."

"Do you come here often?"

"Two, three times a day." The carp, bleeding from large holes on either side, wriggles back into the water. The boy shrugs. "Won't live long," he says. Back at the office, I'm told that shooting carp with a power bow is perfectly legal. Some towns, like Caseville on Lake Huron, even celebrate it with an annual festival.

Note: I became confused about wetlands—everything I read seemed to type them differently. One source divided wetlands into wet meadows (mushy, but without much standing water), wooded wetlands (waterlogged only during certain seasons), coastal marshes (with aquatic plant communities surviving various water depths and conditions), shrub wetlands/marshes (with a few inches to a few feet of water), and bogs (depressions filled with decayed vegetation and standing water). Another source, pointing out that coastal wetlands are affected by wave action and changing water levels, divided them into "zones" similar to the first descriptions but not quite the same. A poster from the Michigan Department of Natural Resources admits that its categories—marsh (flooded grassland), swamp (flooded woodland), and bog (depression filled with decayed vegetation, acidic soil, and standing water)—are vastly oversimplified. I also encountered other descriptive words like "swale," "fen," "strand," "wet meadow," "seasonal wetland," "permanent wetland," "aquatic wetland," "riverine," "delta," "unrestricted bay," "shallow sloping," "pond wetlands," "sedge meadow."

Much of the confusion is due to the fact that until recently, few of us even knew the term "wetland." Those who did tended to be sports persons, or naturalists who described the different areas in terms of their specialities—plants, freshwater ecology, soil, and so on. Then, about twenty-five years ago, the sharp decrease in many bird populations and the polluted condition of the Great Lakes began to alarm everyone. Even the government realized that without wetlands, the Great Lakes couldn't be saved. Wetlands probably produce more wildlife than any other Great Lakes habitat and are also necessary to help clean pollutants from streams and rivers before the water enters the lakes.

Unfortunately, two-thirds of the original Great Lakes wetlands and three-quarters of Michigan's have vanished, most of them drained, filled, and "civilized." Saving wetlands has become a big issue. During the 1970s and 1980s, both federal and state laws were passed protecting our few remaining wetlands. It suddenly became very important to a wide variety of ordinary folks to know exactly what defines a wetland. Could a retiring auto worker build a retirement home on that sometimes soggy piece of real estate bought twenty years ago? Could a farmer sow winter wheat in a dry depression that became a pond in spring? The sport and scientific terms were not clear enough. Legal definitions and very particular descriptions of various wetlands were needed. Today it's politics that influences those definitions most.

AT THE POINTE MOUILLÉE STATE GAME AREA, I discover an unusual attempt to actually build a wetland. "This marsh wouldn't exist without the dikes here," Rex Ainslee, game area manager, tells me. "We're restoring the marsh as best we can." Working with over half of the area's four thousand acres, the U.S. Army Corps of Engineers and the Michigan Department of Natural Resources are cooperating to manipulate water levels and provide vegetation to attract waterfowl, "which is our main objective." Let us not forget, Rex Ainslee reminds me, that this project is paid for by hunters, who are taxed for licenses, guns, ammunition, and other sports equipment.

Outside, I find two men on a tractor on their way to plant corn, millet, and buckwheat for the birds. One of them guesses that this might be the largest project of its kind in the world. "First, they're building a dike here"—he points to a place on a map. "Second, they're putting a dam and a pumping station across Mouillée Creek. Then they're going to divert the water to come back out at the lake down here."

"Woodchucks dig holes through the dikes," observes the second man dryly.

Well, no one said it'd be easy. Building a marsh must be like replacing a rain forest—close to impossible.

THE DETROIT RIVER, LAKE ST. CLAIR, AND THE ST. CLAIR RIVER

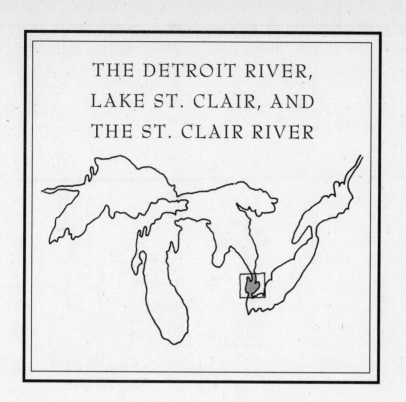

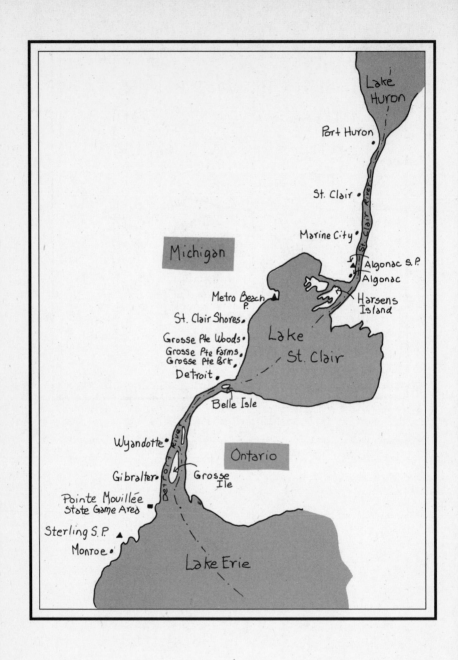

The Detroit River, Lake St. Clair,
and the St. Clair River

JUNE 5

AT THE MOUTH of the Detroit River, which is a strait—a narrow channel connecting two bodies of water (here, Lake Erie and Lake St. Clair)—I become lost in a bewildering maze of water-flanked roads and canals in Venice-like Gibraltar. "You get in, you'll never get out," laughs a clerk at City Hall after my literally narrow escape. "We're not really a tourist town. Most people just come to catch the ferry to Boblo." I'd seen the many billboards announcing this service, but the Canadian island amusement park doesn't interest me. What does are Gibraltar's canals. All three women at the City Hall office claim to have boats tied up in liquid backyards.

"Don't you ever get drowned out?"

The question elicits loud laughter. "Oh, occasionally," the talkative one admits. "I think 1986 was the last time we had floods from the canals. But hey, I'm movin' up north to the woods. I've had it down here. It never used to be like this—used to be so quiet."

I soon see what she means. Heading north, I encounter smokestacks, power towers, a resin plant, factories with massive parking lots. A quaint power plant appears: an old red brick building with a candy-striped smokestack and tile-roofed guardhouse. I pull up to the old wrought-iron gate and roll down the window for a robust, uniformed woman who refuses me admittance. "This is the Detroit Edison Trenton Channel Power Plant," she says, "the oldest power plant in the Detroit system."

"May I photograph the gate?"

"Absolutely not. How do I know you're not a Czechoslovak-ian spy?"

Well, there's an exciting possibility! I dodge over a nearby bridge to Grosse Ile (pronounced, I'm told, "gross ill"), famous retreat of Detroit wealthy. I drive around the island looking for a pleasant spot to eat my sandwich, but search as I may—river on my right; luscious mansions, rolling estates, pillared colonials, and impenetrable castles on my left—I can find not one place to park. Every waterfront street is posted.

Finding Grosse Ile no friendlier than the industrial wastes, I cross back over the one-minute bridge to Jefferson, a street that skewers Detroit between its northern and southern suburbs. In Wyandotte, a busy surburban town, I finally picnic in a lovely downtown boardwalk park along the river. Then it's north on Jefferson through miles and miles of industry on the Detroit River, a scarred, scary land. I go by the Detroit Marine Terminals, a paper company, a cement factory, a steel mill, an exit for the Ambassador Bridge to Canada. I don't dare stop to take pictures: the road feels narrow, the hurtling trucks like attacking tanks, the environs like a war zone. It is with considerable relief that I spy, dominating the skyline of downtown Detroit, the famous five-tower Renaissance Center and soon spiral deep into its concrete gray garage.

I LOVE TALL BUILDINGS. I immediately whisk up an outside glass elevator to the Summit Steak House on the seventy-second floor, where I get the strong impression that I'm seeing Detroit from space. There's a deep roar beneath me, a hum, an odd feeling of movement. "We are revolving," a formally attired waiter explains. "You're hear-ing the motors. We make a complete turn every forty-five minutes." I walk all the way around the ring of elegant, white-tableclothed, upholstered booths, peering out the windows.

The spaceship feeling is reinforced on the floors below, where shops, offices, and a wide selection of ethnic, fast-food, and elegant restaurants mix in a neon twilight, in oddly shaped, mazelike spaces. I feel trapped and I soon tire of it. I manage to find my car and head out for Belle Isle, a nearby island in the Detroit River I'd spotted from the top.

A charming bridge lined with quaint lampposts leads to Belle Isle but I am surprised by the island's shabby, littered, uncared-for appearance. It definitely looks run-down. Still, what a place! At nearly a thousand acres, Belle Isle is one of the largest city parks in the country. From the one-way perimeter road, I watch longboats navigate one of the busiest rivers in the world. A massive, formal fountain crowded with concrete turtles, dolphins, and lionesses appears to drench the Detroit skyline. Squabbling gulls fight for potato chips tossed sky-high by a giggling, pink-hair-ribboned tot. There are picnic tables, lawns, and trees. There are lakes, lagoons, and ducks.

The history museum, aquarium, and botanical gardens share a worn, inviting elegance, accessible and intimate, that makes me want to see them all. The Dossin Great Lakes Museum is closed today, so I begin with the Belle Isle Aquarium, built in 1904, the oldest in North America. Of all the aquariums I've ever seen—including Boston's, Chicago's, and Monterey's—I know I'll like this one best. I pass under vine-covered carved dolphins into a dimly lit hall lined with large glass windows. I move from tiny pupfish to a huge electric eel that, at specified feeding times, can be heard over loudspeakers stunning its lunch with 650 volts. I ogle an iridescent shark, koi, piranhas, several species of stingray, chocolate and redtail catfish. These are all freshwater fish. The place is crowded; voices of children echo in the large hall. I elbow in to see for myself an Australian lungfish. In a free-standing case, tiny tangerine fish appear to fly. This place may not be large, but some of the residents certainly are, including the pale-yellow albino snapping turtles staring at me with pink eyes. An excellent collection of Great Lakes fish includes lake sturgeon, spotted and long-nose gar, species of perch, muskie, bass, salmon, pike, and trout.

I find the curator, Doug Sweet, in a small, tiled office near the entrance. He's a mild-mannered limnologist with brown hair and eyes, wearing glasses, a brown plaid shirt, brown pants, and brown shoes. A limnologist, he explains, specializes in freshwater ecology. Sweet patiently answers my questions. The oldest fish is the short-nosed gar, acquired as an adult in the 1950s. The most valuable is the Australian lungfish, "which you can't get anymore," here since the mid-sixties.

Sweet himself has several special interests. He collects many of the Great Lakes fish himself, preferring to begin with fingerlings and subadults; he breeds several species of freshwater stingray; and he's collected at least twelve species of threatened or endangered fish, one of which is a mouth breeder (incubating eggs and young in its mouth) from Lake Victoria, endangered by a Nile perch that can reach six hundred pounds. When I suggest that Lake Victoria has nothing to do with the Great Lakes, Sweet says, "Africa has great lakes, too."

Racing approaching rain clouds, I check out the giant palms, cacti, ferns, and orchids under the 85-foot glass dome of the Whitcomb Garden Conservatory and stroll outdoor gardens blazing with peonies, iris, columbine, rock roses, southern roses, and poppies. At the zoo, I stride three-quarters of a mile of undulating, elevated boardwalk, looking down on exotic birds and animals. I leave Belle Isle only two dollars (the zoo ticket) lighter.

JUNE 6

I USUALLY DON'T mention negative personal encounters—a person may just be having a bad day and it's no fun writing about nasty people—but today, along the south shore of Lake St. Clair, I am startled by the aggressive contempt for courtesy and the unveiled threats that spokespersons for some of Detroit's wealthiest seem to find an appropriate way to deal with "outsiders." North of Detroit, Jefferson Avenue changes to Lake Shore Drive, edging the affluent suburbs of Grosse Pointe. Just inland, block follows block of large-lawned, several-storied brick houses; enormous estates line Lake St. Clair. Each of the five Grosse Pointe communities has a "residential park," which only residents and their guests may use. Most turn me away, but I am allowed briefly to tour one by a young gate guard. Within the high metal fence, I discover what appears to be a tax-supported country club, a sprawl of pools, tennis courts, a marina, and other facilities.

Finding no lake access for the likes of me, however, I can't wait to get out of here. These wealthy north-side suburbs feel as uncomfortably exclusive as the south-side industry felt intrusive, and it occurs to me that quite possibly the places are connected, the south end in some cases being the shadow side of the north.

An employee of the neighboring, more modest St. Clair Shores offers another perspective. "It really is a problem, being so close to the city. People who don't live here often don't care how they leave it. Even this town keeps its parks more modest than it needs to, fearing that if we develop them, we'll attract so many Detroit users that there'll be no room left for us."

MORE THAN HALFWAY UP Lake St. Clair, on a bull's-head-shaped peninsula, I board a little "trackless train" and tour the vast acres of Metro Beach Metropark: wetlands, playing fields, a marina, a boat ramp, a golf course, shuffleboard courts, a basketball court, a pool, a pavilion, shops, concessions, and a wide, bather-thick beach. Following this, I stroll a delightful nature trail, finishing at a brand-new nature center. "Recreation is a bigger thing here than wildlife," naturalist Leslie Sutton tells me. "But they've just built this nature center and employed me permanently here."

Sutton welcomes my questions. I wonder, for example, about a lop-eared rabbit I saw on the nature trail. It didn't look like any wild rabbit I'd ever seen. Sutton explains that last fall somebody dumped it here, and she hadn't given it a week, what with all the hawks, owls, and foxes in the park, but it survived the winter. "That's no dumb bunny. We hear about the public going right up to it, but we can't catch it—every time it sees somebody in a uniform, it skedaddles."

About power lines in parks, Sutton says that at the park where she worked previously, she used to take a fluorescent tube on night walks and watch it light up when she was under the power lines. "Detroit Edison says that these are nothing compared to the ones out East. Those are the ones that people blame for birth defects. But it makes you wonder. The hair stands up on the back of your neck."

I ask her about the unusual number of swans I'd seen here. "We started with four mute swans—you can tell mute swans by their orange bills—and now we have a hundred and twenty, and they can be a real problem, because mute swans don't migrate," explains Sutton. "They're an alien species, imported from Europe. They're extremely territorial. They can take over an area, chasing out native waterfowl. People like the swans, but we are going to have to move some of them."

Metro Beach Metropark costs less than a movie and is open to all.

IN THE MIDDLE of this peninsula, just south of the Selfridge Air National Guard Base where the Clinton River winds through to the lake, I come upon more boats than I've ever seen in my life. Every other car is pulling a boat. Boats stick out into the road on either side. Huge forklifts lower boats from warehouses where more boats are stacked like toys. Boats float along the river, are tied up at riverside restaurant docks, fill slip after slip in marina after marina. You can even rent a "boat condo," an efficiency built over the water with room for your boat beneath.

"If you want to see something hilarious, just wait for a thunderstorm," laughs a sailor who knows this area well. "You got all these boats out on Lake St. Clair, and all of a sudden ever' one of 'em head back for this little cut where the Clinton River come out. You got big boats, you got big *big* boats, you got little boats, you got itty-bitty boats, and they're all headin' for the same place. These little boats, they got a real problem, because the big boats, they just macho their way through there. 'Course, sometimes the smart thing in a storm is to stay out on the lake—not likely to hit a rock or some other boat out in the middle. These boats all crowding into the river there, I'm surprised more of 'em don't capsize or run into each other."

Trying to find my way around the base, I come upon a lakeside bar called Sail Inn Topless. Across the street, a boat shop advertises PAULA'S TOPS AND COVERS.

TOO SMALL to be a Great Lake itself, Lake St. Clair is sometimes called "the Heart of the Great Lakes," partly because of its position, but mostly because it really is shaped like a heart. On a map, it hangs like a pendant from the St. Clair River, the strait linking Lake Huron with Lake St. Clair. At the top of the heart, the St. Clair River pours into the cleavage, splitting into three channels around a group of island wetlands called the St. Clair Flats. Between the South Channel (the shipping channel and the U.S.–Canadian border) and the Middle Channel lies Harsens Island, just a hop from the mainland town of Algonac and the Harsens Island ferry.

A stone's throw from the ferry, Joyce Bryson, an energetic, upbeat woman, shows me around the Boat (named the *Port Welcome*), one of a few floating restaurants on the east coast of Michigan. She and her son recently bought the three-tiered ex–tour boat in Baltimore and brought it back twenty-six hundred miles, down the St. Lawrence River and across Lakes Ontario, Erie, and St. Clair (tracing, I tell her, by water the journey I just did by land). It's happy hour, and I join a group of friendly women at the gleaming bar, while one describes, with help from the others, who all attended, her wedding on the Boat last Christmas. Finally, I head up the St. Clair River for the Algonac State Park, just minutes north.

The park is crowded, and my van, sited facing a busy road just yards away and crouching between two looming RVs, feels like the little house huddled between skyscrapers in Virginia Burton's children's book *The Little House*. I can see the color TV flickering behind the high picture windows on each side of me, but the older couples aren't watching TV; they're watching me as I cook and eat my spaghetti dinner at the outdoor table between them.

I don't care. Arching over me are exquisite, doming, scudding clouds fired by the sunset. In front of me, just beyond the road, freighters glide by, lights bright along the sides, the last sun slicing across the smokestacks. This narrow twenty-seven-mile river is a fine and intimate place to watch freighters. After dark, lying in the back of the van, I listen for them, purring like big cats, gently rumbling in my guts. I can feel one before I can see it—*purrrrrr, purrrrrrr, purrrrrrr*—and I sit up and watch it slip by. After it passes, Canadian streetlights fall in shining columns across the water, like bar codes of light. All night through my sleep, the ships hum by, trains sigh, and military jets whine home.

JUNE 7

ONE OF THE NICEST things to do on the twelve-by-seven-mile expanse of farm- and wetlands of Harsens Island is hunt wildlife, which I do with binoculars, there being no season on appreciation. In my lens, I capture some fetching red-headed ducks and numerous coots—tiny white-billed black "ducks" that swim like comical wind-up toys, their heads jerking back and forth. Black-capped terns hover before steep dives. Huge carp roil the marshes. Lengthy (nonpoisonous) black snakes live here, says a resident at his roadside mailbox. Mink and muskrats thrive.

I drive by the little year-round town of Sans Souci, past modest cottages along sandy beaches, wild purple and yellow iris, fields, marshes, watery ditches. At a Department of Natural Resources game office, where hunters check in, seventeen pairs of real duck wings have been brought from aloft and are now stuck to a board as an identification tool. I learn that most ducks are legal game here, but not canvasbacks. "Canvasbacks are the best-tasting ducks of all, because their favorite food is wild celery," a helpful summer employee tells me. "But they've been almost annihilated—people shot 'em by the bags—so you can't shoot those anymore." Puddle ducks, like black ducks, teals, and wood ducks, make good eating; unpopular targets are diving ducks. "All fish-eating ducks taste terrible, especially mergansers. They stink—you can't even cook 'em."

Crossing back to Algonac on the bargelike ferry, I head up the St. Clair River. I go through several towns, stop to watch freighters, walk "the longest freshwater boardwalk in the world" in the town of St. Clair, from which I view, across the river, Canadian oil refineries and storage tanks. Then, stopping at Port Huron, I watch a red freighter approaching from under the Blue Water Bridge, which arches to Canada. A young man in a pink shirt, seated by his car next to a camera on a tripod, is watching it, too, through binoculars.

His name is Ron Morgan, he tells me, and the ship is the *Federal St. Laurent*, a 622.7-foot Canadian bulk carrier built in 1978. Morgan knows a lot about freighters—he's been chasing them for ten years. A paramedic from Bay City, he often makes the two-hour trip to count and photograph ships here. He's sighted and photographed most of them, but there's a thousand-footer that's been eluding him, which he'll chase for a hundred miles, checking papers like the *Detroit News* for arrival times. A scanner in the back of his open hatchback is tuned into ship radios.

It's an obsession, Morgan confesses. "Three or four years ago, my wife was in labor and a ship called the *Middletown* was over at the stone dock in Bay City, and I says, 'Gail?' and she says, 'Go ahead.' So I went there, photographed it, and got back in time to see Marcus born. Marcus saw his first freighter—a thousand-footer—three days later." In the seven hours since morning, Morgan has logged nine ships.

Before he heads home to his understanding wife, Morgan tells me that a lot of people around the Great Lakes watch their areas and report to the *Lake Log Ships*, a biweekly publication in Boyne City, Michigan, that publishes information on what ships are doing: "who's laid up where, who's hauling and what, unusual cargoes, things like that."

A few minutes north, at Lakeport State Park, a hulking, chivalrous black-bearded man from a neighboring campsite confesses, as we wave mosquitoes from a canned-soup supper, that although he hunts and eats bear, he can't bring himself to kill deer, which "wouldn't hurt nobody." He's trying out a new gadget the size of a cigarette lighter that's supposed to discourage mosquitoes with a high, irritating whine. Unfortunately, it seems to attract them.

LAKE
HURON

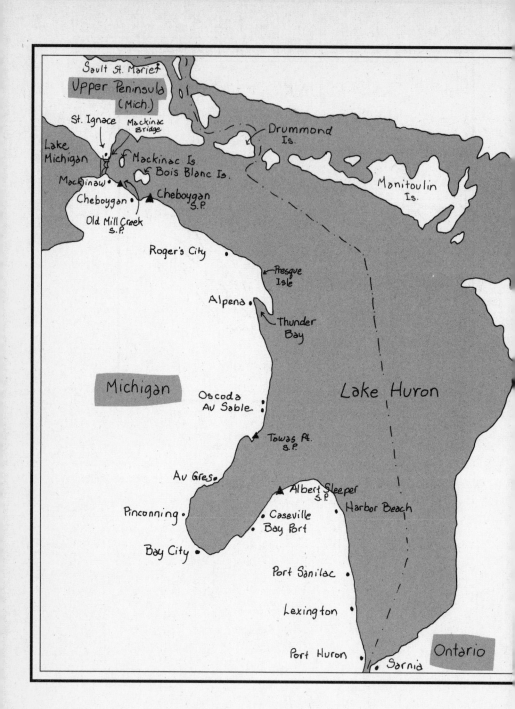

Lake Huron

JUNE 8

DRIVING UP the Lake Huron shore into the area known as "the thumb" of mitt-shaped lower Michigan, I'm aware that something feels different here. I can't quite put my finger on it. Maybe it's the lake, which, even in today's chilly drizzle, seems to reflect a sharper light; whether behind clouds or not, the sun rising instead of setting on that two-tone horizon seems to put a new slant on things. Or perhaps it's the replacement of ostentation and frenzy with a slow, worn homeyness. Or the agricultural landscape: rows and rows of beans, apple trees, sugar beets, each field narrowing into a lesson in perspective. North of Lexington, Tringali Orchard sells produce from a small white frame store crammed with bright fruits and other foods. I pick out some Spies from a slatted basket and ask the aproned Charlie Tringali if the apples came from his orchard.

"Oh, yeah," he says, as he takes a signed blank check and a shopping list from a patron. "They're from last year. Have you ever heard of controlled atmosphere? That's when they shut the door and they don't open it until about this time of year and the apples keep just like they were picked the same day. We store three thousand bushels of apples that way."

Tringali fills in the check, puts it in the cash register, and thanks the man by name before he resumes: "In the thumb area, there's nobody else got an orchard like this. This is an all-apple orchard: Spies, Red and Golden Delicious, McIntosh. My dad was an old produce man from way back. Me and my five brothers, we all had supermarkets in Detroit. I lost the last one in the riot of '67—burnt me to the ground. Back then, this place here was only open on weekends; now we're open all year round."

Tringali sends me to the YWCA camp next door, where I park in front of an old log lodge on a tree-thick lakeshore and am welcomed at the door—from the inside—by five goats, followed by director Jo Laidlaw. "They're going back to the farm this afternoon," she laughs, shooing them out.

To my astonishment, Laidlaw cheerfully drops her preparations for tomorrow's two hundred and fifty arriving guests to treat me to a high-spirited tour. The hardwood floor of the lodge, built in 1929, today supports visiting contradancers as well as summer campers. The tiles in the fireplace were made by girls now grown. Run by the Detroit YWCA, Camp Cavell started taking girls in 1914, says Laidlaw. "It was considered very healthy for Detroit girls. In those days, they stayed all summer. Now we have fifty girls at a time for three or four weeks. There's also a Me and My Mom program: on a typical family vacation, moms work twice as hard as they did at home, but here everything's taken care of. Our Women's Getaway Weekend is really popular, too."

Shouting off the goats, which have tracked us down by climbing an outdoor stairway to the balcony, I notice a nice sandy beach. "Well, you never know about the beach here," Laidlaw warns. "The storms on Lake Huron are legendary—we can lose ten or fifteen feet of beach in one night. You get up one morning and your beach is gone . . . then, another morning, find a whole new one."

The musty smell of wood, varnish, old books, needled woods, lake air, and camp food makes me nostalgic—I spent some of my own youth in places like this. Upstairs, in another huge room, is another stone fireplace and another long screened porch. I envision myself reading away a hot day, horizontal in an old-time swing. Suddenly, the whole place begins smelling like a chocolate factory, and we are drawn through a two-hundred-person dining room into a brightly lit kitchen where three women and a man chat and work. Tim Fenner, a local sculptor, is dipping apple-sized balls of dough with an ice cream scoop and lining them up onto trays. Sheets of preposterously large chocolate chip cookies cool on a large wooden tabletop. "I made the mistake of doing it right once a couple years ago and I've made thousands of them since," sighs Fenner. I eat one with a cup of coffee and time stops. My senses are stunned with rich, hot perfection, a chocolate chip cookie epiphany, a synchronicity of place, taste, and time.

UP THE MICHIGAN "THUMB" on Route 25, through milky fog emerges this sign: WELCOME TO PORT SANILAC: FIRST HARBOR OF REFUGE ON THE GREAT LAKES. It isn't apparent what makes this "harbor of refuge" different from any other harbor. No one here seems to know either, except that it's "man-made."

Confused, I call the Department of Natural Resources. In 1947, I'm told, Congress funded a piece of legislation that enabled the U.S. Army Corps of Engineers, in cooperation with the Michigan DNR, to fill in the gaps between the commercial harbors along Michigan shores. The idea was to provide a refuge during dangerous Great Lakes storms about every thirty miles, so that a boat would never be more than fifteen miles from safety. Although technically any harbor is a harbor of refuge, those built under this program are officially called that. Port Sanilac was the first of these, and, like the others, it's primarily recreational. At least half the slips at most harbors of refuge are available on a first come, first served basis—not rented seasonally or reserved.

NEAR THE THUMB TIP at Harbor Beach—once a thriving commercial port, now largely recreational—I come upon a young woman rocking on the front porch of a small stone lakeshore house. I find so many museums along the lakeshore that I can't write about them all, but Sharon Kramer and this 1874 James and Jane Grice House prove irresistible.

We move through the neat, dense assemblage of art, artifacts, and oddities donated or loaned, Kramer says, by persons in the community. The resonant chimes came from the Catholic church; the ethnic dolls were sent home by sailors who worked the oceans in winter, when ice closes down commerce on the Great Lakes. Stitched on the quilts on the wall are names and dates going back as far as 1834. A "sad iron" was so called because it got too hot to hang on to.

I finger butter churns, a butter bowl, a wooden washing machine, a dry sink (no drain), a weapon-length hat pin, and a porcelain, vase-like hair receiver—"Women saved the hairs from their brush in there for a hairpiece or switch." The raffia cuffs were worn by butchers to protect their wrists; ice skates had to be screwed onto the soles of the wearer's shoes. Upstairs: a room of elegant clothing, linens, and jewelry; a war room with swords, guns, and uniforms; an early-industry room displaying quaint typewriters and adding machines. The marine room holds the crowning jewel: a truly jewellike three-thousand-pound (one source says three-ton) Fresnel lens taken from the squat, round-towered Harbor Beach Lighthouse. Made in France in 1881, the many-faceted lens looks like an elaborate, transparent beehive. (See note, below.)

Outside, we pass the spring promise of an herb garden: spearmint, apple mint, comfrey, basil, sage, pinks, yarrow, dill, garlic, oregano, thyme, aguga (used for blue dye), pennyroyal, and chives. Inside a barn, we walk among old medical equipment (wheelchairs, eye charts, bedpans); lethal-looking farm equipment (a potato sorter, a chopping box for corn, a hog scalder—a huge, cartoon-type black pot on a tripod); a mannikin in a fur-collared coat driving a sleigh. Next to the barn, an old schoolhouse—oiled floors, old blackboards, a pot-bellied stove—until two years ago was actually in use. "Twelve of my ninety-six high-school classmates came from one-room schoolhouses," says Kramer.

Back at the house, I ask for a card—something with the museum name and address on it—and Kramer, who says she's in a hurry to get home to milk the cows, sighs, "Oh lord," and finally finds me a postcard picturing the Fresnel lens. The requested donation is a dollar.

Note: You have to see a Fresnel lens to believe it, but it's a rare sight now. Invented by French physicist Augustin Fresnel in 1822, Fresnel lenses are classified into seven "orders," or sizes, and use prisms to surround and concentrate the light from a single source into a powerful beam. Lenses ranging from two to six (one source claims twelve) feet high, with the largest a first-order lens, were installed in seventy-five Great Lakes lighthouses by 1857, doubling their ranges to ten to fourteen miles, and became standard equipment in new lighthouses. At first the lamps were fueled with sperm-whale oil, but by 1940 most used a single thousand-watt incandescent bulb. Today, nearly all Fresnel lenses have been replaced with plastic lenses or airport-type aerobeacons.

JUNE 9

THIS MORNING, as I ride through the Albert E. Sleeper State Park on the broad tip of the Thumb, I'm kicking myself for succumbing to exhaustion last night and not holding out for a place I really liked. I could camp all summer in one of the sites tucked into the trees here—the place isn't clipped close as a military haircut, as many campgrounds are. There's a deep-woods feel here I'm hungry for; a big, clean, sandy beach with a beautiful boardwalk over the dunes—no rocks or algae, as I saw yesterday. Well, such is life. I drive south down the west side of the Thumb along Saginaw Bay, passing through marshy Caseville—a family-fun town with golf courses, ice cream places, a water slide, even a roller-skating rink—then into wetlands again.

Just before lunch, in Bay Port, I pull up to a warehouse sort of building by a dock and park near an elaborate sign: ". . . The Bay Port Fish Company [was established] in 1895. At [its] peak in the 1920s and 30s [it] shipped tons of whitefish, perch, walleye and carp to New York and Chicago in refrigerated railroad cars. Once known as the largest commercial fish port in the world, Bay Port operates its commercial fishery much as it did in the past."

Inside, a hubbub of customers and workers shout over loud radios. Crates are stacked everywhere. On a white refrigerated counter lie limp, whole smoked herring, smoked trout, walleye fillets, smoked salmon, smoked catfish. Catfish? The woman behind the counter says smoked fish is an area speciality. "Catfish is one of the cheapest"—$3.50 a pound—"but I think it's one of our best smoked fish, that and smoked whitefish."

Do they catch much whitefish here? "So far this year, we've caught over 183,000 pounds of whitefish. We can sell any kind of fish commercially, but some we can't bring in ourselves—for instance, we buy walleye or largemouth bass from the Indians on the Upper Peninsula, who can bring in everything. The DNR regulates where we can fish and what we can fish for. But we do bring in catfish—thousands and thousands of them. We've got a cat hauler [a semi with 'cat tanks' on it] coming in any minute that wants 15,000 pounds for cat tanks in Chicago grocery stores. Cats're the only fish we keep live. The rest are on ice."

One of the men nets a trophy-sized giant from the catfish tank and holds it while I take a picture. I wouldn't touch one myself: once I caught a catfish and it felt slimier than snails. Its skin seemed made of jelly, its bones were like pins and needles, its whiskery, flat-bottomed head was unappetizing. As I leave, however, I'm given a small smoked one to try.

Out on the dock, I consider it: should I eat this fatty bottom-feeder? It must be absolutely loaded with PCBs! Well, I'm not having more kids, and it does seem a part of the adventure, so I pinch off the head, tail, and skin (where the PCBs are said to be concentrated), slowly peel out the skeleton, and eat the remaining fillets, very carefully, with bread and butter and an apple. Mmmmmmm. Greasy, but good—smoked catfish has an intense sweet-saltiness I like. By the time I roll down the Victorian-lined entrance to Bay City, however, I exude fish oil from every pore.

AT BAY CITY, the Thumb's biggest city, I look for an old Peace Corps crony, Frank Starkweather, a first-rate talker, if I remember right. I find him in a crush of small year-round homes on Saginaw Bay with his wife, Julia; daughter, Liberty; and brother, Tom, who is moving back from Los Angeles. Tom and Frank Starkweather grew up here, and I find their fond fun-poking a cross between Garrison Keillor and public radio's "Cartalk" brothers.

Frank (on iceboats): "Back in the thirties, the *Detroit News* published the plans for a new kind of ice boat which was lightweight, a guy could make it at home, it didn't cost much money, and it was a good entry-level boat.

"Well, Saginaw Bay and Tobico Marsh are phenomenal sailing for iceboats, and the Gougeon brothers in town here started making this iceboat called a DN6O, which refers to the *Detroit News* and the number of square feet in the sail. Well, the DN6O caught on until today it is *the* international competition-class boat.

"Then, using a new system of epoxy in wood construction, the

Gougeons started making strong, lightweight sailboats that looked like iceboats, that had a three-point stance, which is what a trimaran is. These boats are fast. Most of your big sailboats will sail six or seven miles an hour on a good strong day. They've never done twenty except when they were being towed down the highway. But I've done eighteen and twenty in my own boat and it was only twenty-four foot long."

Frank, as we bay-watch from the front yard: "There are two conditions to living in this world: there's on the water and there's across the street. And across the street is not on the water."

Me: "But across the street you don't pay waterfront taxes."

"Sitting out here, you know why you pay the taxes. There's just some things that are important. People don't bother even buying a place up here unless they're into boating, sailing, picnicking, beer drinking, ice fishing, ice skating, and snowmobiling. These are the recreational good timers. It probably started in Maine: before Maine got timbered out, a lot of drinking and carousing went on there. Then the trees got thin and the lumber barons discovered Michigan's uncut forests, so the lumberjacks came here. The missionaries tried to gain control of everything to keep out alcohol, so that what happened in Maine wouldn't happen here. Well, fat chance. This is one of the bawdiest places on the face of the earth."

Tom: "I think there should be a one-hundred-yard green belt between the shoreline and a public road, all around any water, except where it's needed for industry. The state, which can afford to take a long-range view, should be buying up lakeshore property as it comes up for sale."

Frank (on area food): "The smoked fish at Gino's—halfway north between Bay City and Pinconning—is the best anywhere. . . . What kind is best? There is no best. Chubs are oily. Whitefish is very light-flavored. Walleye is really better fried, like perch. Salmon is dominated by the salmon flavor, not by the smokiness. Gino's smokes them over corn cobs and they've done it that way for two, three generations.

"Pinconning is also famous for cheese, dark beer, and beans. The bean soup served in the Senate comes from Thumb-area beans. Navy pea beans. Everybody claims it, of course, but you taste it and it comes from here."

Tom: "The food here is phenomenal. You can go to any blue-

collar restaurant—Serendipity or Mama So-and-So's or Miss Patty's—
and eat yourself into a comatose state for under five dollars.

Me: "Better keep eating, Tom. When this book comes out, you'll
have swallowed your last bargain!"

Tom: "Naw. These folks have a lifestyle and they like it and by
God, they're going to do it."

Frank: "The people here are not dumb, but they don't take themselves terribly seriously, and they certainly won't take you very seriously. They're not impressed by an awful lot of stuff, and they're not
afraid to laugh or laugh at themselves. You go other places and people
are concerned about how important they are or someone else is. Hey,
did Tom tell you about the 'plural you'?"

Tom: "The plural of 'you' is 'yous.' It shows up mainly in the
language of waitresses in restaurants: 'What can I get yous?' It's the
area equivalent of the southern 'y'all.' We got infuriated by it at first,
but now we kind of chide those waitresses that don't use it."

Frank: "Have you heard the slogan, 'Say Yes to Michigan?' Well,
a friend who paddles a canoe from Mackinac Island to Bay City—you
know, one of those Voyageur canoes with about sixteen guys, and
they're all singing songs in French and drinking beer—he says, 'What
do you mean, "Say Yes to Michigan?" How 'bout this one: "Say Maybe
to Bay City." ' "

Tom: "The chamber of commerce had a contest for a Bay City
slogan and they chose 'Convenient Harbor Getaway.' "

Frank: "Mine would be 'Bingo, Beer, and Bowling.' Around here
bingo's a contact sport. You ever seen anybody slam-dunk a bingo
card? Go to a Catholic church on a Friday night. I mean, this is serious
stuff here. There are people who arrange their social calendar around
the week's bingo events. These people can play six or eight cards at
a time; they have these tubes that hold the little discs, so when they
get a number, it's like a stamper: plunk, plunk, plunk, plunk. It
automatically discharges each one."

Tom: "When I first came here, I read in the paper that St. Stan-
islaus's was having a Friday-night dinner, 'Earl Kavisto, fryer.' And I
thought they spelled it wrong, that Earl Kavisto was a friar. But Frank
says, 'No no no, he's dippin' the fish, and he has a secret recipe where
he pours in beer and a shot of Tabasco and some pepper and some

mustard seed and he makes the batter and oversees the frying of the fish.' "

Frank: "You probably have a choice of a dozen noncommercial places to have fish on a Friday night in this county. To compete, the local bars and restaurants advertise the fryer. Each fryer has a following, and if one gets mad and moves to another place, a whole bunch of people move with him."

Frank: "Down at the pier the DNR strung a net between some of those pilings and they left it there for two or three days and they caught forty-one kinds of fish and about twenty of them could be classified as game fish. Used to be sturgeon in this river."

Tom: "I remember the sturgeon washing up dead in the springtime. Grandpa would bury them. Eight, ten feet long. Dig a trench, hike 'em over."

Frank: "Yellow-bellied perch here are especially flavorful. But we've got a perch problem in Saginaw Bay—the perch are staying about five inches long—they're not getting up to the one-footers they used to be. The perch seem to go through stages. When they're real small, they eat algae and microscopic krill; then they go into a soft-food stage where they eat larvae; and the third stage they go into hard food—minnows and other perch. But there's such a shortage of larvae, because of the insecticides that are going into the ditches and the destruction of the wetlands, that the perch aren't going through the intermediate stage. The walleye are so happy they can't believe it, because here are all these itty-bitty perch for them to eat. So the DNR put two million mayflies into the bay, hoping that'll help."

Me: "Are walleye and muskie the same thing?"

Frank: "No way! The northern pike can get thirty inches long and maybe twelve pounds, and its cousin, which is the largest of the freshwater carnivores, is the muskallonge, or the muskie, and its minimum keeping size is forty-five inches. You're talking teeth like a barracuda and a mouth that can swallow a volleyball. The walleye, however, is related to the perch."

Frank (on Tobico Marsh): "A wealthy man named Frank Anderson, who's a hundred years old and still active, purchased Tobico Marsh many years ago and kept it as a wildfowl hunting area for him and his buddies, so the trees didn't get cut and the dams didn't get destroyed. Eventually, he bequeathed the land to the state of Michigan, so it's now managed by the state, but it's not part of the state park system."

Tom takes me hiking through part of Tobico Marsh, which in all covers twenty-seven square miles. He explains the algae on the beach as due to excess nitrogen in the soil. "The farmers put nitrogen on their soil, it's washed off into the ditches, and the ditches are pumped into another ditch that gravity feeds into the bay."

As we hike past waist-high ferns, through quiet woods, Tom peels a cattail root for me, which he claims tastes like the heart of an artichoke—and it does: really tender, melts in your mouth. When I apologize for all my picture stops, Tom says, "Hey, this is better'n eatin' popcorn and drinkin' beer. . . . Now this is a swale, which is a small creek that doesn't run. It's a backwater. When the wind blows the water out of Tobico, these swales drain and replenish Tobico. Then when the bay comes up, this is a flood area. So every couple of weeks, this has a chance to flush, and all the bugs and mosquito larvae that grow here get washed into the lake to feed the fish. Except when officials dam off the lower lagoons, which is something we're trying to prevent from happening."

Tom holds up a silk thread from which dangles a gypsy moth caterpillar. "The gypsy moth was brought into the United States in the late 1700s for making silk. Then they escaped, and after a hundred years they made it out here. The problem is that they must taste awful, because the birds won't eat 'em."

I ask Tom if he's worried about Lyme disease and he says, "I'm more concerned about getting run over by a school bus. But have you ever ridden a birch? No? Well, everybody should do it once." We munch on root-beer-flavored sassafras twigs and sweet wintergreen leaves until Tom finds a suitable mount. "What you do is, you shinny up to the top and you start swinging and you take it all the way down to the ground. Works best when you're about fourteen." Well past fourteen, I decline.

Anyway, the leaves on the poplars are turning silver as the wind exposes their light undersides, a sign, Tom says, of a storm. "Storms can come up very rapidly. We may have twenty, thirty minutes to get out of here. Storms from the west that build up over the land are triggered by the cooler atmosphere over the water, and you can get severe thunderstorms, squalls, waterspouts, that kind of thing."

On our way out, a turquoise damselfly lands on my shoulder. "If one lands on the end of your fishing pole," warns Tom, "you know you won't catch any fish." Why? "I don't know why." The farther north I get, the more often I suspect I'm getting my leg pulled.

JUNE 11

AFTER TWO DAYS in Bay City, I'm on the road again. Rounding the top of Saginaw Bay, I chug down a little dirt road and then hike to the end of a spit of land, where I sprawl for an hour watching a pair of bald eagles fish from some offshore rocks. Although I loved the company, it feels good to be alone again, water lapping on three sides of me, egrets and herons spiking through the shallows, lily pads nudging fistlike yellow blooms that, like little buoys, never open.

Then it's into Au Gres (say *O'Gray*) to visit the Bear Track Inn I've read about, but it's not the big log lodge with the stone fireplace and severed, plaqued heads that I expected. It looks more like a nice Italian fine-food establishment. "I was expecting something a little more woodsy," I confess to Frank Storey over a white tablecloth.

"I couldn't believe anybody'd call it that, either," says Storey, whose looks, voice, and manner remind me of Jay Leno. "When I bought this place, I wanted to call it the Captain's Roost or the Sandpiper, some nautical name. When I traveled around the country, I asked people to help, and they'd say, 'What's it called now?' and I'd say, 'Bear Track Inn,' and it didn't matter if I was in Houston or L.A. or Philadelphia, they'd say, 'Oh, I've been there!' So pretty soon I thought I'd better not change it."

I ask him to tell me about the smelt runs Au Gres is famous for. "The smelt are tiny fish that come in from the lake in large schools to spawn in the warmer creeks," explains Storey. "They run in waves from about the middle to the end of April. Twenty years ago when the smelt ran, maybe thirty thousand people'd line up from our parking lot to the Singing Bridge, a place to net them about four miles up the road.

"But it's not like that anymore. I can't really tell you what happened, but the story that I hear blames the salmon that got planted to eat the alewife, which was a junk fish—alewives used to wash up on the shore so thick that you couldn't even walk there, and the odor was horrible—remember that? They'd be three, four inches deep. We haven't seen those in years. Planting the sport fish was supposed to give a lot of fun to the fishermen, but number one, the salmon were supposed to eat up all these alewives. Well, when they finished with the alewives, I think they started on the smelt, because the smelt just don't happen like they used to, and consequently, the people don't happen like they used to.

"Of course a lot of people come and do their dipping at the Bear Track—they just come in and have a few beers, buy some smelt, and go home. There's a lot of that. But the real fishermen wear waders and go into the water and they dip away with these dip nets that look like big butterfly nets, and even now, when the smelt are really running, it's nothing for people to fill up washtubs and hundred-gallon tubs. I've seen 'em fill up the back ends of pickup trucks."

"What do they do with them?"

"They freeze 'em in water in milk cartons, give them to all the neighbors, put 'em in their flower beds for fertilizer."

"Smelt aren't exactly a gourmet fish, are they?"

"No, but they're good. You can can them and make a sort of sardine kind of a thing—that's how I like 'em. And it's kind of a sport going after them. It's often done at night. Very exciting."

"How do you cook them?"

"Well, you snip their heads off with scissors and you clean them out—some people do it with toothbrushes—and you leave the bones and the whole nine yards. Then you bread 'em in pancake flour and deep-fry 'em. That's the way most people eat 'em. Or you make sardines out of 'em."

"Is that how you serve them here?"

"We don't serve smelt at the restaurant," says Frank, grinning a little sheepishly. "We never have. Isn't that funny? The reason is that they're really tough to clean, and if you're going to serve them in a restaurant they have to be fresh. So we'd have to buy them from a fishery already cleaned. There's no way that I can sell smelt."

That's okay. Frank doesn't really need to sell smelt to fill up his inn. Although I'm still not sure why, it seems to be popular by itself.

JUNE 12

I'M CAMPED UNDER a big shade tree at Tawas Point State Park, halfway down a narrow peninsula that hooks south into Lake Huron, offering both eastern and western views over water. I watched a stunning sunset over Tawas Bay last night. Now, up at dawn, I'm trying to photograph the undersides of overhead gulls, brushed Miami pink by a rising sun they catch but I can't see yet. This peninsula is crazy with birds. Hiking to the point and back before breakfast, I follow a catbird's melodic medley and a tiny blue gnatcatcher's *wheezy wheezy wheezy*. I spot sparrows, finches, robins, flycatchers, vireos, warblers, waxwings, kingbirds, and blackbirds. For half an hour, while I make and eat my oatmeal, brush the sand from my sheets, and straighten out my quilts, an American redstart—an inky little warbler with persimmon wing- and tailbars—trills like a bird out of Disney's *Cinderella* in full view, right over my head.

I DON'T SEE many canoes on the Great Lakes, at least not so far, but there sure are a lot of them in the twin towns of Au Sable/Oscoda. Between them flows the paddle-perfect Au Sable River, a challenging canoe course that nevertheless includes an eighteen-mile stretch of clear water (no rapids, no waterfalls) frequented by beginners and birders. Every July since 1947, the fattest ($25,000 in cash and prizes) canoe race in North America, the Au Sable River Canoe Marathon, rips down this river from Grayling to Oscoda, and the most frequent winner is Ralph W. Sawyer, owner of the Sawyer Canoe Company.

Its president, Bob Gramprie, has been filling me in on all this while we tour the several cavernous rooms containing pumps, tubes, tanks, large and small molds, and some spirited workers. I can't hear Bob too well over the rock music and machinery that scream through the place, so I won't attempt a detailed description of Sawyer canoe construction. Leave it to say that tough, woven glass cloth of various weights and strengths, and/or a gold fabric called Kevlar ("also used in bulletproof vests"), are molded with a substance called Gelco into tapered cake pans to form various sleek Sawyer and (less expensive) Oscoda line models. What makes a really good canoe, Gramprie says, is the balance between strength and weight: "As an engineer told me once, any damn fool can build a bridge that's strong enough, but it takes a good engineer to build one that's *just* strong enough."

In the last and largest room, red, green, and white canoes dangle like salamis from the ceiling, an odd perspective that makes them appear alarmingly large, but it's the smallest one I like best. "The Solo is very popular with the ladies," Gramprie confides, "because they don't have to deal with some macho turkey telling them they're doing it all wrong."

I nod knowingly. He's got my number, all right.

KIMCHEE IS NOT a delicacy common to the Fourth Coast, so I am surprised to find, in the Old West–fronted town of Oscoda, a small woman named Yu Pin chopping cabbage in the back of the Oriental Market and Take-Out. My craving for spicy food, however, does not include this particular Korean dish, a hot, fishy mixture of cabbage, tomato, and onions.

"Lotta people are scared to try it," admits Yu Pin, continuing to chop. "A lotta people think that we bury it in the ground. But that's how people *used* to keep it when they didn't have refrigerator. But you'd be surprised. I gotta lotta American people buying it." There's also a substantial Far Eastern population here; many, like herself— Yu Pin is from Thailand—are married to Americans at Wurtsmith Air Force Base.

Next to the door is tacked a handwritten list of frozen items, including squid, wonton, fermented soybean, pig stomach, sea squirt, pollack roe, big mackerel, and small mackerel. A man in uniform picks up a white carton of pat ratna. The phone rings and soon vegetables hiss in a wok. Yu Pin offers me a chair. She is making pancit, she says—Philippine stir-fry. I love Filipino food. Thai food. The smell of lemon grass, curry, tamari. Sauced noodles, sticky rice.

Hunched over the menu in the cramped, steaming kitchen, I reduce the thirty-four choices to four—gang pit, adobo, bulgogi, yakasoba—then leave it to the chef.

About ten miles north, I consume my fragrant take-out in the intimate, heavily wooded Harrisville State Park, under trees so thick that even in the rain, I find a dry haven beneath them. The big evergreens, deeply needled forest floor, thick ferns, and sweet-smelling northern white cedar and balsam fir make me feel as if I'm finally "up north." Closer to Alpena, I discover a state forest campground that's even wilder—outhouses, private sites, woods from which a bear could credibly emerge, mosquito bites big as nickels. I love it here. When I'm up north, something inside me gets free.

Note: I was right on the mark, Alpena astronomer Jim Bruton later told me: that second park, just south of Alpena, is located close to the forty-fifth parallel, the line widely believed, especially by those living north of it, to divide the southern half of Michigan from "up north."

JUNE 13

ALPENA AT FIRST GLANCE seems a dreary city, dominated by large government buildings, a cement plant, factories. Last night, in a smoky coffee shop, a woman confirmed this impression. "Alpena is pretty depressed," she said. "People are always saying, 'I can't do such-and-such because I gotta make my husband his lunch when he comes home from the factory.' In western Michigan, we just say, 'Honey, make your own lunch, I'm going to the beach.'"

I'm about to skip town when I see a sign for a waterfront scuba-diving shop and find myself standing at the edge of the Thunder Bay Underwater Preserve, a 288-square-mile submerged museum. The rocky shoals and islands here have joined forces with Lake Huron's ferocious storms to send over eighty ships to the bottom, earning Alpena the title of "Shipwreck Capital of the Great Lakes."

"In 1981, the state of Michigan established a shipwreck law designating seven areas [now ten] in the state's Great Lakes that would be preserves and nothing could be taken out," explains co-owner Ruthann Beck from behind the counter of Thunder Bay Divers. "The cold, fresh water of the Great Lakes, especially the northern Great Lakes, preserves the wood unusually well. The wrecks become petrified—you can't even get a knife blade in the old oak timbers of some of these ships. Fresh water also preserves the steel. In an ocean, the salt water eats the steel in five or ten years. Sometimes the coral grows on a wreck so fast that in a year, you can't recognize it as a ship. But in the Great Lakes, we're diving ships that sank in the 1800s. They've been down a hundred and fifty years.

"Our shipwrecks are especially interesting because Michigan is the first state to enact laws that prohibit taking anything from our ship- wrecks without a permit. In Wisconsin right now, people can dive wrecks and take anything they want. There's no law that they can't. So there's absolutely nothing left. The wrecks have all been stripped."

"Do people take things here illegally?"

"I think the diving public have changed their attitude. Before the eighties, people thought, 'Nobody will ever see this stuff, so who cares?' Now, people are beginning to see the historic value."

Most of the preserves in Michigan are serviced by a private div- ing center like this one, Beck says, which offers guides, underwater tours, maps, equipment, air, and, in the winter, scuba-diving lessons. A "C-card"—certification card—is required by all reputable diving places.

As we are talking, a wet man drips in and puts a thumbnail-sized, variegated "clam" in Beck's hand. She pales. "This is the first zebra mussel we've seen here," Beck gasps. "It could ruin our shipwrecks. Just one can produce forty thousand eggs a year!"

"Put it on the floor and stomp on it!" suggests the man.

Unfortunately, that won't begin to take care of the problem.

Note: By 1990, the zebra mussel, introduced into Lake St. Clair in about 1986 in a foreign ship's ballast water—lightly loaded ships often carry water to stabilize them, dumped when the ship is loaded —was beginning to cause panic on the lakes. The mussels have since multiplied with astonishing speed, rapidly covering the lake beds, rocks, and underwater structures and clogging city and industrial water-intake pipes. By 1993, zebra mussels had spread to all five Great Lakes but seemed densest in Lake Erie—Detroit Edison's Monroe plant, for example, once reported 700,000 per square meter! The zebra mussel is being taken very seriously. Feeding as it does on microorganisms, the bottom of the food chain, it threatens the entire ecosystem. Can we get rid of it? Not likely. Control it? Not much eats enough zebra mussels to make a dent. Chlorine and pressure spraying help keep intake pipes clear. Divers can scrape them off.

The zebra mussel does have its uses. It filters pollutants, such as phosphorus, through its body. Lake Erie water becomes crystal clear where the zebra mussel cleanup crew has moved in. Unfortunately, crystal-clear water isn't what you want, either: It lacks rich populations of algae, plankton, and other microorganisms that start the food chain going.

"It's really too soon to tell what will happen," Doug Sweet, curator of the Belle Isle Aquarium, tells me in a telephone interview. "But some scientists think it could change the whole balance of wildlife in the Great Lakes."

BECK SENDS ME to Lizette Bison, a slim young woman with a rapid-fire delivery, whom I find in a crammed used-book store. Her voice seems crayon-bright in the drab surroundings. Alpena is a colorful town, Lizette insists enthusiastically. "Once the whole west side was a red-light district. Some of the history they can't write yet because some of the people are still alive, but this town was a rednecked lumberjack town once, rough beyond belief. People settled their fights with Irish shillelaghs—that's a stick about so long and it has a knob on the end, and they hit each other over the head with it. Back around the turn of the century, it wasn't safe to walk down the street during the daytime. Even ten years ago, Alpena was number one in the United States for per-capita consumption of alcohol, based on the tax record. I think it's number three now. We have our minor problems. But there was a lot of money here once. They used to say that for every square foot there was a millionaire.

"I'm fourth-generation Alpena. I'm related to a family of German pharmacists, pharmacists all the way back, but I'm related to the Irish in town, too. But I've said enough. I have to live here, you know." Lizette sends me to the Jesse Besser Museum to meet Robert Haltiner, "who wrote the book on Alpena."

The book is called *The Town That Wouldn't Die*, and soon I sit across from the author, a lanky white-haired gentleman with a courtly manner. Our executive-type chairs in the center of a dark gallery turn 360 degrees, permitting a long, comfortable look at the surrounding twenty thousand artifacts in brightly lit cases.

"This is probably the finest collection of Native American artifacts in the Great Lakes area," begins Haltiner. "My dad started collecting when he was about thirteen years old. At that time there was little interest in the early peoples here, and he discovered many of the sites in this area. Our biggest site was the sandy hill across the street, Alpena's highest point of land. We would go out practically daily, because any slight wind or rain would shift the sand and reveal artifacts. We never dug. We only took surface things. My dad always felt that even though we knew where a number of burials were, we shouldn't disturb them."

"So the Native Americans don't have a problem with this collection?"

"None whatsoever. Their main problem is that so many scientists and archaeologists have desecrated their burial grounds and kept bones or the artifacts buried with the bones, many of which are only several hundred years old. Our sites up here go back thousands of years, so there's no tribal affiliation with the things we find."

Bob Haltiner is a card-carrying Native American, although he downplays the importance of this. "I'm only one-eighth Native American, but it's enough to make me a legal minority."

I spin around in my big, soft chair, taking in the dazzling displays of arrowheads, Copper Culture tools, grooved stone axes, tomahawks, bones and shells, banner stones. "You found most of the things we're looking at?"

"Oh yes. Every one. Many of them are from the early Copper Culture peoples. They mined the copper in the Upper Peninsula for a few short months of the year, but they didn't live there; they transported a lot of the copper to various other sites where they worked it, and they worked a lot of it here. This is one of the places where they fashioned it into weapons and ornaments and other things. The copper cache you see here was found directly across the street, and it's the only one of its kind.

"When my dad retired, he became worried about the safety of the collection—it was kept in our home—so it came here in 1969, and I came with it. This museum is funded by Jesse Besser, who developed the concrete-block-making industry and became the world's largest manufacturer of concrete-block-making machines. A lot of towns died when the lumbering left, but Jesse Besser's machines helped save this one. To this day Alpena is the international authority on concrete-block-making."

"What is your position at this museum?"

"Chief of resources," smiles Haltiner, getting up. "I have no idea what that means. I've never heard of another one anywhere."

I soon retreat to Roy's Campers Cove, a private campground on Alpena's Thunder River, where for six dollars I enjoy an indoor pool and camp facing a spindly collection of birches and maples. I'm napping in the van with the back propped up like an awning when suddenly a fighter plane screams overhead, so low it seems to scrape the trees. I must be camped at the end of a military base landing strip, I think. (I was actually near the local airport.) Here comes another jet, screeching like a demon. And another. They're all coming in, one, two, three, four, directly over the van. I get out and lie on the leaves, facing heaven, feeling the roars crash in like surf. Every twenty seconds, the roar of one melts into the crescendo of the next. Then every ten seconds. I've probably watched fifteen or more, although they may be the same few, circling. Ten more go over. Echoes kaboom like bowling balls rolling down the Thunder Bay River gorge. God, how I love them! Jet fighters should be built without weapons, just for air shows, just for the pilot's astonishing ride, just so I, wingless, can lie on my back and imagine a few of my own kind flying so high they can ride the horizon and see, perhaps, all five Great Lakes at once.

NORTH OF ALPENA, I find another of the many Presque Isles —"almost islands"—on the Great Lakes, but this one, separated from the mainland by a large inland lake, is attached at both ends. There's something else odd here: on the Lake Huron side, a smaller peninsula sprouts, like a chanterelle—a Presque Isle on a Presque Isle. At the south end of the cap, Lorraine Parris welcomes me into the Presque Isle Old Lighthouse and Museum. "This thirty-foot lighthouse was originally built in 1840, but abandoned thirty years later, when it went to ruin," Parris tells me. "The Stebbins family purchased it from the government in the early 1900s, restored it in the thirties, and used it for a summer home until 1956, when they opened it as a historical museum. In 1965 it became a historical marker. Last year we had 17,436 people through here."

I have a hard time imagining that many people here. Maybe it's just the fog, the long drive down the peninsula, or the fact that I'm the sole guest, but it feels awfully remote out here. "There's another lighthouse just a mile up the road," says Parris. "That's a working lighthouse, tallest on Lake Huron. It took this one's place in 1870. You can't climb that one, but you can climb this one. This is also a hands-on museum. You can pick up and handle anything. There's horns to blow, bells to ring, anything you want to do. There's a checkerboard table and a flute and an old turntable."

"How long have you been here?"

"Fourteen years. I love it here. You meet some fantastic people. Some of them are deadbeats, but you get that in any business. And then, of course, there's the ghost. . . ."

"The lighthouse is haunted?"

"It's said that many lighthouses are, but there's only once I had a ghost here. During our first week—our sleeping quarters are upstairs—I woke up at three-thirty in the morning and it sounded like somebody was walking around down here. I woke up my husband and he raised up and listened and he said, 'It's only the old lightkeeper coming back to see how you're running the place.' That was the last time. They say there's been several ghosts at the other lighthouse. They say there's a woman down there that moans.

"My granddaughter, she comes here, but she won't stay in the lighthouse," continues Parris. "She doesn't like that portrait up there of Mr. Stebbins. His eyes follow you everywhere you walk." I head for the door, and she's right: they do. Very creepy. I leave after that and the lighthouse fades into the fog so fast I'm not sure it was ever really there.

IN A LITTLE MARINA off the mowed park at Rogers City, I see a five-digit number—12610—chalked on a blackboard. This, the as-

Date _____ Valid From _____ Area _____

Example of code (see below)									
1	3	5	2	0	9 hrs.	SW	17·21	Fine	3 pm·12 am
CODE					No. of Hours	Wind Direction	Wind Speed in Knots	Condition	Time
1									
1									
1									
1									
1									
1									
1									
1									

North America · Number of Hours · Wind Direction · Wind Speed in Knots · Conditions

0	Now	Calm	0·10	Fine—Mostly Clear
1	3 hrs.	NE	11·16	Risk of Ice
2	6 hrs.	EAST	17·21	Strong Risk of Ice
3	9 hrs.	SE	22·27	Mist—Visibility 5/8·3 miles
4	12 hrs.	SOUTH	28·33	Fog—Visibility less than 5/8 mi.
5	18 hrs.	SW	34·40	Drizzle
6	24 hrs.	WEST	41·47	Rain
7	48 hrs.	NW	48·55	Snow or Rain/Snow
8	72 hrs	NORTH	56·63	Squalls with/without showers
9	Occ.	Variable	64·71	Thundershowers

sistant harbor master tells me, is the Mafor report: a marine weather forecast, for those in the know. According to a three-by-five-inch printed chart he hands me, the fog I've endured all morning will clear up soon: 12610 means it's a North American six-hour forecast with winds west at 11–16 knots and mostly clear skies. The first number represents the continent, the second the number of hours the forecast is good for, the third the wind direction, the fourth the wind speed, and the fifth indicates weather conditions.

I love it. What a tidy concept, I crow. Why not eliminate television weather programs and simply present the Mafor report, like a winning lotto number? It could run twenty-four hours a day in the corner of the screen. The interpretive chart could be printed in the *TV Guide*.

The assistant harbor master looks at me carefully. "Right," he says, without enthusiasm.

A few minutes later, I make a mouthwatering discovery at Nowickis Am See (which means, in German, "Nowickis by the sea"). *"Ja,* there's two, three places here that smoke sausages," says Annamaria Nowicki in a heavy German accent. "This here is fourth-generation. My husband's grandfather started it years ago. Store must be, now, maybe sixty years old. In the olden days there was a lotta German and Polish people living here."

Her husband, Philip, describes their business. "We have fifty kinds of sausage," he says. "We still make the original head cheese, liver sausage, blood sausage, and beef sausage farm-style, which is a little German sausage. We make Landjäger sausage, which is a hunter's sausage. We make ham sausage for Christmas; we make hand-cut sausage the way it was made two, three hundred years ago. We make six different kinds of Polish sausage. We use all the original ways. We make Italian sausage. Then we make five, six kinds of deer sausage, when the hunters come up. One year we made ten thousand pounds of deer sausage." Nowicki waves at a glossy refrigerated meat counter across the back of the store, where a panoply of sausages and meat is neatly stacked. "We also make steak tartare," continues Nowicki. "Ground raw meat. That's a big thing here. Last year we made four hundred and fifty pounds of chopped beef for the parties at the end of bowling season."

This truly is a family business. The Nowickis' son made the 1977 *Guinness Book of World Records* with a mile-and-a-half-long sausage. "We had it on tables in the pavilion down here," reports Mrs. Nowicki. "We started selling it at nine o'clock in the evening and it was gone by the next afternoon."

CHEBOYGAN'S downtown shops and restaurants line both sides of a street perpendicular to Gordon Turner Park, a lakeshore city park—a beach, swings, and a picnic area—that flares into a wetlands full of birds. At lunch hour, workmen drive up, park with a lake view, open metal lunch boxes, and begin chewing. I can see them from the beautiful boardwalk built into the marsh, but in the other three directions I look over acres of cattail marsh and woods. Three sunning turtles amiably share a rock. I hear, then see, the piercing cries of killdeer, blackbirds, mallards, terns, gulls. An osprey—a hawk-sized "sea eagle"—circles the open water, occasionally dropping like a rock. Far away shimmers a postcard-perfect view of the Mackinac Bridge.

I notice a man on one of the swings, not a usual sight, so I join him and we swing higher and higher. He's wearing jeans and a sleeveless jersey. "First time I've done this in years," he says. "I forgot how it hurts."

I soon see what he means. The rubber seat clamps my backside like a vise. We ignore the pain and keep swinging. He's just moved up here, he says. "You always seem to come back home."

From the swings, I'm attracted to some activity on a tugboat pulled up to a dock on a channel. I check it out. At Derosher Dock & Dredge, Raymond Van Antwerp, a courteous worker in his late teens, shows me around the tug, shouting over screaming machines and clanging hammers. Below, several men strong-arm an engine into working order. We tour the neat little galley (a small kitchen), sleeping quarters (sleeps four). It's a houseboat with muscle, scheduled to pull a loaded barge the size of a sawed-off freighter to Erie, Pennsylvania's Presque Isle. I'm reminded of an ant dragging an oak leaf.

THE MACKINAC* STRAITS form a Lake Huron bottleneck, a narrows not just between the upper and lower peninsulas of Michigan, but continuing between the mainland and the large, inhabited island called Bois Blanc (sometimes pronounced *Boblo*, like the Canadian island near Detroit), which lies in Lake Huron off Cheboygan. I don't take the Cheboygan ferry there (an omission I later regret, finding Great Lakes islands particularly eccentric and lovely places). Instead, I head up along the Straits of Mackinac on Route 23 to Mackinaw City, feeling a little sad that I'll soon leave this third Great Lake of the trip, which I've experienced as an affable span of coastline. Although there is industry, I've observed no desolated wastelands. Most of the communities on Lake Huron are struggling to attract more tourists to boost a sagging economy. Everywhere, especially here along

---

* "Mackinac" and "Mackinaw" both are pronounced "Mackinaw." There are Mackinac Island, the Straits of Mackinac, the Mackinac Bridge, Old Mackinac Point; but Mackinaw State Forest (on Bois Blanc Island) and Mackinaw City.

the straits, I see "resorts"—a word that on Lake Huron refers to a scattering of small cabins, modest motels, and camping areas. Lake Huron invites everyone, not just the rich. There's something down-home up here, something nostalgic, behind the times.

Nearing the tip of the Michigan mitten, I come upon a bright display of flags, banners, and posters. Most state parks seem content with an outdoorsy, tasteful sign, but Old Mill Creek State Park is sort of a historical amusement park: a reconstruction of the mill that two hundred years ago provided the lumber (floated across the straits or dragged on the ice) for the fort on Mackinac Island. I stop to take in a contemporary visitors' center; watch costumed participants saw boards with a reproduction of the early stream-powered blade; hike a long trail looping uphill past real beaver dams and through woods. I walk fast to outpace the mosquitoes. Caterpillars are so numerous that they are raining through the trees with a nonstop ticking sound. A thug-sized deerfly begins orbiting my head like a bull roarer. I run, swat, sweat, swear. It's still there, as if tacked to my head on a length of fishing line.

I hate these big flies. This morning, I stopped to lunch in Che-boygan State Park, a wonderfully woodsy place, but had to leave be-cause of the horsefly gangs. I heard from several sources, although authorities will neither deny or confirm the rumor, that the DNR released hordes of these airborne beasts, specially treated not to repro-duce, to help control this year's caterpillar infestation. But they're not eating the caterpillars; they're eating me. Not to worry, assures a Mill Creek ranger. It's a one-year phenomenon. By next year, they'll both be gone.

AT THE CHAMBER OF COMMERCE in Mackinaw City at the northern tip of Lower Michigan, I'm told that three ferry lines, each with a fleet of triple-deckers, deposit as many as four thousand pas-sengers a day on three-mile-long Mackinac Island. I recoil. Although I've never been there, I've always thought of Mackinac Island as the *Jaws* of tourist traps. I'd skip it and head on over to Wilderness State Park, but I'm curious.

I decide to buzz over for a couple of hours and set about picking a ferry. Each promotes a fancy boat—catamaran, hydroplane, or hydrojet—but the cost ($9.50 round trip) and time (sixteen to eigh-teen minutes) are essentially the same. I choose the Star Line, for the name. An enthusiastic fellow named Tracy Smith tours me around the waiting two-year-old *Radisson*—the first hydrojet ever built, he claims. Its two propellers and jet pumps draw the water through the boat and shoot it out the back in two dramatic, hundred-foot rooster tails.

"It's not a hydrofoil?"

"No, a hydrofoil has an air cushion under it. This doesn't. This is like a fire-fighting boat, although we've never used it for that pur-pose. Burns sixty-seven gallons per fifteen-mile round trip." On the water, one seems to talk gallons per mile, not miles per gallon.

Once under way, I ride up top with Captain Mark Brown, a man in his thirties with curly red hair who's already an old hand: "Been at it fifteen years," he says. I ask the four members of his young, red-shirted crew, all from northern Michigan, what they do in winter.

"Sleep 'n' eat," says one.

"Drink a little bit," says another.

"Ho-ho-ho—a little!"

At five-thirty, I step from the hydrojet into a picture-perfect town jammed with little shops, restaurants, and hotels. It feels like a movie set. The buildings look turn-of-the-century but scrubbed; even the fast-food joints could pass for historical landmarks. Lilacs bloom red, lavender, deep purple, pink, cream. Fudge shops advertise themselves as "the original," "the family that made fudge famous," or "since 1887." Bicycles—three-speed, one-speed, tandems—line up like Rockettes before rental shops. Horses go by—*cloppa-cloppa-cloppa*—pulling black carriages or flat-bedded luggage carts, harness bells jan-gling. Cyclists go by. Pedestrians. No cars are allowed here, but I watch where I step—even the full-time shovelers can't seem to keep up. This part of Mackinac Island smells like fudge boiling in a horse barn.

A road circles the island and I start off to the left, toward banked Victorian homes that look down on the street and shore. More horses go by. In minutes I'm in Jack's Livery Stables, inquiring about the many black carriages in front. Co-owner Reggie Gough tells me that for twenty-seven dollars, I can take out a carriage alone, but this makes me nervous—I've never driven a horse and buggy before—so I ask about a horse.

"You been on a horse before?" asks Gough.

"Twenty-five years ago."

"Good enough."

I'm incredulous. Who on earth would insure them? Insurance is a problem, Gough confesses. They use Lloyd's of London, known for its eccentric clients.

I head out of town awfully far from the ground on a mare named Ginger, having persuaded twenty-year-old W. T. Gough (the other owner's son) to accompany me. We ride, keeping to the woodsy island interior. W.T., who rides his horse bareback, talks with enthusiasm. He grew up here, he tells me, pointing out birds and wildflowers, including a surprising number of orchids—puffy yellow lady's-slippers—along the narrow trails. We pass beautiful Victorian homes, some worth millions, including W.T.'s favorite, a white one deep in the woods. He takes me places on paths only islanders know, he says, and he never stops talking. Eighty percent of the island is owned by the state, says W.T. Most of it is undeveloped. He shows me a twenty-five-foot obelisk, a sheer rock his mother—a woman, I gather, to be reckoned with—climbed once. W.T. seems to have inherited her adventurous nature: last February, he walked across the ice to St. Ignace; took him an hour and a half. About eight hundred people winter here, he says. In summer, island kids ride the horses at night and party in the woods.

I feel part of a film, I confess to him—the writer with her Indian guide. W.T. laughs and pulls out a "green card"—this proves he's one-eighth Chippewa, he says. He can hunt and fish where he likes.

It's seven-thirty by the time we get back, and, although I didn't even bring a toothbrush, I'm not ready to leave. I worry about my horsey jeans, but who'll notice? Everything here smells like horse. I check into the Lake View, a huge white Victorian hotel built like a rectangular, four-story O around the island's only indoor pool. For eighty-four dollars I get dinner, breakfast, and an atticlike room up in the treetops with slanting walls and a little window. The king-size bed is covered in pink; the furniture might be Queen Anne; the wallpaper is teal behind pink, yellow, and white flowers big as faces. I take a long, hot shower before lifting the silver covers on cream of broccoli soup, shrimp primavera Alfredo, and a fresh blueberry turnover with strawberry and blueberry sauce, delivered to my room, along with a very cold Heineken, on a heavy oval tray.

JUNE 16

AFTER A BUFFET BREAKFAST —strawberries, cantaloupe, watermelon, muffins, scrambled eggs and bacon—I wander through town. Hundred-year-old French lilacs billow along Fort Mackinac, built on a bluff by the British in 1781. At nine o'clock sharp, a Boy Scout troop ceremoniously raises the flag. A scout bugles without incident. A gun goes off in the fort. "This happens every morning, all summer long," a scoutmaster tells me. "A different Boy Scout or Girl Scout troop takes over each week."

I head up a hill toward the famous Grand Hotel—"the largest hotel on the Great Lakes," with "the longest front porch in the world"—dodging horses and a man shoveling manure into a wheelbarrow. (His T-shirt says, SHIT HAPPENS.) Somewhere along the curved plantation-hotel drive, I find myself back in the movie. A matched set of horses goes by, drawing a boxlike black carriage toward the covered main entrance. Lines of tourists form at a side door. I become Scarlett in disguise, triumphing over a gauntlet of polite, uniformed men who question my appearance (my jeans defy the dress code), try to collect a five-dollar admittance fee (I'm not registered at the Grand), sign me up for a tour. Inside, I'm met with unrelenting Kelly-green carpeting that stretches into something like a turn-of-the-century mall. Someone takes down my name, my publisher's name, and picks up the phone. A graying Rhett appears—tall, charming—and steers me to a table on the hotel's famous porch.

"An early owner once hired an artist to do a drawing of the front of the Grand Hotel to make it look super-long," says the man, whose name is W. T. (Bill) Rabe—he pauses to order coffee from a red-uniformed black waiter—"and he sent this to Robert Ripley and said this 880-foot front porch was the longest porch in the world. And Ripley printed it. Well, about ten years ago, I decided to have a Truth-in-Porches party, and I got some engineering students and professors from Lake Superior State College to chain the front porch, and it wasn't 880 feet—it was 660 feet."

"Is it still the longest porch in the world?"

He smiles like a cat. "Nobody has ever disputed it, so it must be."

I smile back. I have met my match. Bill Rabe, retired from a distinguished career as a professional journalist, knows how to handle writers. I find his candid approach disarming and he knows it. He's going to give me a good story, exactly what I want to hear. Our eyes meet, amused, agreeing to dance, because we do it well and because it's so much fun. Aloud, Rabe asks where I stayed last night and then launches into a story:

"Harry Ryba bought the Lake View about twenty years ago because he wanted the dock in front of it for a ferry line. So he got the hotel by accident, sort of. He's a big man around here, but he got started in Detroit, making fudge in a little shop across the street from the Belle Isle Bridge. Well, one day a man from Mackinac Island asked him for a little corner of the store to make fudge on a slab. Harry'd never seen fudge made on a slab before, so he watched this man do it. One day the guy didn't come in, and it was a holiday and everybody wanted fudge, so Harry started making the fudge himself. He sold it as 'Mackinac Island fudge,' because it was made the Mackinac Island–way, on a slab—they pour this goo on a slab from a big copper kettle, and they walk around with a spatula and keep turning it over until it reaches the end of the table. Then it's set into a long loaf and chopped into pieces. It's a show, a different way of making fudge. Well, Harry started making Mackinac Island fudge at state fairs, auto shows, boat shows, and such, and finally he decided that if he was going to make Mackinac Island fudge, he should have a place on Mackinac Island. So he came up here and started a pancake house and a fudge shop. Now, in spite of the fact that he's pretty much a newcomer—he's only been here forty years—his empire includes the Lake View Hotel, the Star Line, and more."

I laugh. "I can't believe you're pushing a different hotel than the one you work for. What kind of PR man are you, anyway?"

"There used to be many of these huge old hotels on the Great Lakes," says Rabe, ignoring my gibe. "Back in 1887, when this hotel was built, there were already eight or nine hotels flourishing here.

Wealthy families used to come up by boat or train for whole summers. But most of the really big hotels folded when the automobile became common transportation. People could come and go as they liked and they didn't stay as long. But we survived: Today we have 317 rooms that can go for three hundred to five hundred dollars a night.

"We've had to be very imaginative about our publicity to survive. For example, yesterday was World Sauntering Day. We started it about ten years ago, primarily to promote the Grand Hotel. Now it's listed in the *Chase Calendar of Annual Events*. Our annual Stone Skipping Contest is held every Fourth of July. It's become a very big thing. We get about five hundred people skipping stones. *The New Yorker* has covered it. Charles Kuralt did a beautiful thing on it. NBC News covered it on the U.S. Bicentennial broadcast. Then a company did a movie up here with Christopher Reeve called *Somewhere in Time*. It wasn't a great hit, but it went all over the country, and people come here just to see where it was made. It never quits: last Friday, 'Good Morning America' did their weather reports from here. Tomorrow a *National Geographic* film group comes in."

He takes me on a tour, starting with the gardens, where college-age kids are working massive beds. "They just tore out about fourteen thousand tulips big as your fist to put in something new," says Rabe.

"What do they do with them?"

"They throw 'em in the woods. Tulips have to go in with fresh bulbs every year, otherwise they don't bloom well."

The thirteen flags flying along the hotel are new—in this wind, they last about two years. Inside, we tour a tea shop, a wine shop, a bookstore, a magazine store, a candy shop, a toy store, a playroom, a barber shop. Behind the scenes, we look in on a roaring laundry room, a huge sheet laundry with a wall-sized mangle. We practically push our way through milling workers—four hundred people work at the hotel, tending up to seven hundred guests, says Rabe. In the kitchens, crashing dishes and raised voices echo in cavernous rooms. A conveyor belt totes dishes to an enormous dishwashing system. Plates clatter. In the garnishing department, plates of hors d'oeuvres are spread on mirrors. The meat counter could serve a town. The "spice rack" is a room. Bedroom-sized coolers brim with barrels of fat mushrooms, ducklings, enormous hunks of meat. A man is stuffing plum-sized strawberries with tarragon sour cream. Pots big enough to boil a pig in simmer with soup. Half a cow spins on a rotisserie. Rich desserts in a vast display are garnished with fresh flowers.

Back out on the billiard-green carpet, in a vast yellow dining room, we inspect one of the six places where lunch is being served. It's an exquisite buffet: seafood, meats, salads, three kinds of butter, cheese, four or five hot dishes, beef Stroganoff. Someone plays the piano. "We have twenty-two staff musicians," says Rabe. "You can listen to music from four o'clock tea in the parlor through dinner, after which a harpist plays, followed by a pianist and a violinist until nine-thirty, when the doors open to the Terrace Room and a band plays a peppy number to lure all the people up."

Upstairs, we tour some of the recently redecorated rooms on the lake side. The Astor Room, for example, contains furnishings from Lord Astor's private railway car, including a puzzle desk, which turns into a chair. It's a major hike touring the Grand Hotel, and by the time we're through, I can barely walk. I'm freezing up from yesterday's ride. Rabe looks pretty pooped out himself. "You'll stay for lunch?"

"I thought you'd never ask!" Back on the famous front porch, Rabe signals a waiter and I order black bean soup and a salmon-and-asparagus salad, with a cold beer. Rabe, who seems to anticipate most of my questions, answers my next one before I can ask it: "You're wondering why all our waiters are black. Well, the hotel used to run from Memorial Day to Labor Day, and the waiters were American blacks who worked the race track in the off season. There's a whole circuit. But now we're open from early May until Halloween, so that no longer works. We began hiring Jamaican waiters because the Jamaican season is the flipflop of our season, and Jamaican resort hotels have similar service to ours. So we get well-trained waiters who can carry a tray with eight or ten entrees on it. But before we can hire them, we have to advertise extensively to satisfy both the Department of Immigration and the Jamaican government. We've been criticized for having only black waiters. People say we have them in menial positions. But the waiters are the highest-paid hourly employees in the hotel. This year we added fifteen white waiters, but we're already down to ten."

Lunch arrives. I wave some flies away and Rabe says, "When I first came here, there were no flies or mosquitoes to speak of—we had lots of bats on the island and they ate all the bugs. Then somebody decided to use DDT. Well, the bats ate the bugs full of DDT and died. So now you've got to have fly traps, flypaper. There's a fly-control inspector who goes around and inspects and gives you tickets if there are too many flies."

As we eat, a ferry horn toots, dishes clank, gulls scream. I like all the kids I've seen working on the island, I say; they give it a freshness. "The kids make this island," Rabe agrees. "All of our bellhops, doormen, dockhops, and a lot of our desk attendants are young people." Before I leave, he gives me a lifetime pass to the front porch, initialing it himself.

Note: I recently called W. T. Rabe to check on some things and was saddened to learn that he had died. I found him an unusually playful and generous man and hope that those who knew him enjoy this remembrance.

FERRYING BACK, I find Captain Mark Brown again at the helm and we are just in time to see the *Stewart J. Cort* emerge from under the Mackinac Bridge. "That's the first thousand-footer to sail the Great Lakes," Brown tells me. "It's unique because the bow section and stern section were built in Alabama, welded together, sailed up to Lake Erie, then cut in half so the cargo section, built in Erie, Pennsylvania, could be inserted."

When asked if he's ever done the Labor Day Bridge Walk, Brown says, "If I do it again this year—I'm thirty-three years old—it'll be my thirty-third crossing. My parents took me across the year I was born, and our family still does it."

"Maybe I'll do it this year," I say.

"It only takes an hour and a half, but get an early start," Brown advises. "At seven, seven-thirty in the morning, they shut off the northbound lanes and you walk south from St. Ignace to Mackinaw City. About nine-thirty, they take away one more lane for traffic and it's not comfortable anymore. There are thousands of people in Mackinaw City on that day, but by four o'clock in the afternoon, everyone's gone. You could fire a cannon down Main Street."

As I turn the van toward Lake Michigan, I realize I've been traveling a month, completing the first third of my trip. I haven't had a bad day yet.

LAKE
MICHIGAN

THE PIPING PLOVER EGGS hatched today at Wilderness State Park, and the ranger, an otherwise reasonable-looking man, is beside himself. "There's a couple of chicks out there right now," he tells me at the park office. "But this is the roughest time for 'em, because the gulls and crows go after 'em and we only have three nests."

The piping plover—a plump buff-and-white sparrow-sized waterbird with a black brow and collar—is endangered here, reports the ranger. "There's only thirty whole birds in Michigan." A data sheet instructs campers and park visitors to respect the nests, which, dug in the sand and well camouflaged, are easily disturbed or destroyed.

Wilderness State Park reminds me of a small fish pursued by a large fish pursued by a monster's tentacle—two islands off the end of a peninsula. I can wade to the islands, the water's been so low lately, says the ranger. It feels pretty wild here, as well it should with a name like "Wilderness." On the way out, the trees twine over the van like an awning.

AN UNUSUAL NUMBER of homes in tiny Cross Village are built with river stones, culminating in Legs Inn, a large restaurant named for the row of spiky, upside-down stove legs lining the roof. I come to a screeching halt and enter an eccentric tangle of tree roots, branches, knots, stumps, logs, burls, and carved wood, from peaked ceiling to rustic furniture, all of it varnished to a rich, unnatural shine. It represents the thirty-year obsession of the man whose portrait hangs

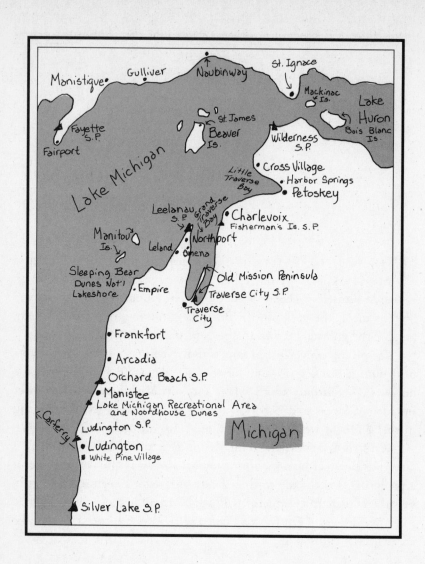

Northeastern Lake Michigan

in the lobby: Stanley Smolak, born in Poland in 1887, settled in Cross Village in 1921, died in 1968.

Today, Legs Inn is a popular summer (May through September) bar and restaurant offering live music and dancing. Four years ago, George Smolak, a nephew of Stanley's, gave up a Chicago structural engineering career to keep Legs Inn in the family. Smolak steals a few minutes from his remote but bustling business to show me a recent letter from the Michigan Historical Commission that designates Legs Inn a historic site, calling it "an excellent and unique expression of vernacular architecture with a colorful history."

This restrained description hardly does justice to the wild one-man museum. Twisted roots reach for my legs under tables; a tall cocktail table's three legs sprout naturally from the top. Across the ceiling appears a contorted display of what could pass for Medusa's wig collection. "Stanley Smolak used to distort the branches of young trees, tie them in place, and wait years for them to grow into the shapes he wanted." Smolak explains the Native American influence—totem poles, paintings of Indians in full regalia. Stanley needed a lot of help with the inn, says Smolak. He became friendly with the Odawas (Ottawas) who lived here in large numbers and who later named him Chief White Cloud.

A Cross Village resident later tells me, "Cross Village was once a sort of United Nations of the area nations; all the peace pipes were kept here. Then the Jesuits showed up, stole the peace pipes, and sent them back to France. An Odawa friend says he has seen some there, in a museum."

JUNE 17

AFTER A DARK and rainy night in a private campground, I follow Route 119, a loopy road between Cross Village and Harbor Springs, touted as "the most beautiful drive in Michigan." The drive is lovely even in the rain. Birch, maple, and beech trees grow to the edge of two winding lanes. Wet, black maple trunks and white birch are sandwiched between green cushions. Now and then a quick view of the churning lake appears through the columns. I drive fifteen minutes before I pass a car or a house.

Lush lawns, big houses, and rolling estates appear. Then Harbor Springs, a beautifully painted town as neat, clean, and well appointed as a yacht: a marina, tasteful restaurants, an expensive shoe store, real estate offices with windows full of photographs, galleries. It is possible to buy a chocolate long-stemmed rose here. I choose from three restaurants on the same corner. A young woman in a red sailor dress gives me the window table that I request with piqued reluctance, but I rush through breakfast to escape a large, voluble woman with a voice like bagpipes at the next table.

Afterward, in a park the size of a house lot, I find a patch of grass, a couple of ducks, and a tall, graceful woman whose three children and big wet dog wait patiently in the station wagon while she explains why I'm having a hard time finding access to the water.

"A lot of property here's owned by people who only use it a couple months out of the year," says Johanna Lund, who, like her husband, works as a nurse at the local hospital. "Most people that really live here can't afford lakefront. There's another beach that's a little bigger than this one, but summer cottage and condo renters use that, so we don't go there much. I feel lucky that we have water a mile away here, but a huge docking area is going in here and this will be turned into parking, so we won't be able to come here much after this summer. It's horrible. It makes me real angry. Until you get to Charlevoix, you'll find the same situation. And you can't really walk along the beach because it's too stony."

She tells me that the entire peninsula on the north side of town is privately owned. "The Harbor Point Club was developed well over a century ago by really big industrialists. Cars aren't allowed in there. They even use horses and buggies to do laundry pickup. Those people are very, very rich—people you don't see much of all year. You should go there; they'll probably let you walk through."

"What do people who live here do all winter?"

"They do real estate. Starve. Now we've got the ski season, which helps." Johanna seems to grow even taller, more gorgeous as she talks.

"You're sure you don't mind if I quote you?" I worry.

"No, I really don't. I'm fairly vocal about the fact that there's so much real estate development here that's aimed at the rich and people that are here for such a short time. I appreciate those folks—they're part of our tax base, and we have wonderful schools here in Harbor

Springs—but there are some disadvantages too. You starve it out all winter, and then when the best time of the year comes, you can hardly enjoy it. You feel like a little guy, but you gotta yell."

Following Johanna's suggestion, I drive to the entrance of the Harbor Point Club, but a guard refuses me entry and calls the supervisor when I point my camera at the arched entrance. I can be sued, I am warned. I drive off quickly, strangely frightened.

PUZZLED BY UNUSUAL STRIATIONS on Little Traverse Bay, I pull into a bluff-top parking area that overlooks a marina and the city of Petoskey. From the shore outward, separate masses of tan, brown, green, and deep blue water abut like paint-by-numbers color groups, edges distinct as horizons. I drive to the marina to inquire about it.

"I've never seen it like this!" exclaims a man from the deck of a sailboat. "It's the goldarn new mall project that has all washed down here. Just go on up the hill and you can't miss it. It's all unearthed. I won't even take my dinghy out in this crap—get that junk in my motor. And their excuse is going to be, 'Hey, you can't expect us to handle a downpour like that.' "

"It really did rain hard last night."

"So what? It really irks you when they can't put their finger on the big guy, but they can on us small guys."

The whole marina is discussing the muddy water. One boat owner says he's been coming here for thirty-eight years and he's never seen anything like it. After a while, I spot a man doing just what I'm doing: talking to boaters in the marina and taking notes. I walk over and introduce myself to Perry Clark, a local news reporter lured out on his day off. "It's happened at least five times," Clark tells me. "It just goes on and on. This is the worst, though."

"So what happens?"

"Nothing. They just point. The city people say they can't do anything because they approved the project, but the approved drainage plan doesn't go into effect until the project's finished. The county people say, 'It's a disgrace, but we can't do anything because it's the city's responsibility.' The contractor doesn't do anything."

"Well, I'll bet there's going to be a hue and cry about it."

Clark scribbles. "Can I quote you on that?"

"Who, me? Sure." I quite enjoy being quoted for a change. We team up. Clark introduces me to Jim Kloostra, commander of the Petoskey State Police force and disgusted boat owner. "I wouldn't run a motor in that crap," says the commander from the back of a power boat. "Wear your engine out about a hundred times faster."

Clark and I retire to the basement bar of an old hotel, where Clark tells stories in a clear, succinct voice. One is about a proposal to turn a nearby abandoned cement plant into possibly the largest resort on the Great Lakes. "My favorite word for it is 'colossal.' It's planned to have thirteen hundred and fifty housing units, two golf courses, resort hotel complex, amphitheater, and inland marina for a thousand boats. It's a half-a-billion-dollar project."

"Are there objections to this?"

"Some. On the other hand, the property is so blighted that if somebody can clean it up . . ." He shrugs. "One of the controversies about that project is whether there's going to be any public access, because it consumes five and a half miles of lakeshore. The developers have promised to keep the shoreline open to people who want to walk along the shore, but it's rock cobble beach, not conducive to walking."

Despite such problems, Clark loves living up here. "I just love to go out and walk along the beach when there's nobody there. I think Petoskey is the most beautiful part of Michigan I've been in. It's still relatively undeveloped: within fifteen, twenty minutes you can be in a woods, if that's your thing, or on an empty lakeshore. Now it's not a great place for mall shopping, although that's going to change. Not a great place for professional sports, but we have great cable TV service. There's all this hilly terrain, water, beaches, and enough civilization to make a perfect balance. But that's changing now."

He tells me the story about the Perry Hotel we're in. "I think it was built around 1899," says Clark. "It's a real Petoskey landmark, the last of our great resort hotels still standing. It went through several owners, but a couple years ago a guy bought it who was one of these high-stakes, risk-taking type stockbrokers. He poured tons of money into this place. Then, all of a sudden, he lost his rating as a broker on the stock exchange, was having problems with his properties, and apparently was at the end of his rope. In March of '89, he kidnapped the wife of an Indiana businessman and held her for ransom: 1.2

million dollars in cash and six hundred thousand dollars in gold bullion. They caught him with this woman tied up with duct tape in the back of his van."

"Where is he today?"

"Prison. After that, the hotel was sold off in bankruptcy court, bought by the local bank at auction, and Stafford Smith—a well-respected guy who owns a bunch of restaurants around the bay—bought the hotel from the bank, and I guess it's just booming."

Perry Clark (whose similar name is a coincidence) drives me down an unmarked public access road to a stony beach, where I soon find a Petoskey stone the size of a small loaf of rye. Petoskey is famous for these gray-brown, ancient coral aggregates, which, polished, resemble interlocking sunbursts. I also find, among round and flat stones, a brick.

"There used to be a brick factory up the beach," Clark explains. "Maybe some weren't quite perfect, so they just dumped them in the lake."

We're in shorts, our legs are getting bit up by blackflies, and we're trying not to step on the thousands of spiders spread over the warm beach stones, feasting on flies. We retreat inland and begin walking down some abandoned railroad tracks. Clark knows the names of everything—trees, flowers, birds. Suddenly, a fawn wobbles to its feet from a grassy nest under our noses and runs into the woods. We stand there, stunned. It was tiny, delicate, utterly new—utterly in contrast with the barren area full of cement kiln dust below us, between the tracks and the lake.

"This is one of the big stories that I've done," Clark comments. "There are areas along the shore where some black water contaminated with heavy metals seeps up from below ground. The same heavy metals are present in this kiln dust. But no one knows whether it's from the coal used to fire the kiln or whether it's naturally occurring in the limestone and shale and gypsum that was used to make the cement, or what."

"And they're going to build condos on top of this?"

"Well, the stuff is going to be moved. That's one of the controversies. They're talking about filling in a quarry and building a golf course on top of it. But the environmentalists say, 'Hey, you don't want to put that stuff in a quarry where there's ground water infiltration and have these heavy metals go into the ground water.' On the other hand, every test they've done so far on this material shows that it cannot leach heavy metals. And so the unresolved question remains, Where are the heavy metals that seep up along the shore right by these kiln dust piles coming from?"

Note: A 1993 U.S. Geological Survey study reports that the 600 million tons of soil eroding annually from farmers' fields, often containing manure, chemical fertilizers, and pesticides, plus the dirt from construction sites and city streets, may pose a greater threat to the Great Lakes than industrial pollution (*Petoskey News-Review*, November 19, 1993).

JUNE 18

ACCORDING TO a map at the visitor center of the Big Rock Point Nuclear Power Plant, there are eleven nuclear power plants on the Great Lakes, grouped as follows: none on Lake Superior, none on Lake Huron, three on Lake Erie, two on Lake Ontario, and six on Lake Michigan. Charlevoix, a charming tourist town set between an inland lake and Lake Michigan, seems an unlikely place to find the oldest of them (its reactor in a big blue bubble), but that's where I am, talking to Charlie MacInnis, the friendly public relations man. Straightforward and undefensive, Charlie MacInnis is impossible not to like.

"This is the first commercial nuclear plant built in Michigan and the first on the Great Lakes, put into service in 1962," he begins, seating me in his office. "We don't have the cooling towers of larger plants. They use a lot more heat; all nuclear power plants borrow water from a lake or river or cooling pond and the water comes back out a little warmer. Ours comes out only about twenty degrees warmer and goes straight into Lake Michigan. That is not considered to be a concern because the volume is not great enough to raise the temperature of the lake. We call this our cute little nuclear plant. A small group of people runs it, and I think we're a pretty friendly bunch.

"Back in the sixties, this was probably one of the largest tourist attractions in Michigan, second only to Greenfield Village. When it was first built, we put one hundred thousand people a year through this place. Then in the seventies, the Consumers Power Company had a kind of a cash crunch, so then we didn't give any tours at all. But after the accident at Three Mile Island, nuclear plants decided to put a public affairs person at each nuclear plant to maintain relationships with the community, governmental bodies, and the news media. So that's why I'm here. I can't give everybody a tour, but I still take through a lot of school kids and people like yourself."

"How much power does this put out compared to a two-tower job?"

"Some of the two-tower jobs might be up between eight hundred and a thousand megawatts, and we're in the range of sixty-seven megawatts. Research was done here for quite a few years. By building the plant small, the researchers could shut it down and start it up again without screwing up the Consumers Power Electric multi-city grid." The phone rings, and MacInnis lets the machine answer it—an unusual courtesy that further endears him to me.

"Now we'll go over to the security building," he says. "They'll check your ID and you'll sign the log book and go through a metal detector and an explosives detector. Then you'll get a badge and a key card that tells security that you're coming in. Then we'll go upstairs to the control room and you can see the operators in there. We'll stop on the way up to pick up a dosimeter, a device that measures radiation exposure."

"How much radiation will I be exposed to?"

"About the same you got already today. Wherever you are in the world, you are exposed to radiation. When you go to the coal plant [my next stop], you'll get a little from the metals picked up with the coal. You'll get a little here, too, but it's not like going into a microwave oven or anything like that. We'll go on the turbine deck and see the generator. Then, we'll go through the air lock and up to the reactor deck so you can look down on the reactor.

"Now, as we start this tour, I have to tell you that one of the security regulations is that you have to stay with me. So if you have to go to the bathroom, we have to go together. So, um, uh, the best thing to do, um . . ."

I laugh, go in the bathroom, but can't turn on the light. I call MacInnis and he can't turn it on, either. "We seem to have a power shortage," he mumbles. I choke back hoots of laughter. A power shortage at a nuclear power plant?

My hard hat has a little crank on the back that clicks until the hat fits my head. As we start toward the security building, I say, "Charlie, being here makes me nervous. In fact, I'm afraid of being near here. I fear a nuclear accident, not to mention the repercussions of storing spent fuel."

"That's a real fear. I believe that the reality is that these nuclear plants are not the environmental threat that some people think they are." MacInnis's response—a pat on the head, not an answer—does nothing to reassure me.

In the security building, all goes as MacInnis predicted and we head for the containment building. "We've got quite a large security operation, most of which you can't see," he says. "What you will see are the swallows that have built mud nests under that track around the middle of the sphere."

Huge numbers of cliff and barn swallows swoop like bees around the creamy turquoise balloon, behind which rises a thin tower candy-cane-striped red and white. The place feels like a child's storybook until we go in. Then it's pure James Bond: a huge, spherical space dominated by uniformed men, massive equipment, and a powerful hum. We go through an air lock, something like a stuck elevator, then climb metal grill steps. Thirty feet up, I look down into the nine-foot-wide reactor filled with long, vertical tubes. Nothing here feels real. When I emerge, which isn't soon enough, I'm not sure how real I feel, either.

"Not to worry," laughs MacInnis. "You'd get more radiation eating a banana."

AN HOUR AFTER leaving the nuclear plant, I attend the first open house ever held by the Top-O-Michigan Power Plant on Lake Charlevoix. Compared with the nuclear plant and its science-fiction ambiance, this coal-fired plant, although only ten or fifteen years older, feels like a place where my grandfather, who once owned a Michigan coal company, would have been quite at home.

I arrive about noon. A small crowd is gathered around a casual buffet of box lunches and soda pop. Earnest plant workers give tours of the several stories, shouting above the chugging, hissing, never-ending noise. It sounds like a 1920s train station in here. Huge boilers and machinery reach through several of the floors. A row of turbines, painted a pale, 1930s yellow enamel, are lined up like fine old cars in a museum. And despite coal piles visible outside, the inside is touchingly clean, so swept and scrubbed my grandmother might have done it.

"This Number Three boiler's on line and running right now!" roars my guide. "It goes up six stories high. It gets hot! This pulverizer grinds the coal that's going into the boiler right now—grinds it almost as fine as talcum powder."

I'm sweating—it's hotter than a summer-camp kitchen in here—but my guide says, heck, I should be here when it really gets hot. He shows me how the steam that runs the turbines is condensed, recycled through a series of heaters before it goes back into the boiler to become steam again. We walk past a lot of concrete and steel. Pipes run everywhere.

I climb metal grill steps to another floor, where everything is painted gray and the noise is even louder. The clock-type dials and other gauges look old-fashioned in this age of liquid crystal readouts. Everybody's yelling. Bill Miller takes over: "I control the large boiler here and the large turbine," yells Miller. "Right now the pressure is about 885 pounds. These are all the temperatures on the auxiliary equipment. It's all hooked up to an alarm system, so if something goes outside the limits, hopefully it will set off an alarm. If it doesn't, we're supposed to catch it anyway. But they have safety interlocks on them too—if it gets within dangerous range, it'll shut the whole thing down."

"How often does that happen?"

"Oh, once we had a tube leak . . . probably about ten years ago, last time that I'm aware of. I've been here almost twelve years. . . . Now, over here's the generator. . . . And this is our stack monitor. If you look at our stack, you'll see there's no smoke coming out. We've got a real good system that takes out all the dust. We haul it to various landfills. Some of it's used in cement." Some harmful gases, however, are invisible.

"How much coal do you burn a day?"

"Probably about two hundred tons."

On a lower level, I sit down at some tables that have been set up in a clear area, where I meet a man from the coal company that supplies the plant. "The coal's mined in east Kentucky," he says. "We load it out in one ship, ten thousand tons at a crack, which takes seven to eight hours, and then it's loaded on the train that goes from Pikeville, Kentucky, up to Toledo inside a minimum—guaranteed by the C & O Railroad—of forty-eight hours."

"So what's the hurry?"

"The hurry is the turnover of the railroad equipment. We've got a hundred and ten railroad cars that are waiting for another train to go someplace else; we need that equipment to be in constant service. So at Toledo, the ten thousand tons are loaded into the boat, and it's anywhere from thirty-six to forty-three hours depending on weather for the trip from the docks at Toledo up through the Detroit River, up through Lake Huron, across the top of Michigan, and down here to Lake Charlevoix."

The freighter, in fact, is presently anchored in Lake Michigan outside the Charlevoix Channel. "It was supposed to be here by now so you could get on and tour it, but it's too rough out there. The freighter is 610 feet long and 60 feet in the beam, but the opening of the channel at the bridge is only 62 feet. Two-foot clearance. You can literally reach out and touch the coal boat from the rail as it's coming into this plant. It's quite an experience. It's a social event in Charlevoix when the coal boat arrives."

I sigh. Sure would have loved to have boarded that freighter.

I ARRIVE AT the narrow, dog-leg channel in Charlevoix, hoping to catch the coal boat going through, but it's still waiting out choppy seas. Wedged between the channel and Lake Michigan, however, is the DNR Great Lakes Fishing Station. No one seems to be around, so I wander among long, narrow, concrete ponds thick with fish sorted by size, then upstairs, where Paul Gelderblom, a tall, soft-spoken researcher who looks as Dutch as his name, appears from an office.

"Most of what we do here is research," Gelderblom tells me. "Mostly we work with lake trout, whitefish, chubs, salmon—game fish. The federal people work more with the forage fish, which is what the big fish feed on, and the lamprey; the universities deal with water chemistry, problems with zebra mussels and things like that."

"I thought whitefish was a commercial, not a sport, fish. I see it all the time in restaurants but rarely hear fisherpersons talk of it."

"It's both," says Gelderblom. "People on Grand Traverse Bay often talk about catching whitefish."

"I thought sport fish couldn't be sold commercially."

"They can be sold commercially only by a commercial fishery."

"You mean a sportsman can't sell his fish to a restaurant?"

"Right. You have to have a special license to do that. We issue those commercial licenses and we keep track of the fish populations in order to set TACs [total allowable catch limits], so we know how many fish can be harvested without damaging the fish population."

"Do you raise fish here and seed them in the lake?"

"Well, whitefish take care of themselves. But lake trout are so slow growing that they don't reproduce themselves fast enough to keep up with the fishing pressure. Those are all lake trout downstairs. This is a state station but those are federal fish, wild fish here temporarily to make sure they don't have any diseases before they go into the hatcheries. If they have a disease and you put them in a hatchery, you can wipe out all the fish in the hatchery. So they have to be here at least two years.

"Now, salmon grow much faster—they'll get as big as those lake trout in two or three years. Usually when they run in the rivers in their third or fourth year, they'll be between fifteen and twenty-five pounds. Then they spawn and die. Except for triploid salmon, which are supposedly sterile, so they can get even bigger."

"I've never heard of triploid salmon."

"Well, regular fish, like regular people, have one set of genes from each parent, making them diploids. But triploid salmon eggs at a certain stage of their development get a third set of genes which makes them sterile. We don't have any idea yet how big these fish will get. Theoretically, a triploid salmon could reach sixty or seventy pounds."

"You mean, there could be monster fish down there!"

Gelderblom smiles patiently. "Quite possibly. This year we're concentrating on salmon. Used to be hatcheries would hatch up and grow them until they were about three, four inches long, plant them in the lake, and then they'd be gone and we didn't have any idea where they'd go. Salmon should be three or four years old before they come back to spawn, but a few, called flashbacks, would come back after one year. After two years, we'd get some jacks—salmon that are mature but only about four, five pounds. Only the males do that."

"Do they come back here to spawn?"

"A few stray off, but most of the mature salmon come back to the Medusa Creek weir, a sort of lock that keeps the salmon from running up the river, or wherever they were planted. Then they're harvested by a private company."

"I thought salmon spawning grounds were like bird migration paths."

"That's some of the research we're doing," Gelderblom explains. "We're keeping them in the weir for a while before we let them go to see if the imprinting will bring more of them back. We also inject microtags—tiny tags about the size of a '1' on a penny—into the nose of the salmon while they're small, before they're released."

"How does anyone know they're there?"

"When we tag a fish, we cut off the adipose fin, which is the fatty fin in back. We just had a bunch of fifth graders come here and I showed them this whole thing about microtags. It's all set up if you'd like to see it."

In a downstairs classroom, we peer at a monitor that lets us read tags through a microscope. "Each stainless steel tag has four sides," says Gelderblom. "The marks are burned in with a laser onto a spool of wire, and a machine at the hatchery cuts a piece off and injects it into the nose of the fish. From these four numbers, I can tell you where the fish came from, where and when it was planted, what kind of food it was fed. If I want to go in the records, I can find out what truck planted the fish, what the driver's name was, and if he had a flat tire on the way. Now, if the fishermen know that that tag is in there, they'll send us the head—"

"You get fish heads in the mail? Old, smelly fish heads?"

"Oh, yes. The finders tell us how big the fish was, how much it weighed, and where the fish was found. Now, once you get all these heads, you've got to find the tag. That's what this metal detector is for." A shrill beep drills into my ears. "You cut the head in half and find out what half it's in. If you put it under this light here, a lotta times you can see the tag and pick it out with a magnet."

"How long has this program been going on?"

"We're just starting to get some of our tagged salmon back. Next year will be a big year for us. This is also the first year that we mark every salmon that goes into Lake Michigan with tetracycline, an antibiotic that is deposited in the bone and glows yellow in black light. So if you put a fish bone under the black light and there's a little circle glowing there, you know it was a hatchery fish. This way we can tell what percentage of salmon out there are reproducing naturally and what are from hatcheries."

I tell Gelderblom that the lake trout I caught in Lake Ontario was missing a fin, but it was one of the two forward lower fins.

"Those fins are used for fish that don't have microtags," says Gelderblom. "Depending on what kind of fish it is, we can tell you how old it is and when it was planted by the different fin clip codes: There's the LP (left pectoral), the RP (right pectoral), and the BV (back vectral) fin. And you can have combinations, like an RV and LP . . ."

"Why would anyone go to the trouble of mailing you fish heads?"

"When I've processed the heads, I send a postcard to each fisherman telling him where his fish came from. It's a lot of work, but the data is worth it."

Paul picks up a neon orange plastic clip. "Now, here's a different kind of tag. Kids get a kick out of this. This is called a spaghetti tag, and it says 'Michigan DNR, Charlevoix,' and a number. Each number is different. You pull the trigger and it sticks in the fish, like giving it a shot."

"You mean it sticks right in the body of the fish? Ouch."

"Did your ears hurt when you got them pierced? So they're swimming around and this is sticking out and you can really see these. We usually get these back. But you can only use spaghetti tags in big fish, which you have to catch before you can put the tags in."

I didn't realize how special these fishing stations are. Gelderblom says there's just one for each lake: "This one is for Lake Michigan, and there's one in Alpena for Lake Huron, one in Marquette for Lake Superior, one on Lake St. Clair for Lake Erie, and there's one on Lake Ontario."

I smile. That last one's in Cape Vincent; I've been there.

JUNE 19

AFTER A PLEASANT NIGHT tucked in the woods at Fisherman's Island State Park near Charlevoix, I'm off with a blast of the *Islander*, a large green-and-white ferry that carries six to eight cars plus freight beneath a passenger deck and lounge to Beaver Island, the largest in a small archipelago thirty-five miles from Charlevoix. I hang over the rail in the sunshine as we pass between the clanging, open jaws of the drawbridge and chug by mainlanders waving from the sidewalk and the condo balconies along the channel.

On the stern, in view of the churning wake, an entomologist from North Carolina, here with her kids, remembers when she took summer courses at Central Michigan University's island science station. "Once about twelve of us banded gulls on one of the smaller islands," she recalls. "The whole island was covered with nesting gulls; it was a really hot day, and we had to wear raincoats and rain hats to keep from getting bird poop all over us. We're running around in all this rain gear trying to catch young gulls. It was one of the nastiest and the craziest things I've ever done."

More than two hours later, about fifty passengers flood onto the dock in downtown St. James, where I observe, on the harbor side of the road, a marina and a modest motel. A vacant white frame building, the Beachcomber Restaurant, and the Shamrock Bar and Restaurant line up on the other. Freight waits in the ferry yard—appliances, lumber, boxes, bicycles, a kayak. Old rusted pickups and boatlike cars roar by. A pontoonless plane with the engine behind the cockpit clings like a dragonfly to the narrow motel beach.

I hadn't planned to stay overnight, but already I know I will. Roy Elsworth signs me into the Erin Motel and offers to take me up later in the amphibious plane I've observed. In the meantime, Jim Willis motions me into the front seat of a dusty tour van and starts up the engine. "I've been coming to the island from Charlevoix since I was thirteen, fourteen years old," Willis begins in a smooth, deep voice, trolling through town in low gear. "I used to work on commercial fishing vessels—a lotta 'em were out here at one time. Worked on the lumber boats and hauled lumber outa here. When I got outa the service in 1946, I worked on the boat that carried the mail and passengers to Beaver Island. For the last fifteen years I've been coming ever' summer. Four years ago I retired here.

"So that's my story. Now, our tour starts here." He shows me a map. A gravel road loops around the edge of the thirteen-mile-long island, enclosing large areas of state forest. We stay at the northern, town end, however, slowly passing the post office, the one grocery store, a dilapidated, to-be-restored fish tug next to a harborside marine museum. Atop a white brick lighthouse at the harbor entrance, a red light flashes. "Immigrant labor built this lighthouse," Willis tells me. "The potato famine was on in Ireland and people wrote home and said, 'Lotsa fish to eat here, lotsa land for potatoes,' and that's how the Irish came to Beaver Island." A plaque commemorates persons lost at sea, the most recent being three commercial fishermen in 1986.

We drive through wooded country on gravel roads with names like Sloptown Road and King's Highway. At Font Lake, I receive a very abbreviated account of the island's famous and strange history. A Mormon calling himself King Strang, who was a state legislator, first came to the island in 1847 and lived a polygamous life here for almost ten years. "King Strang did all his baptisms in this lake. He met his end when he ordered all the women to wear bloomers. A couple of wives rebelled and Strang had their husbands publicly whipped. The next day, the husbands hid behind a woodpile and shot him. Strang died nine days later, but the two men were never tried for the crime."

After the tour, I order lunch at the Shamrock, a darkish, rectangular restaurant with a long wooden bar on one side, a dance floor at the far end, and a picture-perfect view of the harbor. I no sooner begin asking questions at the bar than I am joined by Don Meister, a large, bandannaed man with a handlebar mustache, and Glen Felixson, the harbor master, who, with his gray hair and beard, light-blue eyes, and captain's cap, looks born to the part. They buy me a beer and slip into an earnest but easy island education.

Don* is wearing a lightning-bolt T-shirt and a small leather medicine bag in which he says he keeps a megis shell and some tobacco. He tells me he has been apprenticed to a medicine woman who sum-

---

* It feels ludicrous to call Beaver Island folk, now friends, by their last names.

mers on a nearby island. "Back in the early twenties, thirties, if you followed the old ways, you were scum," he says. "Many of the old ways are lost because they have to be passed from person to person, so that the wrong person won't get the knowledge."

Glen was born and raised in Chicago but has been coming here since he was ten. "You know the Wrigley Building? The bridge where you get the boat rides? I ran one of those tour boats for ten years."

Don (raising his voice over jukebox country music): "I used to run a company, but the day after my youngest son finished school, I went into the plant, gave everybody their check a day early, closed out all the books, and locked the whole thing up. They said, 'You can't just do that!' And I says, 'I'm doing it.' And they says, 'Where you goin'?' and I says, 'North.' Hasn't been a day that I regretted it."

Glen: "If you're going to live on this island, you have to love the island itself, because there isn't much else to keep you here. There isn't any nightlife, you can't go to the show, and you don't come here to make money. In the winter there's such a thing as cabin fever out here."

Don: "A lot of the island is Irish. You should see it on St. Patrick's Day. We have a tug of war in the snow, shopping-cart races, pitch-the-pike. The next day, everybody's got a king-size hangover."

The ferry toots. I watch it pull away through the picture window.

Glen: "When I was a kid in the fifties, this harbor was like something out of a picture book—old net sheds, piers, wrecked boats, fish-net reels. You'd look around and your jaw would drop, it was so beautiful. Then in the sixties, somebody said, 'We gotta beautify this place,' and they ripped out a lot of the most beautiful stuff. But although I like to go back to Chicago about once a year, I absolutely love this place. It's in my blood."

Don: "I'll probably make a trip to Charlevoix sometime this fall."

Glen: "There's a local joke around here: 'We're going to the United States today.'" He cackles.

Don: "The water can get pretty bad in hunting season."

Glen: "I've got a twenty-five-foot Steelcraft built in 1946, and one year Don and I took it to a neighboring island and went deer huntin' for a week. When we got back to the boat, it was iced in. I was bound and determined to get back under my own power—if I had to be pulled out, I'd a never lived it down. We broke out of the ice all right, but then the darn water pump broke down. I disconnected it and put a big funnel in and handed Don a bucket."

Don: "Took us three hours to do a forty-five-minute run. The Coast Guard icebreaker *Mesquite* was going past us with all its life preservers and stuff—this huge ship, right? And here him and I are dippin' over the side with a five-gallon bucket and we're freezin'. Crew's lookin' down at us and laughin'. Three weeks later, the *Mesquite* sunk in Lake Superior."

Glen: "Less than two years that we've had a cop here. You can leave your camera on the front seat of your car, go across for two weeks, come back, and it'll still be there. But a six-packa beer, that'll be gone."

The above is just a sampling. These guys can go on all day.

ROY ELSWORTH STARTS the engine in his amphibious plane and we roll into the water. Suddenly he retracts the wheels and slams a keel through a slot next to me. "Now we're a boat!" shouts Roy over the propeller roaring behind the cockpit. "The body is the pontoon!" We putt out toward the lighthouse, turn, and roar over the chop toward town. "Pull up the keel!" yells Roy, which I do, and we clear the Shamrock.

Seeing no windsock on the motel, I ask Roy how he knows which way the wind's blowing, and he says sailboats at anchor always point into the wind. I don't see any sailboats today, I say. No comment from Roy. Somehow he knows the wind direction.

We begin skimming the scalloped island perimeter, flying first over a black-and-white commercial fishing tug trailing a screaming speech balloon of gulls. Milky green waves curl beneath us; farther out, emerald water swirls with purple shadows. Inland, small lakes gleam in deep woods. As we dip toward one, a couple waves from a canoe. Back out over the lake, Roy grins wickedly as he sneaks up behind a green tug pulling a barge. "He can't hear us," shouts Roy. "He's going along at five miles an hour, bored to hell, and boom, here comes an airplane right by his window! Scare the hell right out of him!" Indeed, the startled pilot laughs and waves as we shoot past nearly at deck level, and shortly thereafter we land back in the harbor, the engine subdues some, and we're a boat again. I shove the keel down, we chug back to the motel, Roy puts down the wheels, I pull up the keel, and we park back on the beach. Didn't even get my feet wet.

JUNE 20

I SLEPT IN my clothes last night in a room with a bay-view picture window, which by morning has become a runway for over a hundred mosquitoes revving for takeoff. I shower, redress, and venture across the street to the Beachcomber, a restaurant with a counter, knotty-pine everything, and a waitress in a T-shirt that proclaims, under a rendering of a chest-sized mosquito: I GAVE AT BEAVER ISLAND.

Then it's down the road to the St. James Boat Shop, where a black Lab lavishes me with attention and sawdust. "That's Bear," says a lanky, white-bearded man, who's knotting a thick rope handle onto a wooden bucket. Bill Freese works at a large workbench that fills the middle of a sawdusty, high-ceilinged room. Lumber cut to various widths is stacked against the walls; sawdust covers the floor; buckets gleam in the window; birch and cherry canoes invite stroking in an adjoining room.

"Is that a kayak?" I ask about an oddly shaped small one.

"That's a canoe. Coffee's back there if you'd care for a cup." I wander into a gloomy back room and pour from an automatic pot on a once-white sink.

Back at the bench, I tell Bill I'm a writer and ask if I may tape him. "I don't give two hoots and a holler what you write," Bill says. "Writers around here are a dime a dozen. Same sort of things you're doing. Not a bit uncommon." I catch a glint in his eye and decide he's teasing. I ask about paddles.

Paddles, Bill allows, go for about one hundred dollars—"if I ever get around to making them." People wander in and out, asking pretty much what I have asked or intend to. Canoes sell for about forty-five hundred, Bill tells them. About white-water canoeing: "That's a modern sport. That's outa Hollywood. Those old-time traders, they'd come down loaded with furs, there's no way they were going to take those canoes down white water."

"Not many shops to cater to the tourists here," I observe.

"There's not many tourists. You get a lot of different sorts of people here. As for me, after the military I had to strike out and make my big mark in the world. Pay off the mortgage, raise the kids. Finally I got tired of all that rat race. But for a long time, I didn't realize I could quit."

On my way out, I notice that the hours posted on the door suggest that if he's here, he's open; if he's not, he's closed. I'll remember that.

NEXT DOOR CARL FELIX, who, like his son Glen, looks like an old-time sea captain, is carefully constructing customized models from pictures of yachts and sailboats. I continue my walk around the harbor to the Beaver Island Toy Museum, where Mary Scholl, a forthright, curly-haired woman, is taking quarters and dimes from small hands in exchange for bagsful of toys. She moved here from Chicago ten years ago and didn't leave the island for nine, Mary tells me as I gape at her impressive collection of old metal toy trucks, airplanes, and other antique toys hanging from the walls, ceiling, and rafters. Below them, vacationing children swarm among bins, baskets, jars, and drawers of pea shooters, ARCHIE BUNKER FOR PRESIDENT buttons, 1948 German-made cowboys, ten-cent monkeys, rub-on tattoos, rings (thirteen for a dollar), necklaces, planes, dolls, cars, whistles, and much, much more.

Glen Felixson is sitting on the weathered porch overlooking a little wetland. "Kids go completely out of their minds when they come in here," he tells me while Mary tends her customers. "They come in here with a coupla of quarters and leave with a bagful of stuff—rubber pencils, whoopee cushions. Glow bugs for a dime, sharks for a dime. A knife that the blade goes in so it looks like you're stabbing yourself. Antique cards, two for five cents. Beaver Island Monopoly that she drew herself. Compass rings for fifty cents. Candy lips."

"It's the last five-cent store in America," claims Mary, joining us. "How do I know that? Who else would do it?"

"How do you get all this stuff?"

"I brought a lot with. I used to buy out old stores and warehouses that had wonderful stock all the way back to the twenties. I also buy stuff from carnival suppliers, stuff that isn't wind-up or needs batteries."

Mary leads me behind the store into a parklike garden fragrant and rich with two hundred kinds of roses. A rowboat planted with hundreds of hen-and-chick varieties. Thirty-two types of lilacs have just passed their prime. Fantasies of cement and found art—a gym shoe overflowing with hens and chicks, a wedding cake with bride and groom, concrete studded with bits of broken glass, jewelry and pottery—pop up between plants. A bench is bowered with roses, an arch draped by a weeping tamarack.

Back on the ferry, I can think of nothing else.

SOUTH OF CHARLEVOIX, hills roll on as if behind a Renaissance Madonna until I get to Traverse City, where the splendid views of Grand Traverse Bay are blocked by mile after mile of development. I pay for a site at the woodsy but urban Traverse City State Park, then maneuver the van across the bordering five-lane highway to picnic on a surprisingly quiet beach. Mid-munch, a brilliant parachute drifts like a balloon across the waterscape. A parasail! When the boat pulling it turns back, I note where it's heading, stuff my deli strawberries and smoked whitefish back in their plastic tubs, jump into the van, and screech around the bay on the busy highway—past the campground, motel after motel, restaurant after restaurant—park on a side street, and run up the sandy, condo-lined beach, down a dock, breathless but in time.

The two parasail guys allow me to join several other passengers on a water-ski-type boat for twenty-five dollars (usual price: forty), and then we're out on the water. Suddenly, reality sets in. I can't believe I'm doing this. I watch two other brave souls go up before I climb nervously into the strap contraption on the back of the open power boat, the ski-bright parachute blooming behind, and then up I go at the end of a long line, into a shining pink-and-gold sky. It's sunset over Grand Traverse Bay, and I'm in it, dangling below my billowing parachute, clinging with both hands. Higher and higher I go, so far up I can see over the Old Mission Peninsula that splits the bay like a wishbone. After ten thrilling minutes, I'm cranked back in, teasingly close to the water, but my shoes hit the landing pad dry.

JUNE 21

AFTER A NIGHT in crowded Traverse City State Park, I tour the skinny Mission Peninsula, looking for breakfast. Twice I cross the forty-fifth parallel, which, a sign informs me, also intersects Yellowstone Park, Minneapolis, Bordeaux, Italy, Yugoslavia, the mouth of the Danube, the Caspian Sea, the Black Sea, Mongolia, the tip of Japan, and the Great Wall of China. The hilly farmland and orchards here feel peacefully remote after brash, busy Traverse City, but the shoreline parks are tiny, and I can't find a waterfront restaurant. I end up back in Traverse City at a fast-food joint, seated next to the Biggses, a retired couple with a bee in their bonnets:

He: "We came to this area because for years we looked for places where we could get to Lake Michigan and play. Which are getting few and far between. You're losing more with each year, especially here. Used to hunt and fish in this area. Now you can't put a boat in unless you pay."

She: "They started the motels at only one story. Now they're putting second and third stories on them. Driving along this shore, you can't hardly see the bay for the homes, motels, and the condos."

He: "In Sweden, any property on the water has to recess so that the shoreline belongs to everybody. To me that's a wonderful thing. But all they see here is what glimmers and glitters—dollars."

She: "Developers are trying to get a permit to build condos and a big golf course in a wetland area west of town here. Environmentalists are fighting it, but I think the condo people will win out."

He: "There's a saying they have up here: 'After you pay, there's a view of the bay.' That disgusts me. By the time the young people realize what's happening, it'll be too late, and by that generation"— he points to his six-year-old granddaughter—"there won't be anything left. Huntin', fishin', outdoors, won't be nothin'. They already got a program where they raise pheasants and turn 'em loose. Turn 'em loose today and shoot 'em tomorrow."

Mr. Biggs pauses, then breaks into a wide smile. "Well, that's a relief. Got it off my chest for today. I get pretty warmed up about this stuff."

Note: Government acquisition of shoreline for public access and environmental protection is now being suggested by experts. In 1993, the International (U.S.–Canadian) Joint Commission appointed to study the possibility of increased regulation of Great Lakes water levels* recommended to state and provincial governments that instead of investing in expensive and potentially environmentally damaging water level controls, they buy waterfront property wherever possible and keep new development a greater distance from the waterline.

I WOULD ALSO like to see development pushed back from the shore, but I have to admit that I enjoy the variety that some coastline development can bring, and I like the energy and fun of Traverse City and the large numbers of young people who find summer work and play here—and schooling. At the Great Lakes Maritime Academy (part of Northwestern Michigan College), I'm ushered into the office of Rear Admiral James F. McNulty, whose beard and bearing remind me of former surgeon general C. Everett Koop. "When the St. Lawrence Seaway was opened, this was in fact referred to as the Fourth Coast," the admiral assured me upon hearing the title of my book.

Although qualifying licensed graduates of the school may sign aboard any American vessel an an engineer, the Great Lakes Maritime Academy is the only maritime college in the United States serving the special needs of freshwater transport, says McNulty. Graduates earn from $18,000 to $30,000 their first year; an experienced freighter captain may earn $100,000. A Great Lakes freighter is typically run by eight officers—a captain, three mates, three engineers, and a chief engineer—who work sixty-days-on / thirty-days-off shifts. "Except for ferries, there are no passenger ships left," says McNulty. "Twelve is the greatest number of passengers a freighter can carry without getting into a different category of ship and having to carry medical staff, and so on."

---

* Although the flow from Lakes Superior and Ontario are now controlled, there are no controls on the middle three lakes.

About women: "The first woman was admitted here in 1977. Since then, twenty-three have graduated, and thirteen are presently active in the fleet. It takes a certain amount of grit for a woman to succeed here. A lot of guys can sort of coast through, because it's a male world and they don't have to prove anything. On board, everything functions in a neat framework. A lot of guys like it because they don't have to talk—they just grunt."

I smile. A perfect place for some husbands I know, I amuse myself thinking, until my wandering gaze discovers a tall ship outside the office window. The volunteers renovating this vessel are not officially affiliated with the school, McNulty tells me, but the school has lent them the dock.

Reluctantly leaving the rear admiral, whose gallantry made me feel I'd slipped back in history, I wander over to the cluster of people in a small yard near the ship's wooden hull. The setup looks motley compared with the elaborate, state-funded *Niagara* renovation.

A man pours molten metal into triangular-shaped molds from a claw-footed bathtub that looks incongruous next to the lake. He's making ingots for ballast, he tells me. The bathtub is cast iron. Works like a charm.

"We've been working on the *Madeline* for five years," explains one of the organizers, Edwin P. Brown. "She's a replica of a schooner built in Fairport, Ohio, in 1845 that sailed this area and disappeared off Milwaukee in the 1860s. She'll be sailing by fall—we've even got an 1845 penny and a this year's silver dollar to put under the masts." He smiles at my puzzled look. "In olden times sailors put coins under the mast to pay their way across the river Styx to heaven," he explains. "Sailing's always been risky business."

JUST MINUTES from the *Madeline*, I find a second, even bigger tall ship, the *Malabar*, a hundred-ton working reproduction of a two-masted, freight-carrying schooner. The sun's out and the wind's kicked up. "This is the best sailing weather I've seen in weeks," says owner John Elder as I buy a twenty-dollar ticket for the afternoon sail. "A hundred, hundred fifty years ago, there were probably a thousand vessels like this on Lake Michigan alone. Before roads and rails, everything was moved by ship—dry goods, lumber, passengers. But fresh water rots wood very quickly, so almost all these vessels have disappeared."

"I thought salt water ate sunken ships."

"Salt water eats steel, but it actually pickles wood. We brine our decks every day to keep them from rotting."

About twenty passengers and a crew of six file aboard the big wooden ship, sails unfurl dramatically, and suddenly we're creaking and flapping down the west side of Grand Traverse Bay, an elegant one-ship parade. What a glorious sight we must be, I think—people should pay just to look at us. From the animated conversation around me, I learn that one person's here to escape the deer-fly invasion; another claims that, unlike on the oceans, there's no drinking age on the Great Lakes. A startling facsimile of Captain Ahab holds court in the bow, but the wind is whistling into my tape-recorder mike, so I go below, finding myself in a closet-sized galley with the only female crew member: short, blond Karen Barrows.

"It's difficult to cook down here," Barrows says in a soft southern drawl, "because as you can see right now, we're heeling. When I hear the captain holler 'Comin' about!'—these pans are pitchin' the wrong way—I have to turn 'em, like this, so the spouts don't dump. When he calls 'Ready about!' I have to switch them all again. The stove has rails, and it's on gimbals to keep it level, but stuff'll come loose anyway. It's a diesel stove. I call him Fred. Fred operates a lot like a wood stove—takes forty-five minutes to get him to full temperature. Also I've got a propane stove, which goes right off the bat. Hortense—this red pump here—is hooked up to a two-hundred-gallon holding tank."

While she talks, Barrows adjusts pots and stirs chili for the crew, which eats and sleeps on board. "This certainly is not a high-paying occupation—room and board plus about a dollar an hour—but it's more fun than anything I've ever done," Barrows tells me. "I was in the army for four years—I was a Russian linguist, then drove a tank in West Germany. I came here in 1987. It's hard hours, difficult conditions, and low pay. But there's just nothing like it. It's very immediate."

Note: The 106-foot *Malabar*, in addition to providing daily summer sails and romantic overnight accommodations, participates in a student "Schoolship" program, as does the fifty-foot *Madeline*.

I'M DRIVING up the woodsy east side of the Leelanau Peninsula when what should appear in the tiny village of Omena but a large, sophisticated art gallery. I fall in love. I want everything. The Tamarack Gallery, with its choice, fresh selection from midwestern artists, has thrived for years, a clue that, despite its remote appearance, the Leelanau Peninsula attracts the wealthy.

I continue north through Northport to the very end of the peninsula and tuck myself into the Leelanau State Park woods, where the knotty-pine outhouses, lack of electricity, few RVs, stony beaches, loons, and raccoons afford me an overwhelming feeling of peace. Clowning on the beach are what I've nicknamed BBDs—big brown ducks, the females of most duck species looking alike to me. Heaven has to be something like sitting on a log on a quiet, pebbly beach watching BBDs and eating apple pie from a deli box, unless, like me, you drop your gummy plastic fork in the sand. (Don't do this. You think you've wiped all the sand off, but you haven't.)

Before turning in, I follow a flashing light to the old Traverse Bay Lighthouse and its working replacement, an ugly contraption attached to a bare metal frame. The caretaker, an older man who's wandering around a tidy lawn full of stone walls and sculptures, lives in the old lighthouse and grew up here. He remembers how life was when his father was lightkeeper. "Had to keep things spick-and-span," he tells me. "Couldn't throw your clothes around." He points to several huge maples. "I helped plant these trees in 1923. Left for fifty years and came back in '85. Place was a mess—windows boarded up, roof all gone. But we're restoring it—probably put eighty-five, ninety thousand in it in the last three years. All volunteer help. Well, make yourself to home."

It's summer solstice, the longest day of the year. Parked at the northern tip of a spit of land with a view both east and west, I watch the sun set from one side of my van, then, at dawn, rise from the other.

JUNE 22

QUAINT FISHTOWN (part of the prim town of Leland) squats picturesquely on the western shore of the Leelanau Peninsula. "This commercial fishing district has provided a livelihood for the residents . . . for over a century," begins an elaborate sign. "Fishermen reached the fishgrounds . . . using small sailboats until the introduction of primitive gas-powered oak boats around 1900. Small fishing shanties and related buildings such as ice and smoke houses were constructed during the peak years of the industry which spanned the first three decades of the 20th century. Now gray and weatherbeaten, some buildings still serve their original purpose. Leland continues to be a commercial fishing area as well as the headquarters for transportation to the Manitou Islands."

In one of the ex–fish shanties, I find a little bakery featuring aromatic oatmeal-cherry muffins. "When my great-grandfather first began fishing here, they were using sailboats," says owner Eloise Fahs. "In those days, they would take the fish out of the nets on their way in and then clean them in the shanty. The nets would be rolled out on huge reels like that one." She points to an antique one displayed outside. "They used to mend nets off these reels.

"A lot of men died at sea. Both my great-grandfather and my grandfather died. My grandfather and uncle were on one of the original motor fishing boats when it exploded out in the middle of the lake and they were thrown into the water with their life jackets. My uncle survived twenty-nine hours in the lake, but his father—my grandfather—died in his arms. They were picked up in the middle of the night by two men who were out searching for them. When they were right next to him, one man said to the other, "Stop the motor, I hear one of them calling." But my uncle did not have a voice to call. He could only whisper. Isn't that something?"

I'm waiting for the ferry to take me on a day trip to South Manitou Island, because, as one backpacking woman tells me, "One can't just day-trip on North Manitou. It's a wilderness area, more secluded. Nothing's there. Rangers' quarters, that's it. Only forty or sixty people are allowed on at once." (The Manitou Islands are part of the Sleeping Bear National Lakeshore.)

Once at sea on the rough-and-ready boat, Captain George Grovenor, who's run the ferry for forty-two years, tells me that South Manitou was settled long before the surrounding mainland. "It was inconvenient in those days to settle on the mainland, because all transportation was by water. To travel by land, you had to bushwhack through the wilderness."

After a brisk ninety-minute ride, we debark, queue for the only flush toilet on the island, then head for the South Manitou Lighthouse, led by National Park Service ranger Chuck Kruch. "Back in the 1830s, this was the main commerce area for Lake Michigan," Kruch begins. "Between the 1860s and 1880s, it was the busiest waterway in the world. Just imagine the steamers going up and down the shore-line! There were about fifty wrecks a day on the Great Lakes then, most of them here on Lake Michigan: lacking good harbors, Lake Michigan had more shipwrecks than all the other Great Lakes combined. The route around the lake from Chicago was called the Horse-shoe Route, considered unlucky because it was upside-down, so the luck could run out, which it often did. Most of the ships and schooners lasted no more than a dozen years. Those that did had already sunk once or twice and were sailing under new names.

"This tower was only fifty-five feet when it was built in 1840. There was so much traffic that in 1871, it was rebuilt to one hundred feet high, the second-highest tower on the Great Lakes. The foundation—seventy-five feet deep—took a year to build: a hundred pil-ings, sixteen logs driven down into the ground, and fifteen feet of limestone piled on top of it. It took another year to do the tower. The walls, five and a half feet thick at the bottom with two feet of air space, taper to two feet four inches at the top. If this wind was about twenty knots [24 mph] faster, you'd feel the tower sway. But the 125-step spiral stairway is free-standing—it's not bolted into the wall. So if the tower sways a little, it doesn't affect the stairway."

We stomp the sand off our feet so it doesn't fall through the metal grill steps into the eyes of people below us as we begin climbing single-file. The first floor is a wreck: plaster bashed, lathe exposed, graffiti everywhere. "In 1937, this lighthouse was replaced by the new one that you can see through the passage there. Since it was decom-missioned in 1958, this lighthouse unfortunately has been vandalized, mostly by people coming over on private boats." Although he must have given this talk hundreds of times, the ranger sounds genuinely distressed. Looking around, I understand. The interior feels violated, as if someone had hated the place. "They tore out the shutters, broke all the windows, threw rocks through the roof," continues the ranger. "The National Park Service acquired it in 1970 and started cleaning it up. I've been working on it for three years."

The damage continues as we ascend. "If you were a lighthouse keeper, you'd be coming up these stairs with a brass bucket holding at least three and a half gallons of kerosene, weighing as much as forty pounds. . . . Watch your head as you come to the metal hatch door." I bump my head anyway. I've raised several goose eggs on lighthouse hatch doors. At the top, we crowd onto a windy catwalk. "We're not sure what happened to the light that was up here," says Kruch. "Some say it was broken, others that the Coast Guard has it in a warehouse. This was a third-order light—about four and a half by two and a half feet. We probably won't get another Fresnel lens because they're too valuable—the Coast Guard requires twenty-four hour security on them."

Moving inside, I ask Kruch if the keeper had to be up here all the time, like a forest-fire observer. "No, generally the keeper was down below, manning the foghorn and steam whistle," Kruch says. "If he saw the light flickering, then he'd run up the stairs to adjust the light. He controlled the air flow by closing the hatch. Sometimes he'd have to climb out on the upper catwalk and scrape off the ice and snow. Although no one lost his life inside this tower, one light-house keeper did die out in the lake. The lighthouse keeper would make rescues, which was very dangerous, particularly if he just had a rowboat. The coming of the United States Lifesaving Service in 1901, 1902, made the lighthouse keeper's job much safer."

"The Lifesaving Service was the Coast Guard?"

"Early Coast Guard. In the 1930s, the Lighthouse and the Life-saving services joined forces to become the Coast Guard."

On the way down, I bang my head again on the heavy trapdoor. Our voices echo in the tall chamber, Kruch's dominating: "There were weights suspended down these hollow walls. One of the keeper's duties was to crank them up to the top. As they came down, they would turn the light."

After the tour, we choose between walking trails and touring some old abandoned farms from the back of a pickup. I crave time alone, so I stroll the cool, shady dirt roads. There are no deer on the island, so wildflowers thrive here. I identify, among the dense roadside ferns bordering thick woods, ballooning white campion, white clusters of cow parsnip, and fringed, marigold coreopsis. An insistent bird call sounds like a digital watch alarm going off in church.

Before we leave, the young man who drove the pickup offers to show me where the wood lilies bloom. The two of us and two women I met on the ferry climb a steep, sandy dune, and nibbling on wild strawberries. Our guide points out cinquefoil, calling it "no buzz," because it looks like marijuana but "doesn't do anything."

We finally stagger, panting, to the top of the dune, and look way, way down on a sparkling blue bay. Grass plants fountain individually around us, scattered over light, bright sand embroidered with wildflowers. Big orange monarch butterflies flutter above slick yellow hairy puccoon, mahogany-red wood lilies, wild onions, white false Solomon's-seal, green jack-in-the-pulpits. The sharpness of color, vastness of panorama, and height of view send chills down my dripping, sun-soaked spine.

Note: The Manitou Passage—the once heavily traveled stretch of water between the Manitou Islands and the mainland—has been state-designated a wreck-rich Michigan underwater preserve.

JUNE 23

EVEN IN THE RAIN, the forty-mile-long Sleeping Bear Dunes National Lakeshore (the first of five Great Lakes national parks I will visit: two on Lake Michigan, three in or on Lake Superior) is stop-the-car-I-want-to-get-out beautiful. Here begins the longest stretch of freshwater dunes in the world—a 90-percent-quartz sand beach that continues down the entire coast of western Michigan to the Indiana Dunes National Lakeshore. It's been called "the Golden Crescent," "the Midwest's best-kept secret," "America's hidden Riviera." So where are all the people? Maybe it's the soggy day or the pre–July Fourth season, or perhaps those who live here take it for granted and those who don't never heard of it, but today I have this nationally protected natural opulence almost to myself.

I begin with the Pierce Stocking Scenic Drive. A brochure from a covered box at the entrance describes the wonders along this sweeping, intimate, one-way paved road that includes seven miles of very tall trees, a covered bridge, breathtaking views, and white daisies. Within minutes, the forest and mist close over the van and whisk me from the real world.

It's still drizzling when I emerge, so I do my laundry in the tiny town of Empire while lunching next door at a gourmet restaurant, and then head back to the dunes. Driving to one of the many trails, I don raincoat and boots and strike out through a glistening meadow past plump, long-needled pines growing so fast their lime-green branch ends are corkscrewed. The air is earthy, the birches white, the maple trunks black, the ferns dense. When I reach the shore panorama, I'm astonished to discover that most of the dunes, some towering over four hundred feet, look more hirsute than bald.

"A lot of people think sand dunes are dry, but we get about thirty inches of precipitation a year here," explains a ranger at the visitors' center. "All but the most active part of the dunes, where there's a lot of human activity, are pretty densely vegetated."

The rain stops and I spend the rest of the day outdoors, collecting memories: a freckled fawn tailgating a doe through a tunnel of trees . . . cathedral-like red pines slim and straight as palms . . . fragrant balsam firs brushing my face with soft, pawlike branches . . . yellow silverweed, black-eyed Susans, orange hawkweed, white campion, something purple, lilies glowing like lamps against a Gothic wood. Wild pink roses, poison ivy, flame-shaped red cedars, white anemones, sunflowers. A mosquito whines; an iridescent beetle crawls up my arm. A deer stomps. Another deer splashes through a glossy black pond. Muskrat lodges; another deer. The beach, screaming with gulls, is dense as a printed page with bird, bug, mouse, and canine (fox?) tracks. When I sit on a clump of beach grass, a cloud of mosquitoes rises and adopts my head. The sun comes out. On either side of me, a pair of bluebirds call from separate jack pines. I pad at last through a damp, dappled wood waist-high with ferns and echoing with loud evening birdsong.

The commercial campground I stay in here is cramped, but I'm too exhilarated, and too tired, to care. I put on my Paul Horn tape, engage in a mosquito safari (even one whiner can keep me awake for hours), then tumble, as if down the highest, softest dune, into sleep.

Note: An excellent guide to the Sleeping Bear Dunes National Lakeshore can be found in *Hunt's Highlights of Michigan*.

JUNE 24

THE *CITY OF MILWAUKEE*, a fifty-nine-year-old ship-sized ferry, has just been declared a National Historic Vessel, according to Frankfort's local newspaper. The last of a "mighty fleet" that ferried railroad freight cars to Wisconsin from 1892 to 1981, the *City of Milwaukee* is being turned into a museum. I drive to the far side of the harbor to tour it, but the place is deserted.

On the town side of the harbor, JoAnn Frary, cook and owner of the Car Frary Restaurant (since renamed JoAnn's Restaurant and Catering), has just pulled a spiky banana-cream meringue pie out of the oven. I wait at the counter in the unbearable fragrance for the pie to cool while Karen Nielsen Lupton, a deep-voiced woman sitting next to me, informs me that she's a Frankfort native, born and raised here. "I've been here twenty years and I'm still considered an outsider," Frary claims. "Newcomers are real outsiders, and then there are summer people and tourists." Enjoying the company after yesterday's solitary adventures, I encourage the women to reminisce:

Lupton (in a Lauren Bacall voice): "When I was young, there were five boats runnin' outa here. Everyone grew up sailing. The men were on twenty days and off eight, so there were a lot of boat widows. The ladies had their own societies and kept things going, but when the men came home, everything stopped. Every summer we rented our home to a family from Chicago. We moved out and they moved in. We had an apartment downtown. Everybody did that; it was just a way of life. There used to be a factory on the bay that processed cherry juice—northern West Michigan is big cherry country—and we still see a few cherry pits on the shores when a storm comes in."

Frary: "That goes back about fifty years, and cherry pits are still coming up! It's like *The Witches of Eastwick*." We all laugh. "It used to be so nice when the ferries ran. We'd hear the signal—a long and a short whistle—we could tell by the sound which boat it was—and we'd go watch the boat leave. Everybody did. The turnaround down at the beach was always just packed. I miss the old foghorn, too."

Lupton: "I loved that old foghorn. We've got a new one, but the old one was better. Nyaaaaaaaaaaa. When we were kids, the challenge of the century was to go out to the lighthouse and stand there when they cranked that sucker up. Or we'd run the breakwall when the waves were comin' in so hard they'd wipe you right off. It's a wonder we didn't all die. But we didn't lose anybody there. We lost people other ways."

Frary: "We used to call the inside of the pier 'the polio side.' You never swam on the polio side. We swam outside the pier. Still do."

Lupton: "Years ago, the boats dumped their trash in the harbor and the water inside the pier'd get stagnant. Grapefruit floating around. Seagull city."

Me: "Do you keep the restaurant open all year?"

Frary: "I used to, but the times have changed. Since the car ferries quit, the railroad stopped coming, and now there's about a quarter of the activity. But in winter people here are very dedicated to the school sporting events. There's always a good turnout. We just won the girl's state softball championship, and we're gonna have a sign at the edge of town to say so."

Me: "I've noticed a lot of town signs like that in northern Michigan."

Lupton: "It's big in the UP [Upper Peninsula] too. The UP was going to secede, you know. People up there don't feel that the government ever thinks about them. There was a time they wanted to become another state. Going to call themselves Superior. Well, it didn't happen, but they still call themselves Yoopenites. My father was born and raised there. Called himself a stump chopper. Ever eat a pasty [rhymes with 'nasty,' not 'hasty']? You know, those stew-filled turnovers?"

Me: "Yes, in Mackinaw City. Tasted better than I thought it would."

Lupton: "They're not as good as they used to be. Miners used to take pasties down in the UP mines because, being a meat pie, they'd stay warm most of the day. That's how they originated."

Me: "Do you live here now?"

Lupton: "I lived twenty-nine years in California and retired to Arizona, but I come back every summer and it's always home. When I'm gone, I miss the country, the pattern of speech, the way the time is, all the little things."

Frary: "Like in late June, we pick baby's breath along the roadside. We dry it, use it in arrangements, put it on the Christmas tree."

Lupton (spelling her name): "Be sure to get the 'Nielsen' right, because that's the Danish spelling. Spelled another way it's Finnish. There are lots of Scandinavians here. They all got along well, but they stuck to their own groups. They'd lay awake nights thinking up ways to insult each other. My father used to say that a Swede was a Norwegian turned inside out."

At last, I fork into a big piece of pie. Ahhhhh. Best I ever ate.

ONE OF THE THINGS I promised myself when I began this trip was that I would do some things I've always been too timorous to try, which is how I got strapped into the nose of a tiny, soon-to-be-airborne glider. I feel like a pair of panty hose stuffed in a plastic egg. From the seat behind me, John House, my pilot, tries to reassure me. "We have better control over where we're going than powered planes do," he insists. Still, there's no parachute in here. John instructs me to keep my feet off the pedals, "and if you get sick, don't throw up in your own cap." (I'm supposed to ask for his?)

And then we are being towed into a gentian-blue sky by a single-engine, peppermint-striped plane. I see the Manitous ahead and below; straight down, a magical mix of woolly trees, inland lakes, an azure Lake Michigan. At two thousand feet, the cable snaps and suddenly there's silence, only a soft whoosh as we ride the invisible thermals. I look down on a toy freighter, float over Frankfort. My heart thumps at the bumps. But oh, it's beautiful up here, the lake flashing sunlight, the Betsie River sunning like a snake on green velvet. After fifteen minutes, House, whose longest ride has been about five hours, says he's running out of thermals: "No thermals, no lift." We descend very, *very* fast, about eight hundred feet a minute, skimming a cemetery, heading for a landing, snubbing the single asphalt strip for the grass. WHAM! We slow to a stop, get out, and push the glider into position for the next trip.

I really don't advise following a large piece of banana-cream pie with a glider ride, but I wouldn't miss either one.

TINY, trim Arcadia is so quiet, you could hear a pun drop—no boutiques, no tourist attractions, just town. I figure there'll be no lines at *this* post office, so I drop in to mail my tapes and head on south. While there, however, I meet Eugene Bischoff—township treasurer, church organist, and passionate historian—who for two hours fills me in on local people and places, ending up at the 102-year-old Trinity Lutheran church, where I get a crick in my neck observing three steeplejacks.

"The man that used to do this kind of work is in the hospital—fell off the Guardian Angels clock in Manistee," Bischoff tells me. An accident at Guardian Angels Church? That's sort of like no lights at the nuclear power plant, isn't it? But of course it isn't funny. "The clock on our tower was installed in 1901 and has never stopped running," Bischoff continues. "Chimes every hour. My brother-in-law winds it every Sunday. The front entrance has been remodeled so we can get a coffin through."

Inside the intimate sanctuary, I throw my head back once again to take in the seven-sided pulpit. "It used to be even higher," says Bischoff. "The minister was practically at the ceiling." We climb back stairs to an exquisite antique pipe organ, its prettily painted pipes crowding the balcony wall. Bischoff slides onto a bench so close to the one-foot rail, I wonder he doesn't tumble backward into the pews below. "The lady before me played this organ for fifty years," Bischoff says. Music bursts from the back wall, resonating as if in a cathedral.

Before I leave town, I stop at Arcadia's tidy harbor, where I learn from harbor master Nick Goutziers that people who like quiet come back here every year. Birders come to see the sandhill cranes; boaters come in for gas, water, or to get their holding tanks pumped out. "Can't empty tanks in the lake like they used to," he adds. "Even the freighters used to do that. Now it's punishable by jail and a fine."

A thirty-two-foot cruiser docks smoothly, and Goutziers begins filling its two-hundred-gallon tank. "We probably use twenty gallons an hour—that's about a gallon a mile," the owner tells me. "If we hit heavy seas, it's worse. From Indiana to Charlevoix and back, we'll go through as much as fifteen hundred dollars' worth of gas." I can't believe this—by road, I could do the same trip for about thirty dollars—but Goutziers confirms the claim, saying, "That sounds about right. The gas bill for a couple of fifty-footers we had in here recently came to almost a thousand bucks."

IT'S NOT EVEN four-thirty and I'm already installed in the pleasantly lawned Orchard Beach State Park, which crowns a bluff two
miles north of Manistee. Although the park isn't foresty, it has a
Sunday-afternoon-in-the-park atmosphere I like. For a dollar, I board
a red-enameled trolley that chugs from the rangers' station to Manistee
for an hour's tour of the town.

"Orchard Beach State Park was once a model farm," our guide,
Ed Katabaczka, begins. "The previous owner brought the tracks out
here so people from town could enjoy the place, and eventually it
became a park." The trolley squeaks past black oil pumps that munch
the shore like grasshoppers from hell, and in town we are hit by the
stench of billowing smokestacks. A massive swinging bridge at the
channel allows both freighters and railroad cars to service the paper
mill, power plant, and other industrial endeavors crowding Manistee
Lake, which swells behind the shore, more industry than I've seen
since Detroit.

"In 1898 the city of Manistee had a population of twenty-four
thousand, with more millionaires per capita than any city in the
United States," Katabaczka tells us. "Today it's one-third that." The
onetime wealth is reflected in wondrous architecture. We trolley by a
carefully renovated, predominantly Victorian historical district boasting a theater presenting live productions, several impressive stone
churches, and a voluptuous brick Victorian firehouse painted, turrets
and all, a knock-'em-dead cherry red.

"At one time Manistee exported enough lumber in one year to
build thirty thousand average-size homes," says Katabaczka, returning
us to industry. "Shortly after, we became known as the world shingle
capital. In the late 1880s, salt was discovered of such quantity and
purity that we became known as Salt City of the Inland Seas." Salt is
still recovered in Manistee, not from mines, but from wells "maybe
twenty-five hundred to thirty-five hundred feet deep. Water is
pumped down; the salt is brought up as brine and then processed by
evaporation." Another plant recovers magnesium by a similar process.
How many wells can a piece of ground take?, I wonder. By now this
county must resemble a frozen lake hole-punched shore to shore by
ice fishermen.

Katabaczka moves on to the unusually pure sand here, valued for its high silicon content, telling of a big sand dune called Creeping Joe, most of which has been hauled by boat and rail to Toledo and Detroit for automotive glass. We pass (and smell) a "gas-sweetening plant, where the naturally odorless gas is treated so you can detect the gas if it leaks. Manistee sets on one of the richest oil bases in Michigan. For the past twelve to fifteen years, our biggest export has been oil and natural gas."

One of Manistee's few remaining undeveloped dune areas (not counting the two swimming beaches) is scheduled to become "our North Shore Development Project," which will include a "retail complex."

"Manistee is turning its only remaining shoreline into a mall?"

"I do hear a lot of comments like the one you have just made," responds our diplomatic guide.

Back at the state park, craving fresh air, I set out along a sandy pebbled beach lined with steep, badly eroding bluffs consisting of reddish, battered-looking mud. Trees are falling down the bank. A black locust in full bloom lies across the beach, roots violently exposed. This kind of erosion often is caused as much by run-off from heavy rains as by wave action. Still, the place is beautiful. Wildflowers proliferate: daisies, nightshade, something pink. A bluff polka-dotted with holes swarms with bank swallows. The beach glows peach in the setting sun.

I walk back along the road, past thousands of wild roses blooming among tall, glossy buttercups, then through the park's Beech-Hemlock Nature Trail, trotting to outpace mosquitoes. It's romantic in here—shredded bark trail, ferns, labeled trees, gray-skinned beeches. Just the place to bring your honey and a lot of Skin So Soft.

By the time I stagger back to the van, it's dark and I'm exhausted, but the neighbor on my left, a twenty-eight-year-old cyclist from Milwaukee named Dave Weir, has a nice fire going and offers to share brats and beer. A woman of similar age, Deirdre Savage, emerges from a round yellow tent only slightly bigger than a beanie, pitched on my other side. Hunkering around the fire, we three discover that we are all lone adventurers: Dave is cycling to and along Lake Superior, "until my money runs out"; Deirdre, a New Yorker, quit her job and is on her way to Alaska in a bug-sized Subaru with 192,000 miles on it; and after describing my trip, I announce that "I've been everywhere

behind me and nowhere in front," which we all find hilarious. Deirdre
is the first woman I've met so far camping alone. "There's nothin'
better!" she declares. "Friends I just visited in Chicago gave me a
Mace gun, but I left it behind. I told them they needed it more than
I did."

Gathered around a spitting, smoky fire, we celebrate ourselves and
our adventures far into the starry night. By sheer coincidence, Dave
has spent five years in Alaska and is full of contacts and advice for
Deirdre. He went there out of high school with eight hundred dollars,
he says, did a variety of jobs, and ended up panning for gold to survive
and "keep me in brewskis."

I ask Dave how he manages with just a pack and a bicycle, and
he says, "I carry a tent (the tent is rather big and heavy but it's worth
it), a sweatshirt, two shirts, the pants I'm wearing, two pairs of shorts,
some underwear, three pairs of socks, and that's it. A little knife."

"He doesn't have a stove, a pot, a pan, or a fork," adds Deirdre.

"Why'd you come back from Alaska?" I ask Dave.

"I don't know why, to be honest with you. To see my family, I
guess."

Deirdre laughs. "And they were all just the same as when you
left! Hey! You gotta make things happen to you."

JUNE 25

BETWEEN MANISTEE AND LUDINGTON I'm blocked from
the shoreline by the luxurious stretch of the Manistee National Forest,
followed by the Lake Michigan Recreation Area, the Nordhouse
Dunes, and, finally, the dune-lined Ludington State Park. I venture
into this unusually vast wild area along ditches brimming with cattails
and wild iris, ending at the Lake Michigan Recreation Area and an
extraordinary campground: private sites tucked into trees, some on
paved loops providing "modern" facilities (flush toilets), some not.
Emerging from a trailer on one of the loops, camp host Ruth Gaida
tells me that the campground is leased for the summer.

"This campground is private?" I ask.

"Sorta," replies the ebullient woman. "Most of the U.S. Forest
Service campgrounds are that way now. It's what we call semiprimitive

here. *Family Circle* listed us with the twenty best family campgrounds in the United States. We offer beautiful hiking trails and wheelchair access to a dock and the fire rings."

Gaida takes me behind the trailer to inspect her semiprimitive shower—homemade from hula hoops, a bright blue tarp, and a solar bag—hanging in the woods. Deeper into the forest, I come upon a woman sitting at a sewing machine. I consider demanding three wishes, until I see the orange extension cord twisting toward Ruth's trailer. The seamstress is a visiting friend, and it's hard to say which of us is the more startled.

Bordering the campground is Nordhouse Dunes, the only wilderness area in Lower Michigan (not counting North Manitou Island). I climb the beautiful boardwalk that spirals up a dune—189 steps!—to a deck that overlooks a generous, deserted, crescent-shaped beach, then hike along a Nordhouse Dunes bluff. Despite a trail map, I become hopelessly lost. Am I using the right map? (By now, my vest pockets are stuffed with old folded trail maps.) Why aren't there any trail markers? Well, I can't remain lost long with a "landmark" (watermark?) like a Great Lake. When I finally get back to the overlook, an elflike woman resting there explains that all the trail markers have been removed so the Nordhouse Dunes can relax back into wilderness. The barely-more-than-four-foot, seventy-four-year-old Eleanor Wescott has just completed a ten-mile hike. *Ten miles?* "I hike that far every day," she says. "As a volunteer for the U.S. Forest Service, I measure every five hundred feet or so to make sure the trails aren't too wide."

I'm losing my sense of reality. The deep woods, the woman sewing there, Wescott's Puck-like stamina, a park going wild, and the sugar-cookie beach are starting to feel like a midsummer's day dream.

EXTENDING FROM the huge beach at the end of the city of Ludington's main street is a long concrete pier, tipped with a lighthouse and lined with fisherpersons. My heart leaps at the sight of it. I hike out onto the pier, nearly losing my cap in the wind, past kids and adults tending poles and lines, feeling, for the first time all summer, at home. In my early teens, my uncle Joe took me fishing for perch off a similar pier in Holland, Michigan, and last year I foolishly raced the breakers on the Grand Haven pier.

There's something special about West Michigan piers (which by now I know are really jetties, but I still call them piers), because there's something special about the way our rivers behave when they hit this state-long ridge of dunes. Sand, drifting as it does along the coastline, tends to block river outlets, forming inland lakes. All along the West Michigan shoreline these little lakes balloon behind the dunes, forming exceptionally fine harbors. But to utilize such a harbor, often a channel must be dug, regularly dredged, and protected by one, sometimes two, long jetties.

Indeed, what should be pumping just off the end of the Ludington pier but a big blue dredger connected to a fat tube that snakes up and along the length of the pier and disappears behind the beach. I ask a man fishing next to the lighthouse if he knows where the sand goes. "Goes through that tube to somewhere," he says. "That dredger's a sand sucker. It's got like a big vacuum down there. About every year they hafta do that to keep the channel clear for Dow Chemical and the Carferry. That there's a private company, but used to be that the Army Corps of Engineers did it. It's the government's responsibility to keep the channels open."

Tom Langford, who lives in Grand Haven, a couple of towns south, works for the railroad and often lays over here. He can't believe what I'm doing. "That's all you do? Just write?"

"That's what I do," I say.

"Well," says Langford, "you live here, you take it all for granted. People don't understand what they have here, and I think they're going to have a hard time protecting it."

A dilapidated black-and-white fish tug chugs into the channel. "That's the only fish tug left outa here," Langford says. "I think it sunk once and they got it going again. There used to be twenty-one fish tugs out of Grand Haven. None now. Only Indians can fish now. But for a lotta years, when I was young, I worked those fish tugs." Langford, who's compact, wiry, and tough, speaks in a deep, smooth voice. "I used to get terrible sick on those fish tugs," he continues. "You're down in there, bobbin' around, and there's no deck, hardly. They feed the nets out the back and then a power lifter brings 'em back in. If your nets have been out there a few days, the fish drown —that's why some people are opposed to gill nets, because those fish just bloat. You can imagine, rollin' in the seas down there. Then you got the fumes off the lifters hittin' you in the face and you're tryin' to pick the rotten fish outa those nets. And you gotta get 'em outa there, because a fisherman without his nets, he's outa business."

"Why would they leave the nets out that long?"

"Well, if a storm hits, you can't get back out to get 'em, you know. You just wait it out. See, that's the trouble with gill nets: the fish swim into 'em and can't get back out—they're caught with their gills. If they're in there overnight even, you get a lotta bloaters. You have a thing with a hook on it to snap 'em outa that net, and you hit 'em with a pick and they go *pop*."

I gulp. We've moved into a booth in a bar and grill, and I'm glad I didn't order dinner. "What an awful job!"

"Oh, I loved it."

"So how many fish can you catch in a gill net?"

"Depending on the length of your net, I've seen 'em bring in a ton. Your holes in the nets are diamond-shaped, and they're regulated for sizes. There're sizes for perch, for chubs, for lake trout, for white-fish. Like if you're settin' for perch, that's pretty much all you're gonna get in that net. If you're settin' for chubs, that's all you're gonna get. You know what tatting is? That's how a net is made. When you stretch 'em, the holes have to measure so many inches, and that's what makes it legal. Now the DNR is starting to require trap nets. Traps nets don't drown fish, but they're more expensive."

After his fishing years, Langford worked on the railroad crew that loads the famous Carferry, so that's where we go next, strolling past bright gardens planted down the main boulevard. " 'Carferry' actually means 'boxcar ferry,' " Tom says. "It has nothing to do with auto-mobiles. They were called carferries way back in the early 1900s. See those ramps? That's where the autos go." The ramps curve to a high deck on the ship-sized ferry. Below, boxcars bump noisily into a large ship's cavernous hold, the rails on the ground fitting into those on the boat.

"Loading boxcars is not something you just walk up and do," Langford continues. "You can't put too much weight on one side, because you'll tip that boat over. It has to be loaded so many cars on this track, so many on that. You load it seesaw like, bring that boat up level. It's very interesting. People don't realize the brain work that goes into switching boxcars and loading boats."

Today, Langford works as the brakeman on a three-person crew that brings the cars in.

"The ferries run in the winter?"

"Oh yeah. All winter. They're built for that. Used to be seven boats going. Used to be so busy. Maybe fifteen years ago, they had eight hundred and some people workin' here."

About the rumors I'd heard that the ferry might close down, Langford says, "Well, I think it takes a crew of about forty to operate one of these boats that carries maybe twenty-five boxcars. But you can take a train of a hundred fifty cars with a crew of three and run it up to Chicago, through the yard there, and then to Milwaukee. Much cheaper. It's sad to see the ferries go, though."

JUNE 26

I SPENT LAST NIGHT jammed next to the rest rooms in a seething sea of campers at Ludington State Park. I'm annoyed by parks that offer, as this one does, a vast stretch of dunes, spacious beaches, luxurious forests, an inland lake, a creek, and more, but pack campers in so tight, I could hear one neighbor snoring and, at five A.M., a couple in the next tent quarreling. It's easy to be fooled by visual privacy into forgetting you can be heard, so I said in a very quiet voice, "Excuse me, but your voices are carrying." There was a stunned silence and then a truck started up and I guess they left to fight the next round somewhere else. I slept a couple more hours, and now hastily depart, stopping briefly to dump my trash. I remember when campgrounds provided a trash can by each site, but not anymore. Now I'm given a plastic bag to deposit in a Dumpster on the way out.

I'd hoped to ride the ferry to Wisconsin and back today, but the weather's so dismal that instead, I head out of Ludington, driving around Pere Marquette Lake (Ludington's "dune balloon") to get back to the lakeshore, where, in serene contrast to Ludington's heavily trafficked streets, a re-creation of a late-nineteenth-century village appears called White Pine Village, run by the Ludington Historical Society and funded by the village and county. "Everything here has been donated," a pleasant woman in a new, carpeted office tells me. "The courthouse sits on original ground, but most of the buildings have been moved or built here."

Upstairs, behind a large desk, young-looking executive director Tom Hawley elaborates: "White Pine Village is the second- or third-largest historical restoration in the state. We were the first historical society in the United States to pass a millage for preservation of this kind, in which tax money is turned over to a nonprofit corporation for preservation.

"This side of the river was developed before the other [Ludington]. The courthouse served for about six years before following a timber baron [and the larger part of the population] north of here. Some say that when Michigan became a state in 1837, the trees here were so dense that when you walked in the forest it was like dusk—the trees then were hundreds, perhaps thousands, of years old. What was thought to be a five-hundred-year dream to remove the lumber from Michigan ended in forty years, because technology improved so rapidly. Of course, we're looking at second and third growth now."

"These trees seem older than the ones I saw on Lake Erie."

"It's easier to get to Lake Erie, so the population centers are larger. When lumber grew up there, it was soon taken down. But you have to make an effort to come to northern Michigan, because it isn't on your way anywhere. After the lumber in Michigan was taken, much of the industry left. Some replanting went on—a lot of it in the 1930s during the Great Depression—so what we have here is largely second growth. People started to buy up the land; restrictions were enacted. I hope some lessons were learned from the decimation of the forests of Michigan."

I begin my tour and find the historically attired guides in each building young and interesting. "Out of necessity, if the men left, like during wartimes, and the women had to fix something, they'd pick up the hammer and they'd do it," declares a young woman apprentice in the blacksmith shop. She's got a real fire going and is pounding on a piece of wrought iron. A man who had done blacksmithing in the area for seventy years donated all the tools.

I pass an antique fire engine in a fire station and wander into the general store. Someone's sitting on the porch, ripping rags into strips and rolling them into balls. Inside, I'm told that the cabin was built in the 1830s by a fur trapper from Quebec who became trader, doctor, and postmaster. "The bed is made with ropes," explains a young man. "The expression 'Sleep tight' meant 'Tighten the ropes before you go to bed so you don't fall through,' and 'Don't let the bedbugs bite' meant 'Be sure no straw will poke through the mattress and give you a little welt.' The bed is also very short, because people were shorter then, but some people didn't want to sleep completely lying down, lest they breathe their own air. And nobody wanted to sleep too deeply, because that was the touch of death."

In the freshly repainted white courthouse, a young woman sits at a large loom in the back room, weaving place mats from rag strips. The loom, 150 years old, still looks good. It's called a barn loom, "because it's too big to have in the house," explains the weaver. "Many barn looms would be huge—twelve or fifteen feet high. During the summer a traveling weaver would weave everything the women had spun during the winter for bed and board and enough money to get to the next town."

Of the sixteen buildings here, my favorite is a softwood chapel so small and sweet, with its rose(bud) window and small pump organ, it seems like a child's. Musing in the little cemetery outside, I suddenly realize that the sun's out and the delicately decorated white chocolate salmon I bought at downtown Ludington's Anna Bach Company* might melt before I can get them home to my family and friends in Saugatuck, two hours south of here. (I'm taking a couple of days off from this trip to sleep in a bed and check into my "real world.")

I race back to the van.

JULY 1

I'VE NEVER SEEN Silver Lake before today, but the name evokes paradise for me: for years I have imagined its silvery water, magical skies, and fairy-tale forests, images inspired by a girlhood friend whose

---

* Where the best chocolates I have ever tasted are made by a Danish candy maker in his eighties.

family summered here and who raved so often about it that I felt cheated when my family didn't come here, too.

Well, here I am, and what a shock. If it ever fit my fantasy, it doesn't anymore. Silver Lake takes the cake as the rowdiest, tackiest, most deafening town of my substantial experience. Silver Lake State Park, I have just discovered, provides the only legal playground for ORVs (off-road vehicles) in the state, a mammoth sandbox attracting dune buggies, pickup trucks, and motorcycles from all over the Midwest and probably farther. Nearby, miniature golf, go-cart rides, Jellystone Park, water slides, dune-buggy rentals, arcades, swimming beaches, and other hot spots add to a lakeside ambiance of unrivaled playtime intensity.

Round yellow smiley faces appear on signs, decals, and in rows on tough-looking monster trucks. I follow one of these astonishing vehicles to the state park entrance, bypass a mile-long line of ORVs waiting their turn to play, and arrive at a huge parking lot where triangular orange flags wave on thin poles like a field of flowers, each attached to the back of an ORV.

Some folks have come from quite a distance. "It's about a hundred sixty miles for me," says the driver of a seventies boat-style sedan resting on massive tires a yard off the asphalt. "I came up last night; first one in line. Slept in the back." The line, he tells me, can grow three to five miles long on holidays.

"It was ten miles on Memorial Day," says Ranger L. H. Prim. Despite the noise and high spirits around him, he has everything under control. "They're good people. You don't have people at cross-purposes here. This is the only place the Michigan DNR allows ORVs on the sand dunes." A turquoise three-wheel buggy roars up the steep, chutelike entrance and vanishes over the top. "You gotta be at least sixteen years old to do that," Prim tells me. "You can rent dune buggies, but you should be familiar with the machine before you drive one. We have about three miles of dunes here. The northern part is for the ORVs; the center—about six hundred acres—for pedestrians; and the southern part we lease to Mac Wood's Dune Rides." He looks me over and recommends I walk up the observation path or take the dune tour.

I do both. First I walk the border between the pedestrian and ORV designated areas. The sand shivers under my feet as I labor up the dune. Two-, three-, and four-wheeled vehicles rev by on my right; pleasant woods of sassafras and wildflowers provide shade on my left. On top, the bare sand stretches about half a mile to Lake Michigan: at last, dunes the way I always thought they'd look. ORVs shoot like pinballs off the top of the hill onto the vast sands, spread out, spin out, spit rooster tails. Two that get stuck together look like insects mating.

Next I visit Mac Wood's Dune Rides, run by Pete Wood, son of founder and dune-buggy inventor Malcom Wood. "My dad started sixty-one years ago with a Model T Ford," Wood tells me. "He took people on the roads and hills around here, but the narrow tires wouldn't work on the beach. So he put ten wheels on a Model A and that was our first dune buggy. We've been at this location for about thirty-one years now. There're only two other dune rides in the country, one in Saugatuck and one in Oregon."

Today's dune buggy, a fat-wheeled red flatbed with four rows of benches occupied by me and eight other passengers, is driven by Chuck Persenaire. Persenaire zooms down a hill to the tune of a light patter: "This is Termite Bridge," he sings out. "Take a deep breath. Makes the car lighter." Persenaire is trucking—this is no Sunday drive. After a spate of woods, the sand goes on and on. "Used to be a white pine forest ran through here," he tells us. "Most of the trees were cut down in the late 1800s to help rebuild Chicago after the fire. At that time this was probably one of the largest logging areas in the world. The stumps left behind are what we call dune wood, which is different from driftwood. Driftwood gets rounded off on the edges from being in the water and ground down along the bottom. Dune wood has sharp points and edges, from years of being sandblasted."

When we take a break at Little Point Sable, I ask Persenaire if the environmentalists have a problem with this operation. "No, we stick to the trail," he reports. "We grade it out every morning. When it's windy I can spend five, six hours a day grading, just to keep the trail passable. Now this place here's about as close to Wisconsin as you can get—about fifty-seven miles. If you're going to swim Lake Michigan, this is a good place to start." On the way back, he thrills us, careening down the hills, everyone screaming.

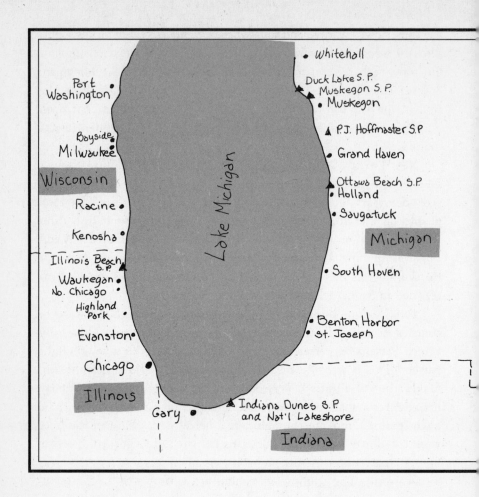

Southern Lake Michigan

JULY 2

MY FAVORITE LAKE MICHIGAN drive traces the shore between White Lake and Muskegon. I have done it many times, living
as I do only an hour and a half south. I usually wait for a day like
today—bright and brisk—for the heightened contrast of whitecaps
on dark swells and the drama of waves crashing unusually close to the
road. I breakfast before I start, knowing I'll not find a restaurant—
there's little development on Scenic Drive, but many surprises, like
the curve that never fails to stun me with its vista of power and
splendor; hidden forest trails; miles of white sand; and three beautiful
parks.

At peaceful Duck Lake State Park, I stroll a short boardwalk along
tiny Duck Lake, then cross the road to dodge booming breakers on
Lake Michigan. I pass up Pioneer Park, a lovely camping and picnic
place, for my favorite park of all—the enormous Muskegon State
Park—climbing the hill to the blockhouse, a reproduction of a stacked
two-room fort resembling a square mushroom. Upstairs, 791 feet
above sea level, I peer through musket slits onto four panoramas: the
entrance to Muskegon's harbor (south); thirty miles out on Lake Michigan (west); a solid green canopy of forty-to-fifty-foot second-growth
white oak and white pine (north and east). Today, I discover something I hadn't noticed before: a network of soft woodland trails in the
dune valley behind the blockhouse. For an hour, I pad around in
dappled sunlight, protected from the wind, shaded from the summer
swelter.

If I were camping (this week I'm driving home to Saugatuck each
night), I'd stay at one of Muskegon State Park's three campgrounds:
the tree-canopied bluff-top campground, with its showers, camp store,
and miles of beach and trails; the quiet tent campground tucked back
in the woods across the road; or the sunny beach campground, where
I almost get stuck in the sand that has drifted over the road like snow.
The parking lot at the nearby swimming beach is buried, too—I can't
tell where the lot stops and the beach begins. Apparently, neither
could the young man who is struggling to free his red sports car.
When six of us can't push it out, I go for help, locating a large college
fellow sweeping sand off a sidewalk, who lopes cheerfully to the rescue,

single-handedly frees the wheels, and sets the car back on the asphalt. Cheers go up: we are all amazed.

"Does this happen often?" I ask wunderkind Richard Gunderson. "Oh, God, yes," he says. "We had four or five people stuck yesterday." When I wonder what's to be done about the sand problem, Gunderson replies with the firmness of a parent: "The wind did it; the wind can clean it up."

IT'S CLEAR from the difficulty I have finding a parking space in Muskegon that something special's going on. I have arrived on the last day of the annual Great Lumbertown Music Festival, a summer celebration that includes a full schedule of polka and other musical events, a maze of art and craft booths in a city square, an entire floor of model trains hurtling and whistling through a wraparound, hand-painted local landscape, a lakeside traveling carnival, a visiting naval frigate, a basketball tournament on the beach, and tours of a World War II submarine.

The basketball tournament—played on a long row of courts, each outfitted with backboards and portable baskets—has been set up on a city beach parking lot to benefit the Ronald McDonald Houses. The place swarms with players and cheering sections, all out in full sun within breathing and hearing distance of big lake surf. "It's a Three on Three Round Ball Classic," player Stacy Cummings explains to me, "and there are brackets for age and height. My team's from the Kalamazoo area. We heard about the tournament from radio advertisements, so we put together a team. There're teams here from Indiana, Chicago, all over."

"You mean anybody from anywhere can play?"

"I think so, yeah."

A member of a team called Forty Something, playing on Court 3, tells me his son is playing on Court 8. A block away, Mark Hughes, a Muskegon resident, a captain of the University of Michigan's national championship basketball team, and maybe the tallest man I ever have seen in person, is signing autographs amid a press of fans. I can't find the tournament organizers, although the mother of one of them—she is running the pizza booth—instructs me to "just go look for someone tall, dark, and handsome." But there must be a hundred men here fitting that description. I learn from an assistant organizer that twelve hundred boys, girls, men, and women between the ages of nine and forty-five are participating here. The tournament is held a couple of times a year, "but this is the first one held on the beach. It's such a success that we'll probably make it an annual event."

A few blocks away, on the Muskegon Lake channel, I tour the U.S.S. *Silversides*, "the most famous World War Two submarine still afloat," claims Michigan Youth Corps participant William Grandsynn, herding about ten of us into the submarine. "The U.S.S. *Silversides* was ranked third for tonnage sunk out of 250 submarines. Later this submarine was used by the National Guard in Chicago for training, although it was never fully operational—the U.S. has an agreement with Canada that no submerged submarines will function in the Great Lakes. So although the boat is eighty percent operational, it no longer can dive."

We inspect the tubes from which twenty-one-foot, ton-and-a-half torpedoes were launched at targets as distant as three miles. I find it unthinkable that sixty to eighty men lived and worked in these cramped quarters on patrols averaging two months. Water was so precious, our guide informs us, that only the captain, the two cooks, and the baker showered daily, the seven other officers showering every three or four days, the sixty-nine enlisted men every fourteen days. "They washed their clothes in the ocean and dried them over the engines, which took about a minute."

The submarine is owned by the nonprofit U.S.S. *Silversides* Maritime Museum, operations manager Ilmar Sinivee tells me after the tour. Groups such as Girl Scouts or Boy Scouts are booked on weekends through October. "They come in at six in the evening and we take them on an extended tour. Then we give them educational games and puzzles, an honorary-crew-member certificate, and a patch like the logo on the *Silversides* there, which was designed by Walt Disney. He did a lot of those during the war." Disney's logo is a cartoonlike submarine/dolphin with a torpedo tucked under one flipper.

JULY 3

MIDWAY BETWEEN MUSKEGON and the fun-loving tourist
town of Grand Haven, I stride up and down the dunes on P. J. Hoffmaster State Park's elaborate boardwalk. But the heart of this pristine
park—which also offers secluded picnic areas and woodsy trails—is
the Gillette Nature Center, set snugly into a dune, with the first full-
time naturalist I've seen since Lake Huron.

Earl Wolf, a wiry, dark-haired, high-intensity man who calls himself a "salesman for nature," takes a few minutes before his ten o'clock
snake-and-turtle talk to tell me about the dunes. "It has been the
belief of naturalists and biologists for over a hundred years that the
sand dunes of Lake Michigan are unique in the world," begins Wolf.
"The father of ecology, Dr. Henry Cowles of the University of Chicago, did his original studies [in the 1890s] on Lake Michigan dunes.
His theory of succession—which applies to deserts, rain forests, and
all areas—is laid out here, from beach to forest, like a book. The idea
that things are related in a growing, changing scheme was at the time
quite revolutionary. Before its acceptance, nature was viewed as a kind
of inventory, as reflected in the Victorian museums—the Hall of Butterflies, the Hall of Fish.

"We are in an ideal location here in that we are halfway up the
Lake Michigan shore, where the northern dunes and the southern
dunes intersect. The southern, wind-formed dunes are totally different
in how they came to be and what they're made of from the northern
Sleeping Bear Dunes and the dunes up on Lake Superior. The northern
part of the southern peninsula is a fabulous handprint of the last
receding glacier—our hills and dales are a series of moraines (gravels
and sands) laid down during its retreat. The bluffs on the Sleeping
Bear Dunes are moraines as well. If you were to cut one in half, you'd
see layers of gravel, clay, rock, all that sort of thing, which is why
you have a four-hundred-foot bluff that looks knifed off. The wind off
the lake pounds that bluff, picks up the sand, blows it across the top,
and drops it on the back.

"In contrast, what we have here—the southern dunes—started
from point zero and built up, wind-formed, from sand off the beach.
That two-hundred-foot dune you see out there is wind-formed top to
bottom, all sand. These wind-formed dunes are characteristic of dunes

from Indiana to Ludington. They're one of the natural wonders of the world as far as I am concerned, because, except for the lava formations from the volcanoes, there aren't any newer geology formations in the world. A couple thousand years, what's that? That's nothin'. That's like a split second of geologic time.

"However, anything that grows quickly can erode quickly. And that's the second part of the story—finding a way people can enjoy the dunes, and hike and camp, without wrecking the place. That's just proper park management. Which sometimes brings us to some touchy decisions, such as our latest unpopular mountain-bike ban on the trails. As environmentally cool as mountain bikes are, they are not cool enough in highly erosive areas, and nothing is more erosive than a dune. Any machine on a terrain like this just tears it to nothing. That was a tough decision. Of course the age-old problem is keeping the ORVs from where they're not supposed to be."

"That's still a problem?"

"Always. Now, Silver Lake was a good choice of a site because there wasn't much to erode to begin with."

"Those were the only dunes that looked the way I expected dunes to look—like the Sahara," I confide.

"That's right. And that's odd. You don't often have something that's barren in Michigan. People theorize about fires, overgrazing."

Wolf has run out of time. I follow him downstairs to a room crowded with birds, animals, amphibians, and reptiles (live and stuffed). Aquariums line the walls. Turtles swim in tanks. The glass eyes of hawks and owls gaze down from high perches. There are games to play, questions to answer. Amid these tempting distractions, Wolf holds a medium-sized live turtle before a small group of children, a few parents, and me.

"Turtles are garbage collectors," Wolf announces, getting our attention. "They keep the lakes clean and scrubbed. They can't catch a fish very well. This one here is a snapping turtle. And you know what? When he's in the water, he doesn't hurt anybody. But once he's lifted out of the water, he seems mean. And you know why? Because he's scared to death! He can't close his shell around himself like other turtles can. So raccoons and skunks and just about anything can flip him over and eat that delicious meat inside his shell. Look at that tail—I think it looks like a dinosaur's."

Earl returns the snapping turtle to its aquarium and holds up a smooth spotted turtle. "Turtles are having a hard time in the world," he tells us. "Their population is being reduced drastically. This is Michigan's rarest turtle, called the spotted turtle. Isn't he beautiful? That's one reason he's rare. If you see one of these out in the woods, you should call the DNR, which is trying to find out where the last of them live so no one puts condos or something there. Spotted turtles are called a special concern. There's hardly any place left in Michigan where their habitat hasn't been destroyed."

Next, a hand-size tortoise: "This is called a box turtle because he can close up tight. He can float in the water, but he'd rather walk in the woods. Except for a few people, box turtles are the oldest living creatures in Michigan. Some have been found to be a hundred years old. Now, isn't it a shame if one walks out into the road and gets squished and he's eighty-nine years old? That bothers me. Now, it bothers me when a rabbit gets squished, too, but a rabbit has twenty million brothers and sisters and more comin' every second. The turtle is all alone. He hardly ever has kids. If you see a box turtle in a neighborhood, you take him to a woods someplace. Don't keep it in the wintertime."

Now a slim, striped snake curls around Wolf's wrist: "This eastern garter snake just shed his skin and he's feeling kinda handsome today. He's nice and soft. This is a reptile, not a worm with a head. He's got a skeleton just like you. He's got lungs, stomach, all the organs you've got, but in a different arrangement. He's not just a big tail with a head on top. Garter snakes like to eat earthworms and little frogs. They can live right in the big city, and that's why there's so of many of them, because they're adaptable.

"Now here's a water snake. His eyes are big bubbles so he can see underwater. All snakes can swim, but none can swim underwater as fast as this one. There're no poisonous water snakes in Michigan. Just a big ol' nasty-tempered water snake. Now don't move, just freeze. Then he thinks you've disappeared." Earl feeds the snake a fish. "Some people think it's gross, a snake swallowing food whole. Well, I think it's gross the way my kitty tears a mouse apart.

"Here's a little hognose snake. Watch him do his cobra act." The snake spreads out a hood. It really does look like a cobra. "Looks real fierce. But would he bite? Doesn't even think about it. The hognose snake's the perfect sand dune animal, because he's short, fat, and he blends right in. Only problem is, he does his act so well that a camper might see him and his dad might say, 'Oh my God, get the shovel!' And stupid Dad saves the day. But make no mistake, if you ever see a Michigan snake that hisses at you, it's the eastern hognose snake, and he won't bite you at all. He's soft, like a big noodle, probably the weakest snake there is, because he doesn't need muscles for climbing—he just wiggles along the sand.

"Here's a handsome snake. He's called a milk snake, and he's a climber. In the old days, people would see the snake crawling around the barn and think he wanted milk from the cows. But he was looking for mice. He has a little head for snooping in small places." The slim, mottled brown-and-white head slips under Wolf's cuff at his wrist, crawls up his sleeve, and comes out his collar. The children scream with laughter. "He's a snooper, see?" resumes Wolf. "Milk snakes only hunt at night. They've been living in people's houses for years and the people don't even know.

"Now, this is the only Michigan snake you don't want to handle: the massasauga rattler. If you see one, just walk away. He won't chase you. You're not the food of any snake. There's no other snake in Michigan with rattles on its tail except the rattlesnake. If you get bit by one of these, get to a doctor right away. He's a viper. This one's real hungry. He ate about two weeks ago and now he's ready to eat again."

Wolf puts an enormous black rat snake on the carpet: "She's uncomfortable on the smooth floor, because she's a climber. The rat snake eats mice and even chipmunks. This one's name is Amy. She's really big. In the old days, if you were a farmer, you'd love to have an ol' rat snake livin' in your barnyard, because it'd eat more mice and rats than your cats would. So anybody who'd bother the old rat snake was in big trouble. This snake is becoming quite rare in Michigan now."

Wolf asks one boy to stand up with his arms out like a tree and Amy drapes herself over the boy's arm. He gasps. "She's not going to bite you, she just has a fear of falling," assures Wolf. "And she's not going for your neck. Snakes don't know a neck from a tree stump. Now, what's a big mouse that lives in a tree? A squirrel! A rat snake will climb up trees and get into squirrel nests." To the happy squeals of us all, Amy loops from kid-tree to kid-tree but resists one of the dads, who confesses to wearing mosquito repellent. "Snake probably says, 'Ooh, worst-smelling tree I ever smelled,'" Wolf guesses. Everybody's giggling. Me, too.

Upstairs in the exhibit hall, I discover a transparent, irregular model grain of sand the size of a child's bowling ball. "Dune sand has unique properties not found in common sand," the display reads. "It's composed almost entirely of a silicon mineral called quartz. Silica content may reach 97 percent in some dune sands, as opposed to 50 percent or less in common sand."

Another exhibit, divided into four "zones," explains how these dunes demonstrate Cowles's theory of succession:

> The BEACH zone comprises three subzones: (1) The *shoreline,* or the wet beach, at the water's edge, where the wave action washes the sand; (2) the *storm beach,* identified by the debris and detritus; and (3) *an area between the storm beach and the grasses of the foredune.*
>
> The FOREDUNE (the second zone) has two subzones: (1) *grasses,* from the base of the foredune up the side; (2) a *cottonwood and grass foredune* at the top.
>
> The TROUGH is the small valley between the fore- and the back dune: (1) the *pond* subzone at the deepest part of the valley and (2) the *pine* subzone that surrounds it.
>
> Three overlapping hardwoods make up the BACKDUNE zone: (1) the *black oak* subzone; (2) then the *mixed oak* subzone; and finally (3) the *maple/beech/hemlock* subzone.

"THIS IS the most beautiful day for sailing I've seen this summer," declares tan, athletic-looking James Hartger, a family friend I'm visiting at his Grand Haven lakeside cottage. "Let's get wet."

We jump into a sailboat just big enough for two and zip out to the end of the nearby Grand Haven pier. For an hour, we tack back and forth, slipping across the white-capped swells. It would be a perfect afternoon if the Grand River, which empties into Lake Michigan between the long Grand Haven piers, didn't surge into the deep blue lake an oddly unsavory brown. I watch strollers along the blue-railed channel continue out the pier, first to a bright red tower, then along a spidery black metal catwalk to the small red house at the end. What a dashing sight this lighthouse pair makes against the water! Just beyond the pier, high above the sandy beach at the Grand Haven State Park, rainbow-hued power kites dart and buzz like birds. For years I've loved this place, coming to play, stroll, shop, eat. Grand Haven's one of my favorite Michigan play towns.

An hour later, at the Tri-Cities Historical Museum, Kenneth Schultz, museum curator, tells me that not only has Grand Haven officially been dubbed "America's Coast Guard City," but it is presently celebrating the United States Coast Guard's two hundredth anniversary, with, among other things, an impressive museum display and a coast-related quilt show. "Grand Haven's the only city in the United States to hold a Coast Guard festival every year."

From the museum, I drive south to the Bil-Mar Restaurant, the only Michigan restaurant I've ever found on Lake Michigan proper besides Legs Inn. I used to come here from Grand Rapids for dinner with high-school and college beaux. How many sunsets have I watched from the Bil-Mar's picture windows over a plate of whitefish? How many times have I been kissed at the end of the Grand Haven pier?

DRIVING SOUTH to Holland, I become even more nostalgic. Lake Shore Drive curves through woods, with occasional glimpses of Lake Michigan between cottages and trees. There's the driveway to Aunt Jean's cottage, now my cousin's; the sign for the DeBoers', from which Uncle Joe and Aunt Maude took me fishing, is still there; and the black mailbox put up by my father about twenty years ago accepts someone else's mail. Most of the names along the road are, like my own, Dutch. Lots of Vans and Vanders, lots of names ending in "a." I've been in all the parks: quiet, wheelchair-accessible Kirk Park; little Tunnel Park, which used to be free; and Holland's Ottawa Beach State Park, the biggest, from which extends yet another pier-protected channel, tipped with another lighthouse.

Near Ottawa Beach, I stop at a shack called Fun Incorporated, where I recognize, renting Rollerblades, a friend of my son's. Michael Vanden Brink, probably a high-school senior, claims he can jump over cars on Rollerblades and persuades me to try a pair.

I've never skated on Rollerblades before, but I find that the three wheels in a row instead of four squared off are a surprisingly stable arrangement; I just have trouble stopping. Nevertheless, I glide without incident along Lake Shore Drive beside warm, sweet-smelling woods all the way to Tunnel Park—a couple of miles—and back, a glorious, late-afternoon skate.

JULY 5

JUST OVER a dune on the other side of the Holland pier, there's a restaurant, a five- or ten-minute walk if there'd been a bridge. As it is, I must drive all the way around Lake Macatawa, Holland's "dune balloon." Halfway, I stop at a power plant. Unlike most cities, Holland supplies half of its own power, I'm told by Loren Howard, superintendent for Holland's Board of Public Works. "We buy the rest from Consumers Power and the City of Lansing. We burn coal here, brought in by ship, about two hundred thousand tons, fifteen shiploads a year. You just missed one, came in this morning."

"I don't see anything coming out of your stack. Is that typical?"

"Two things you're looking for coming out of the stack: one is the particulates, the ash, and the other is the oxides that make acid rain. Power plants take out pretty much all of the particulate now; our recovery of that ash is upwards of ninty-nine percent. Then there's the nitrous oxide and sulfur dioxide, and there're different ways of dealing with those. One is to burn low-sulfur coal, which is what we do. Another is to desulfurize the flue gas before it goes up the stack, a process that allows the plant to burn a higher-sulfur-content coal." The process is expensive to install and maintain, however, and is not yet universally used.

The road around the south side of Lake Macatawa ends at Point West, a brick restaurant nestled below precarious-looking old frame cottages scattered across a high, steep dune. I've come to find out why the Oz Festival has been an annual event here. Manager Paul Terbeek sits me at a dark table at the back of the bar and I "taste-test" a bowl of velvety mushroom bisque while he explains that L. Frank Baum wrote *The Wizard of Oz* here, in a cottage that has since burned down. But the Yellow Brick Road and the Emerald Forest are still up there on the dune. Even a real Dorothy, a summer friend of Baum's, once played there.

"The big attraction for the festival was the Munchkins," Terbeek says. "Several of the actual actors from the movie would come—they were really nice people—and you could have lunch with them. But almost all of the Munchkins have died. Last year was the fiftieth anniversary of [the movie] *The Wizard of Oz,* and the last remaining Munchkin was in so much demand that a high-school drama troupe from Detroit performed here instead."

A FEW MINUTES and blocks away, Brian Dekkinga of Eldean Boat Sales, Ltd., leans behind his desk in a Macatawa lakeside office resembling a classy car dealer's and, looking appalled at the limit of my boat smarts, tells me that what I want to know about boats is "acquired information." I ask him to help me acquire some, beginning with dollar outlay.

"A typical thirty-foot sailboat might sell for $80,000 to $150,000," Dekkinga sighs, giving in with a hint of a smile. "Used, $25,000 to $75,000. If you were going to start out, you might start with something like that."

"How would I learn to sail it?"

"You have friends. Either that or we can set up private instruction here. Or you can look in the back of just about any sailing magazine for week-long sailing schools, although there aren't many on the Great Lakes. Yacht clubs don't offer a whole lot of instruction, either."

"What tests must I pass to take my boat out on the lake?"

"None. You can buy a boat today and take it out tomorrow. No instruction is required."

"You don't have to learn the rules of the waves? Like, if two boats approach each other, which side you go on? You don't need to know that?"

"You don't have to know anything. You can spend half a million dollars on a big yacht, get on, and drive it away."

"Is this true in all states or just Michigan?"

"I believe it's all states. At least now."

"Are there any alcohol regulations?"

"Yeah. You can still drink while running a boat, but it's

now illegal to be intoxicated. This is the first year the regulations have been in effect. There are government publications that spell them out."

"Do these regulations differ from state to state?"

"No, it's pretty much the same wherever you go."

"The women I see on boats are generally passengers. Do women buy boats from you?"

"Very seldom. In the twelve years that I've been selling boats, I've sold boats to women twice—a sailboat and a mid-size sport boat. However, the interiors of boats are definitely laid out for women. The guy nine times out of ten could care less what it looks like, but companies have understood that a cute little interior is important."

"Okay, I've got my boat now. Where do I store it?"

"Winter storage would be $1,000 to $2,000, depending on the length of the boat, and whether you want inside or outside storage. And the bottom has to be painted every year."

JULY 6

SAUGATUCK OFFERS the the classiest bunch of shops, restaurants, boutiques, galleries, deckside dinners, dune rides, boat tours, and marinas you'll ever throw your money at, but, living here, I've been to most of these. What intrigues me is a boat I've never noticed before: a cross between a tug and a yacht docked along the Saugatuck channel at the edge of town. "That's the *Cisco*, a U.S. Fish and Wildlife Service research boat," explains Richard Eichler in his modest channelside station. "We have five boats, one on each Great Lake, reporting to a central laboratory in Ann Arbor. We primarily assess the forage base in the lakes—the little fish that the big fish eat. We've been working this lake for thirty years."

Eichler points to a large map dotted with push pins. "We repeatedly fish these established index stations through the years to see what's happening, either pulling a net on the bottom, which is trawling—not to be confused with trolling—or setting gill nets, which are very much like cyclone fences that sit on the bottom. We use a graduated mesh—one hundred feet of one size and one hundred feet of another size, so we can catch all sizes of fish. Now, this is the area known as the Treaty Water Rights for the Indians."

"I thought Native Americans could fish anywhere, anytime."

"No. I don't know about the other states, but in order to avoid certain conflicts they agreed to give up rights to some areas to get exclusive rights to other areas. When the Indians came down here, there were a lot of problems because of the sport fishermen. There was some real concern about bodily injury being done. So now they fish exclusively in these agreed-upon areas, which put white commercial fishermen outa business."

"How long has it been since this happened?"

"Quite a while. Maybe eight years."

"Aren't gill nets illegal now?"

"Technically, no one except Indians in Michigan can use gill nets. Wisconsin and Illinois, however, are still engaged in gill-net fishing. And it doesn't hurt nothing. They have very avid commercial and sport fishing there. But Michigan and Wisconsin went different ways. State of Michigan said many years ago that whenever there's a conflict of interest, sport fishing will take precedence. And so after twenty years of fighting, they pretty much got rid of the commercial fishing. Wisconsin had a similar law, but that was changed in 1975 or '76, and now all decisions are made on biological data, not political."

"Is there still a conflict between the sport and commercial fishermen?"

"There still is, but it's not as bad as it used to be. I know because I was a commercial fisherman, so you get a very biased opinion from me. But the Wisconsin shoreline is fished both commercially and by sportsmen. There's commercial fishing in Door County; you'll see fish tugs in Kewaunee, Two Rivers, Algoma. As you go south, though, they're harder to find. Big money has taken over so much of the waterfront property."

We tour the sixty-foot, thirty-nine-year-old *Cisco*. "A crew of six goes out for seventeen days at a time," says Eichler. "There's a deck, with living space underneath, four berths in the front end of the boat and four in back. And we've got a full-size kitchen." When I ask what the crane on the back is for, Eichler says, "A log in the net can measure forty feet and weigh over a ton. And occasionally we'll get a large load of fish."

What do they do with the fish when they've finished examining them? "Well, we gotta slit 'em open, so they go back in the water. It's all biodegradable material."

ART'S THE THING in Saugatuck, right down to the outside walls of the public rest room, all four of which are pointedly muraled with a park scene à la Seurat. Nearby, across a carpet of grass, a group of students in a hexagonal white gazebo sketch a summer's idyll: mallards waddling down the sidewalk; a white gingerbread, canopy-bed-like "chainferry" being loudly hand-cranked across the channel; gliding boats and swans; sailboat masts clinking on the opposite shore. Ellen Wilt is teaching a drawing class here, but it's almost over. "Come back tomorrow," she urges. "I'll give you a photograph and you will hold it upside down and draw it, so you just see shapes and values. And let me tell you, you'll be so proud. We have such satisfied customers." Everyone laughs.

Ellen Wilt is in her element. Retired from university teaching, she actively paints, shows, and teaches. Here, on this languid summer morning, students of all ages bask in her congenial, low-key style. Wilt started this community program in conjunction with Ox-Bow, the Art Institute of Chicago's summer school (see p. 194).

JOHN FRUTH'S sleek white sailboat, moored at a marina on Kalamazoo Lake (Saugatuck's dune balloon), is a sloop, he tells me as I step aboard. "That means there's one jib [forward sail] and one mainsail. A cutter would have two jibs and one main. And then you get into split rigs, which have two masts—typically yawls or ketches." We settle inside on comfortable, upholstered benches, amid shining woodwork and background music that Fruth tells me is sung by Jimmy Buffett.

When I confess I have never heard of Jimmy Buffett, Fruth is stunned. "Jimmy Buffett typically writes about the sea," he says. "He appears to be a free spirit and has great appeal among sailors. His songs don't get much play on the radio, but there's kind of a cult. Last Saturday I went to a Jimmy Buffett concert in Chicago. There must have been twelve thousand people in the seats and another ten thousand in the grass area, and everyone knew all the words to all the songs that he sang. It was one big sing-along.

"I've been sailing probably forty years," claims Fruth, an automobile company executive who looks no older than that. "I've built three sailboats. The first one was a wooden sunfish, a little board boat. That's the way to learn to sail. You learn how a sailboat moves through the water and how sensitive it is to anything you do. If a sunfish capsizes, you just flip it back up, get back on, and sail some more. Anyway, I had that for several years. Then I helped build a wooden catamaran when I was in Sea Scouts."

"Sea Scouts?"

"It's part of the Boy Scouts. Then I built a sixteen-foot fiberglass pit boat. After that, I bought boats. Before this one, I had a Catalina 22, a very popular cruising boat that hauls well on a trailer. Now, this boat here weighs almost six tons. It's got about four thousand pounds of lead in the keel. There are two ways to handle ballast—externally and internally. Mine is external—the lead weight is bolted to the outside, so if I hit bottom—and I have—it's metal hitting bottom. With internal ballast, the fiberglass is molded around the lead, so if you go aground, you might scuff through the fiberglass. If water gets in the ballast cavity, you have to haul the boat out of the water, drain, and repair it. But this boat can take about anything. It has a motor, but I probably don't use more than twenty gallons of diesel in a season."

Fruth takes cheese from a small ice-cooled icebox, pours some wine, and we move onto the deck to lounge in the afternoon sun. A nice breeze has whipped up. We discuss the age-old rift between powerboaters and sailors, how marinas sometimes claim that sailors (as opposed to yachters) are tight with money. I ask Fruth if he races. He shrugs. "There are three kinds of racers: the super-dead-serious, who put a lot of money into it, which is what it takes to win races; the middle of the fleet, who're pretty good but not passionately committed; and the stragglers that just enjoy the party. I'd like to keep it at the last level."

The day is fresh and dazzling. Hundreds of sailboats line both sides of long docks, masts rocking. "I drive three hours to get here," says Fruth, "and every time, I say, 'Lake Michigan's a phenomenal wonder of the world. And no sharks!'" I don't take him up on a sail, having twisted my ankle last night. It's enough to enjoy this gentle rocking, the fishy air, and the forest of shining masts clanking happily around us.

Ox-Bow, the School of the Art Institute of Chicago's summer campus, swells at the end of a winding woodsy road: a half-circle of modest buildings around a lawn, overlooking a lagoon and the opposite dune. Standing there, I take in a fantasy of brilliant outdoor sculptures: netted hoops hang from trees, flashing white light from dangling silver discs; a wind-shimmery, fence-high Mylar fringe dances across a clearing; a room-sized balloon sways on the lawn; towering, helium-filled tentacles reach out across the lagoon like huge fingers, a joyous display resulting from a class taught by visiting "environmental artist" Lou Rizzolo.

"I'm not an ecological artist; I don't use natural materials particularly," Rizzolo tells me. "To celebrate the environment, my students and I use bright materials that intensify an area—that Mylar disk, for instance, catches the wind, reflects the sun like a little strobe light, and is designed to fit into a tree. The tubes that extend from the lagoon 110 feet in the sky are to me very gentle works, a kind of a dance. Here at Ox-Bow we can work on the land, in the water, and in the sky."

A few minutes later, I look out on the puzzle-shaped backwater from co-director Jennifer Hereth's rustic cabin. "In 1907, when the Kalamazoo River was straightened, the lagoon took the ox-bow shape you see now—hence our name," Hereth explains. "Our 110 acres include dunes, marshes, swamps, a view of Lake Michigan and woods. Around 350 students from all over the country—college students working on their BFAs, high-school teachers, local artists—attend summer classes in glassblowing, papermaking, printmaking, ceramics, painting, fiber, and others, taught by fellowship students from many of the better art schools. It's an intensive art-making experience. At the end of the summer we build a twenty-two-hundred-degree furnace on the beach out of a garbage can and a vacuum-cleaner hose. We pour iron into molds for twenty-four hours straight. It's spectacular to see."

JULY 7

THIS MORNING, as I rev up the van, I find myself resisting my scheduled dip around the bottom of Lake Michigan, a lake that, on the map, hangs from the Mackinac Bridge like a swarm of bees, all the way to Gary, Indiana. My heart seems to have acquired a needle that always points north, and Saugatuck is about as far south as I want to go. I take a few minutes to reestablish faith in my overall plan and, reminding myself that perseverance pays, buckle up and head south.

About twenty minutes out of Saugatuck, I stop at the Golden Brown Bakery in downtown South Haven, selected from among the modest buildings lining a main street perpendicular to the shore. I breakfast with some amiable locals who are chatting around a large table about a recent accident: three kids were recently swept off the end of the South Haven pier; a boy drowned, one girl is in a coma, and one girl is better. "People from inland don't realize how treacherous it can be out there," says a woman. "Once I watched fireworks blow back on a boy at the end of that pier and kill him."

"I used to swim the channel when I was a kid," volunteers another. "All of our crowd did. But it's dangerous—against the law."

"Are you going to remain here long enough to see a storm?" asks a man. "Because it's beautiful when a storm hits the lighthouse. The waves just almost drown it." Everyone agrees: a bad summer storm is not to be missed. "We used to always go down and watch the yachts crowd in when a storm was coming."

No one denies this story: "Once, around the turn of the century, a crowded passenger boat was docked at the South Haven pier. Suddenly, all the people rushed to the same side of the boat to look at something and the ship capsized. Two hundred people drowned in the harbor." (See Note, p. 196.)

Most of those present are helping to restore the spidery black catwalk on the South Haven pier. When I mention that theirs is the third catwalk I've seen in western Michigan, I'm told, "But ours is the best! We're all donating money!"

This small-town warmth and eagerness to please seems an honest reflection of South Haven, which is spiffing up an area along the channel with shops and more kinds of boat rides than I've ever seen in one place: charter fishing expeditions with Captain Ray (a woman); a catamaran sail; a pontoon boat river cruise; perch fishing on Captain Nichols's party boat; a meal aboard the lavishly restored *Idler* river-boat. I choose the last, eating a bowl of seafood bisque on a sunny deck. Earlier, before the restaurant opened, the fullback-sized chef, hunched earnestly over a steaming pot of this soup in his cramped galley, promised that it'd be good enough to come back for. It was.

Note: The capsized-ship story demonstrates why it can be so difficult to separate Great Lakes history from yarn. I'd never heard of a ship capsizing from a passenger rush, and neither had the reference librarian at South Haven's public library, but she did know about the steamship *Eastland,* which did frequent runs to South Haven but capsized in Chicago in July 1915, drowning 868 people. David D. Swayze in *Shipwreck!* confirms that the *Eastland* had picked up twenty-five hundred picnickers along the Chicago River, became topheavy, and capsized. It was the largest loss of life from any Great Lakes disaster.

IN THE SMALL Great Lakes Maritime Museum, across the channel from the *Idler,* presides one of the few Great Lakes professional marine archaeologists with permission and enough funding to excavate a Lake Michigan shipwreck. Seating me in the museum library, museum director Kenneth Pott tells me that unlike Wisconsin, the state of Michigan has no full-time marine archaeologist, but that unlike Michigan, Wisconsin has no underwater preserves, a state of underwater affairs I find rather odd.

Pott has been working for several years on the *Rockaway,* a small lumber-carrying schooner that sank off South Haven in what is today the Southwestern Underwater Preserve. "We have a major research project going on out here," begins Pott. "It's a schooner, built in 1866 in Oswego, lost in 1891 off South Haven, and discovered in September of 1983. It was a virgin wreck [no divers had found it yet]. In cooperation with the state, we began an archaeological study of the wreck, and there's since been a PBS documentary, a traveling exhibit, and an exhibit on this wreck and the subject of underwater archaeology in the state historical museum." The *Rockaway* sank in water so deep and cold, Pott says, that nearly everything has been preserved. He has even found traces of salted meat in the galley.

"The underwater wrecks in the Great Lakes are not affected much by oxygen, or by acids in the soil," Pott explains. "The only other places that preserve as effectively are bogs and deserts. So we have this incredible environment out there. And not only are the ships preserved, but much of their cargoes as well. On the *Rockaway*, we've found clothing, canned goods, bone material. We've even done a pamphlet on the conservation of archaeological artifacts from freshwater environments."

Note: More than five thousand ships are estimated to have sunk in the Great Lakes, of which fewer than half have been found and fewer still have survived recognizably intact. Researchers, divers, and, unfortunately, piranhalike treasure hunters (who, despite laws to the contrary, may strip their victims to the bone), scan for these with sonar. Now there's a new device—an ultrasound scanner—newly adapted for marine use by Marty Wilcox, the same person who developed ultrasound for medical purposes. One hopes this technological advance won't lead to even more thefts from sunken ships.

BENTON HARBOR AND ST. JOSEPH seem halves of one city, divided by the St. Joseph River, with St. Joseph dominating the shoreline. The place feels moneyed. I cruise a bluff between a row of sedate buildings—including an art gallery and a hands-on children's museum cushioned in well-established greenery—and an open space sloping a length of several blocks to the lake. Impressive monuments are positioned on thick lawn between solid benches facing the water.

I take time to stroll and read plaques. One claims that the two-hundred-pound cannonballs now welded into a neat pyramid next to a cannon could be hurled over two miles by the eleven-inch Dahlgren, which, built for service in the Civil War, weighs 15,800 pounds.

The cannon points toward the large, sadly vacant area between the lake and the road, a site I once heard discussed at a historical-society gathering: in the early years of this century, music and laughter rose from an extraordinary amusement park located here, run by a religious community called the House of David. It attracted thousands with its luxurious gardens, musical and dramatic entertainment, rides, famous bearded baseball team, and rich ice cream, which some old-timers still yearn for.

When I glance up, I spot a tall, impressively mustachioed man across from the public library, as if conjured there by my thoughts. But he is real: Michael Ferguson, a member of the International Jugglers Association, is juggling four bright yellow balls . . . now five, six, seven, eight! As the apple-sized spheres soar a good twelve feet aloft, he wonders aloud to me, "Do we want people to come in here and enjoy our coast, or do we want to keep it for ourselves?"

While I consider this, a car goes by and beeps. "That may just be a positive beep," analyzes Ferguson. "The ones interested in giving me a hard time, they usually don't stop the car. They just drive by and yell"—he yells—" 'Hey, dork! Drop it!' " His eyes remain on the sky-looping balls while another car goes by, beeping and beeping. It sounds to me like applause.

JULY 8

WHO'D EXPECT to find a national park on Indiana's steel-mill-belted coast? Well, here it is: the Indiana Dunes National Lakeshore. At least I think that's where I am, gaping at a huge mound of hot, gasping sand. "Mount Baldy is known as a smoking dune," a sign explains. "The winds pick up the sand grains from the beach and blow them inland. The sand grains roll and bounce around in a process referred to as saltation. . . . Viewed from a distance, the sand blowing off the top of Mount Baldy looks like smoke. . . . One of the largest dunes on the southern shore of Lake Michigan (135 feet above the lake), Mount Baldy is advancing inland at four to five feet per year . . . slowly burying the forest just south of the dune."

This must be the third or fourth Mount Baldy I've encountered on Lake Michigan (Holland's Mount Baldy and Saugatuck's Mount Baldhead were my most recent encounters); it's time I climbed one. I take the trail at a good clip up some railroad-tie stairs, then lope along a pleasant trail under a roof of green. I hear crickets in the shrub oak, a warbler riff I can't identify. Farther up, pines appear oddly short, trunks buried alive beneath the shifting dune, as if up to their armpits. Ladybugs congregate on marigold-orange butterfly weed; yellow petals shine from low strawberry-plant-like clumps of silverweed.

The trail vanishes and I slip-step arduously up the sliding sand, collapsing, sweating, and panting.

The summit, except for some curly green earlocks, really is bald. Below me a river of vacationers, mostly people of color, is streaming onto the wide, soft beach, making me suddenly conscious of how "white" most Great Lakes beaches so far have been. Tropical beachwear blooms on the sand. Sharp white sails cut across a swath of wrinkled blue. Aloof to the north, two nuclear-power-plant cooling towers loiter like voyeurs.

At a U.S. Park Service station, I'm told that the area includes both the Indiana Dunes National Lakeshore and the Indiana Dunes State Park. The confusion goes back to 1909, when the Prairie Club of Chicago, a group of nature lovers that included Carl Sandburg and Jane Addams, worried that industry would dismantle these dunes and transport them, carload by railroad carload, to Chicago for fill, leaving what was left to the questionable mercy of the steel mills. Long years of efforts to stir public and congressional support for a national park failed, so park advocates appealed to the state. In 1927, 3.5 square miles of dunes were purchased for the Indiana Dunes State Park. It took nearly fifty more years of agitation by conservationists before Congress authorized, in 1966, the Indiana Dunes National Lakeshore, purchased in four separate properties, with more added later. Meanwhile, some industry prevailed: the mile-and-a-half-wide, fourteen-mile stretch between Michigan City and Gary is today a patchwork of federal and state parkland, private residences, businesses, and steel mills (Midwest, U.S., and Bethlehem Steel). Highway 12, which runs through it, appears scarred and depressed, although a turn on a cross street often spells instant, sweet green relief.

I cool off gratefully in an air-conditioned U.S. Park Service office, while Ranger Rawl Hesserbalt tells me that it's the plant variation more than the dunes themselves that has attracted the scientific community here. "A person just walking through these forested dunes doesn't say, 'Wow, look at that dune!' very often. There are much taller dunes elsewhere. But the famous Dr. Cowles [see p. 182] did his studies in plant succession here. More plant species are found in our twelve to thirteen thousand acres than in Yellowstone Park, which is ten times as big."

I ask Hesserbalt, who specializes in plant ecology, how he feels about wildflower picking. "There's been an idea that picking wild-flowers kills the plant," he responds. "This usually is not true. The problem with picking wild plants is that you reduce the seed source. But seeds are a food source for birds and other creatures, so plants produce many seeds. Unless you pick the only one, another wildflower will provide the seed. Still, it's best to recommend against picking. Some species have been picked to near extinction.

"Of course, within national parks, it's illegal to pick anything. You can get permits to allow you to do so for research purposes, but you have to apply through the superintendent of the individual park. I think this is generally true for most state parks as well."

About birds: "You'll see a lot of birds here, especially waterbirds. Most birds don't like to fly across Lake Michigan, so during fall migration, the birds flying south along the western shore and birds following the eastern shore funnel together here." For birdwatching, he recommends the Indiana Dunes State Park, which, having been left largely undisturbed several decades longer than the U.S. National Lakeshore areas, offers trails through a greater variety of wildlife and habitat—woods, dunes, open marsh, wooded swamp.

I drive to a trailhead outside the Nature Center at the state park and begin a short, one-mile loop. Trail 9 starts out hot and buggy. I get out the suntan oil and the insect repellent, anguish over which to put on first—when you dress a salad, does the oil go first or the vinegar?—then realize I'm serving myself up like a meal.

So here I am, on a weekend just after the July Fourth holiday, at the peak of the day, padding through ferns and sun-dappled oaks, wondering how Gary, Hammond, and Chicago could be within an hour's drive when I have yet to encounter company. Maybe the sweltering heat's to blame. I drink half the water in my canteen and pour the rest over my head, expecting to be back any minute, but somehow I take a wrong turn—I have an awful time reading the squiggly trail maps most parks distribute—and I'm out half an hour longer before I stagger into the icy air of the Nature Center and slump into a chair.

In front of me, a small boy stands with his arms out, backed up against a painting of a life-size, open-winged blue heron, entitled "How Big Is Your Wingspan?" A variety of wingspans have been marked along the heron wings, labeled with the names of birds. The boy has the wingspan of a loon, his brother that of a turkey vulture. "What's yours?" they ask.

I heave out of the chair and spread-eagle against the wall. I have a sixty-six-inch wingspan, the boy informs me—same as a Canada goose.

AN HOUR OR TWO LATER, just inside the Gary city limits, Linda Seamon, a tall, athletic-looking woman with a blond ponytail, laughs when I tell her that I'm nervous about driving in Gary. "I've been a firefighter here for twelve years—six for Bethlehem Steel," claims Seamon. "I feel very safe here. I guess I have a lot of faith in humanity."

She's waiting for her young son outside the beautiful Paul H. Douglas Center for Environmental Education at the southern edge of the Indiana Dunes National Lakeshore, and she is the first person I've met who has already done what I'm in the middle of. "When I get time off, the kids and I hit the road," she says. "We just throw out the maps and keep the water on our left. We did the Great Lakes when my daughter was eight or nine. Our last big vacation was along the East Coast, hunting islands."

Seamon suggests I explore the Lake Street Beach. "From there you can walk the shore almost to U.S. Steel; that's where you'll see the slag and residue from tourists, mills, and boats. And the perch fishermen will be out," she adds, noting a west wind. "This is the season for perch. There's an old saying: 'Wind out of north, they bite the least; from the south, they bite in the mouth; from the east, they bite like a beast; from the west, they bite the best.'"

And what does a steel mill firefighter do?

"I fight fires. A lotta fires. They can start during maintenance work, or from grease, oils, or by-products. Used to be we didn't know what we were fighting, but fire departments are becoming very health-conscious. Those diamonds on the trucks tell exactly what's inside by the number. At Bethlehem Steel, we're very conscientious. We report any spill to the EPA, dock it off, bring sand, and dig it out."

Inside, Michael Dale, a high-school teacher in his fourteenth summer at the park, smiles when I say the center seems enormous. "It feels a little cramped to me," he says. "Nine or ten of us work out of here, and sometimes we're doubled up on desk space. We have computers, microscopes, and a very fancy audiovisual theater, but our real role is helping kids—preschool to college age—improve their relationships to each other and the natural world. And we're trying to attract more inner-city people. Nature is often a new experience for them."

"Is this area still famous for its pollutants?"

"The chemicals released have not been corrected to any great degree, but eighty or ninety percent of the particulates are now taken out," Dale says. "I used to wonder, when I drove here in the sixties, why so many houses were painted such an odd shade of orange. After a few years I realized they had been painted white, then oxidized orange from the air pollution. But that doesn't happen anymore. Water quality is improving as well, except after a torrential rainfall, when the Grand Calumet River can carry a whole variety of raw sewage and toxic waste into the lake, bypassing Hammond's ancient sewage plant.

"Otherwise, Lake Michigan is probably clean enough to swim in. Chicago, which gets its water from the lake, doesn't want to pollute the source, so it brings it in one end and shoots it out the other. Most of the effluent ends up in the Mississippi Basin, not in the Great Lakes. But then it becomes St. Louis's problem, or New Orleans's problem. It isn't over."

MY DRIVE from Gary through Hammond and East Chicago is so unpleasant, I hate to talk about it. I resist making unflattering generalizations about a place; after all, I see only a few blocks of anywhere, and a good number of people call it home. Furthermore, I'd been strongly advised to take the Skyway, "unless you have a lot of confidence in your car." Instead, I take 41 north, which subjects me to a stackland so vastly blighted and phallic that I am reminded of a back room full of bleary old men smoking cigars. After Hammond, I am detoured in East Chicago and become lost in a maze of narrow streets lined with barred, padlocked shops and surging holiday crowds. I roll up the windows. *Chugga-chugga* goes the air-conditioner. A voice shrieks directions from a microphone set into a bulletproof convenience-store window. I feel like a Pacperson, scuttling from ghosts.

I keep doggedly driving until, suddenly, I am in Chicago, three blocks from the first apartment I shared with my first husband, and then, at last, at the lakeshore. What a relief to hum along the many-laned Lake Shore Drive. I pass a nice park—tennis courts, golf course, sailboats, yachts—then another, and another. Chicago's shoreline appears to be almost all public land. It's a steamy holiday Sunday and the beaches are jammed.

On a small peninsula, along the boulevard leading to Grant Park and the Adler Planetarium, I find a prize parking place in the shade. Grant Park is abuzz. Cars not parked bumper-to-bumper prowl for a spot. Planes landing at Meigs Field skim the bobbing heads at the crowded swimming beach, vendor music tinkling between roars. Across a swatch of blue water, a glossy skyline flaunts its famous architecture, postcard-perfect under a spotlight sun.

JULY 9

I SURVIVE a night in a sixty-dollar room the size and temperature of a walk-in freezer, returning to the planetarium to ask about a tiny observatory I noticed on the lakeshore. A longtime Chicago astronomer, the scholarly-looking Dr. Eric Carlson, teeters on the edge of his busy schedule, then brakes good-naturedly. The observatory has been operating for twenty years, he informs me, gesturing me into his office. Its purpose is to allow the public to look at the real night sky.

We seat ourselves. "When we first got it, we used to trundle two to four hundred people outside Friday evenings after the Sky Show," Carlson tells me. "They would wait in a line, then climb a little ladder and stand in there for a few seconds. It was an awfully long wait for not very much. Then someone gave us enough money to get a device which is basically an electronic recording screen. Now we can project onto the planetarium sky dome a twenty-four-foot picture of the sky as it is seen through the observatory telescope at that exact moment."

Carlson, despite his wonderful dignity, reminds me of the Little Prince, exuding Saint-Exupéry delight. The electronic eye can see right through big-city haze and lights, he marvels. "One night I went out and there were just two stars coming through the haze. Two stars!

Period! But through the haze, we picked up a picture of a galaxy. How is this possible? It's not radio." Carlson looks at me as if I might know this, then explains that basically, the haze of the city light is "filling up all the buckets out there more or less equally, and the galaxy is just adding its light on top of that. Your eye just sees the glare, but using electronics, we can start slicing off all the uniform brightness, until we're left with the sky beyond. But we will soon escape even the city lights, because we are now connected with a 140-inch telescope on a dark mountaintop in Mexico, so sometime next year we'll start getting live pictures straight from Apache Point."

I share Carlson's excitement. I've always wished planetarium shows were more immediate, less canned, I confess. I've always wanted to look at a live sky through a real telescope.

"Yes, but it's also nice to be able to tape sky events," says Carlson. "Then, if it's cloudy or raining on a Friday night, we can display a past night. Or if Saturn was visible at seven o'clock but the audience won't be viewing until later, we can film it and show the sky as it looked before Saturn set."

UNABLE TO SEE this live show myself, it being only Monday, I walk to the John G. Shedd Aquarium and join a swarm of school-children pouring from yellow buses into the huge lakeside museum. They practically push me along the live exhibits that glow, bubble, glide, stare, or writhe behind glass along the walls of dark rooms. The Great Lakes section is less crowded. High halls amplify already-loud voices. On a balcony over the lobby, CBS is broadcasting its morning show live. Sorry, I'm told regretfully. No way we can talk to you today.

So I walk to the third museum in this impressive coastal cluster, encountering inside the Field Museum of Natural History a contrasting, templelike hush. A few echoing voices arc briefly under towering ceilings and fade like falling stars. Here the exhibits, natural and anthropological artifacts from around the world, are inanimate or dead, some for centuries: dug-up, stuffed, stretched, collected, sorted, analyzed, or preserved. Quiet observers scrutinize what must be millions of objects in glass case after glass case in hall after hall on floor after floor.

Although my inquiries about the Great Lakes are met with wrinkled brows, some in-house calls are made, and in minutes I'm name-tagged and emerging from an elevator onto a mazelike upper floor of little offices. There's an old-library feel to this hall of wood and glass, a Victorian, academic hush even thicker than the one below.

Dr. Scott Lidgard—the tall, red-haired associate curator of invertebrate paleontology—confesses as he escorts me to his earth-toned office that he doesn't often deal with the public. Perhaps he needed a moment of distraction, or was simply curious; but whatever his motive for assenting to see me, he is exceptionally gracious and courteous, meeting my gaze directly through horn-rimmed glasses.

I ask about Petoskey stones, feeling as if I were asking Einstein the sum of two and two. Without hesitation, in a very soft voice, Lidgard explains: "Petoskey stones were formed in the Paleozoic ancient fossil ocean of the Devonian period, several hundred million years ago. At that time, the region around the Great Lakes was largely covered by shallow epicontinental seas, and its position in the world, because of the movements of the plates on the surface of the earth, was much more subtropical than it is today. In these warm, shallow seas, among the many organisms that were growing were corals, and these corals formed calcareous hard skeletons which were preserved in the rocks. Through the eons, as those rocks were lithofied in stone and are now being eroded by the Great Lakes, the skeletons of the corals are exposed. What you see in the Petoskey stone is a cross-section through the corals. The variation in patterns is due to a variation in coral species and a difference in the column growth form and the difference in the angle of cut. Even in the living world today, the diversity of reef coral can often be quite high in a relatively small reef tract. Not all of those corals have skeletons that are robust enough to be preserved in that way, but some are, and in the Devonian period the same thing was true."

"Are there other fossils to be found around the Great Lakes?"

"Certainly. Because of glaciation, topography around the Great Lakes is low, so not much of the underlying sediments are exposed. But where river cuts and mines expose the underlying areas, there's a transition going from south to north into older and older and older sediments that are all lapped onto a stable platform called the Canadian Shield. In upstate New York and surrounding areas, it's common to find an enormous variety of sea life, including trilobites, corals, brozomes, crinoids, blastoids."

"You can just pick these up along the lakeshore?"

"Yes. Not all the counties are well exposed. The problem is that glaciation in the, geologically speaking, relatively recent ice ages planed off the surface so that not much of an outcrop can be seen. What tends to be on the surface of much of the Midwest and upstate New York are the evident workings of glaciation—glacial till, fine-ground kinds of sediments, glacial moraines, glacial stones dropped by the glacier, which may not be from the area where they are found at all. Erratics (boulders or stones dropped as the glacier recedes) containing fossils may have traveled a great many hundreds of miles within a moving glacier.

"What I tend to see here in Chicago from lakefront collecting are primarily corals, brachiopods, and trilobites from areas where Silurian reef rocks are exposed. But sometimes riprap erodes and produces fossils that wash up on the beach, and people find them and say, 'What is this? I found this on the South Shore beach!' and I say, 'It didn't come from there.' Often it will be from a quarry in downstate Illinois or Indiana, brought here for use as building material or roadbed or lake protection boulders."

WHILE STANDING in a fresh, hair-tousling breeze on a skyline boat ride from Grant Park, I learn from a tour tape that, in a manner of speaking, Chicago owes its miles of recreational shoreline to Mrs. O'Leary's cow: the massive rubble from the Great Fire of 1871, which the animal allegedly started, had to go somewhere, and where it went was in the lake, pushing the shoreline out several blocks. Today, most of Lake Shore Drive's 124 blocks are dedicated to the recreation of the people of Chicago (see Note, p. 207).

"We dug all this material from the Chicago Historical Society," the amiable Captain Charles Collopy informs me. "Our family's been giving boat rides in Grant Park for fifty years. My uncles started it in '39 or '40 with speedboats, and they had as many as nine boats running at one time. In 1951 we moved the business into these big cruisers."

We pass the enormous Navy Pier, covered almost entirely by long, dilapidated, shedlike buildings. "Navy Pier was completed in 1916 as an amusement pier," Collopy tells me. "During World War II the Navy took it over. Three thousand men occupied the top floor of those two long sheds. After the war, the University of Illinois took over, and it was called Harvard on the Rocks. Both ends have been declared historically significant buildings. They're going to tear out those middle sheds and decide what to do. But first they have to fix the pier so it won't fall in the lake."

Note: Actually, although fill from the Great Fire did create new lakeshore property, it was an excellent plan created by Chicago architect Daniel H. Burnham in 1909, backed by a group of prominent citizens, that saved Chicago's shoreline from going the way of Gary's, Hammond's, and other Great Lakes cities'. Officially adopted in 1910, the Burnham plan's recommendation that the lakefront be developed as a recreational site available to all is influential even today. The story that Mrs. O'Leary's cow started the Chicago fire by kicking over a lantern is, however, apparently largely folklore.

JULY 10

AFTER A SOUND SNUBBING by the north-side Chicago Historical Society library, I nose the van onto Outer Lake Shore Drive and whiz out of town beneath a canyon wall of old brick condominiums. "We're gonna drive till we can smell the flowers," I promise my trusty vehicle.

Lake Shore Drive becomes Sheridan Road, which continues through wealthy lakeshore residential communities for miles; as in Detroit, Chicago's north side contrasts with its south. I drive through Evanston, a dense, moneyed suburb boasting Northwestern University; Wilmette, home of the Taj Mahal–like Bahai House of Worship and Gilson Park, the largest park on the north shore; Winnetka, a well-heeled suburb where the only car I see at one manicured little park is a big black limo; Glencoe, with a tabernacle next door to the Lake Shore Country Club; Highland Park, home of the Ravinia Summer Music Festival, famous for its cultural events; Fort Sheridan, Fourth U.S. Army, which enjoys a golf course inside the base; and

Lake Forest, where to use the beach, I'm told, I have to buy a sticker somewhere else.

The glitz ends abruptly at the Great Lakes Naval Training Center in North Chicago. I trace a foul smell to Abbott Laboratories, its buildings filling blocks and blocks behind a high fence. The sad, depressed-looking area feels shocking so close to the miles of mansions.

But I like the next town up: Waukegan seems an earnest, hard-working town with a big old brick hotel and a recreational, cultural, and senior center begun years ago by Jane Addams as a camp for Chicago's underprivileged kids. "Waukegan's on a natural harbor, so it has thrived on maritime-type industries," says Mary Jane Anderson at the public library. "We're more a blue-collar than a white-collar town. We've made boat loaders here for years. And we have a gorgeous shoreline."

"You do?"

"Well, it's been allowed to run down. But the whole area's being renovated. It's going to be lovely. We don't have the tall buildings or condos here like they do further south. And we do band concerts in the park—John Philip Sousa is very popular here."

To find Waukegan's beach, on euphemistically named Seahorse Drive, I curve around mountains of sand, silos, a cement company, railroad tracks, and a boat-building operation before reaching the long, flat stretch of sand near an old brick power station with four stacks. But Waukegan likes its industry; many here find this beautiful. And Illinois Beach State Park, gorgeous by anyone's standards, lies only a few miles north, where I soon camp amid small trees, facing a paradise of wildflowers blooming in a wide lush marsh.

JULY 11

I'M WAKENED early by Ranger Paul Richardson: seems I forgot to post my registration card in front of my campsite last night. I hand it to him as I emerge and tell him of my project.

"I've worked in the park five years and lived here all my sixty-three years," the big ranger responds. "According to Indian lore, this land was once called Buffalo Wallows—the Indians would drive the buffalo into the marsh, take what they needed, and let the rest go.

Used to be wild turkeys down here. Back in World War I, marijuana and hemp were grown here. Then it became farmland for a while. Nineteen forty-two to 1945, the army had tanks racing up and down and we still find fifty-caliber bullets. Found one right on your site here about two months ago."

After he leaves, I slip happily back into my much-missed morning routine, boiling water on my little stove, brushing my teeth with water from a plastic pop bottle, spitting into poison ivy. The park seems quiet—amazing to me, given its urban proximity. After breakfast, I drive to an unpretentious building overlooking the beach amid wildflowers, benches, and a martin house. Susan Wright, park naturalist, and her dog face me from behind a desk in a large, pleasant office. On the bulletin board, Rosie the Riveter flexes a biceps. I ask Wright why a nuclear power station has been allowed in the middle of this glorious park.

"Isn't that horrible?" asks Wright. "And this park has the only dunes left in Illinois! We have over 650 plant species in a mile stretch from the lake. The land here was purchased back in the forties and established as a state park in 1954. In the fifties, a group called the Dunesland Preservation Society fought to have a law passed—and it wasn't easy—to make this a nature preserve. It became the first nature preserve in the country. All the other nature preserves are patterned after ours.

"But in the early seventies, the power plant was built at the north end of the park; at that time, there were no laws against locating a nuclear power plant next to a campground. After a second reactor was built, we purchased the land north of it to the Wisconsin line, so we now have six and a half miles of lakefront. Eighty percent of this park is nature preserve or natural area. Although over two million people visit every year, we try to keep them to the picnic areas, beaches, and the marina at the north end, which is the largest small-craft marina on Lake Michigan. You can go to the hiking area, find the parking lot full of cars, but see only a few people on the trails."

Wright is right: from the beginning of the Dead River Trail—a misnomer if there ever was one—I am deep into my wildflower book, identifying orange butterfly weed, fat purple field thistle, blue spiderwort, sweet white clover, pink roses, yellow goatsbeard, hot-pink crown vetch. A prairie lily. Selfheal. Flowering spurge. A tall stalk of lavender flowers called pale spike lobelia. Full-blown yellow prickly pear cactus, bright as skirts. Grass pink orchids, each over an inch across, on the stem about a foot tall. Calamint, tubular lavender flowers, wafting mint. Winged loosestrife. Black-eyed Susans. I'm in heaven—and I haven't progressed farther than a stone's throw from the parking lot.

I advance along a comfortable, four-foot-wide barked path past a patch of white meadow anemones, behind it pink starry prairie phlox. Here's an asterlike flower called daisy fleabane. Velvety yellow coreopsis. Butterfly weed. Hoary puccoon. Blackbirds swoop out of the grass, stirring up little brown fritillaries. I'm wearing my khaki vest with all the pockets in it, which are full of maps of other parks. As usual, I can't find the right one. Oh, well. I poke at some shrubby cinquefoil, watch a chipmunk play in the weak sunlight, a swallowtail butterfly, a blue jay. A robin is singing. A rabbit skitters by. A cedar waxwing leads me along the path, staying just ahead. I've only seen one other person, a pale, stout man in a tank-type undershirt, slapping mosquitoes. I continue, smug and snug in my sweatshirt.

From a lookout, I can see the Dead River sloshing through the rich marsh. A treeful of speckled blackbird mamas scream at a stoic kingbird. A tern loops past. Something makes a tremendous splash.

I live for mornings like this. Back on the path, I find a wren's nest. Meadowsweet (a woody shrub from the rose family), a yellow sand primrose, and an awful outhouse with no paper. I find a use for old maps, then circle back on a narrow path that goes through a stubby oak forest. Mosquitoes like it here, as do dragonflies so big they rustle leaves on takeoff. Milkweed blooms pink and violet under orange monarchs. Something smells like mint. As I approach the parking lot, I scare up about fifty blackbirds. Big flap of wings. Shrieking.

It's almost noon.

JUST NORTH of the Wisconsin line I brake for a deer in somebody's yard before I realize it's plastic. Sigh. It's been a long time since I saw a deer. In the harbor town of Kenosha, beyond piles of riprap on a rubbled shore near a U.S. Dismantlement Corporation sign, I see a lighthouse and pier.

At the Kenosha County Historical Museum, located in a converted brick mansion, pink-suited Lois Stein explains that the streets here start with Second Avenue because First Avenue washed away. "And last Friday, the smokestack came down," she adds sadly. "Everybody was really disappointed. We wanted to save it." She shows me a picture: the lone stack was quite handsome, the last remnant of Kenosha's downtown industry. It explained the rubble I saw.

"So Kenosha used to be more industrial than it is now?"

"We were totally industry," says Stein.

Nevertheless, there is no shortage of parkland in Kenosha. I pass Eichelman Park, a grassy spread with shade trees and beach, then drive through seemingly endless Simmons Island Park, where I find a No Loitering sign (isn't loitering what parks are for?); a red-brick lighthouse; a red-brick municipal bathhouse (1934); a bike path curling through clumps of trees; vast playing fields; a long, wide, sandy beach; picnic tables; more playing fields; a brand-new bandshell; and finally, the end, and the beginning of Kennedy Park, which runs into Pennover Park, which connects with Alford Park. Kenosha knows how to play.

I'M BEGINNING to like these scrappy west-shore industrial towns; their determination to survive is impressive. In Racine, population pushing one hundred thousand, banners instructing me to DISCOVER DOWNTOWN: RACINE ON THE LAKE flap above an urban street on which nearly every third storefront is vacant. When I try to buy a window-displayed beach towel embroidered with RACINE: THE RIGHT PLACE TO LIVE!, I find the place is closed. A new, blue-roofed Festival Hall sprawls within sight of a downtown marina. Looming over everything is Lakeshore Towers of Racine, ten or eleven stacks of ritzy-looking, brown-and-white condominiums, with a similar project rising behind high scaffolding next door. A more ambitious rebuilding of an urban shoreline I have never seen.

But almost no one is out here. A mother tending the several children hanging from a crayon-bright play structure allows that evenings are livelier. A graying man dipping for minnows off a newly built fishing pier, when asked what he thinks of all the development, says mildly, "It's fine if you can afford a boat and a condo. We used to fish from a pier that stuck way out. Used to catch salmon, lake trout, all kinds of fish, but we're lucky to get a few small fish offa this one." He doesn't seem mad, just sad. Nearby, hoses dangle over a covered brick cleaning station. Men stand around it, gutting their catch.

Downtown, a chamber of commerce employee tells me that "up until about five years ago, Racine was part of the rust belt—mid-western cities with declining industries. Like many towns along the lakeshore, Racine had turned its back on its lakefront area. But our whole harbor has been redesigned and dredged, and today we have a 931-foot marina, a thirteen-acre park, and a new Festival Hall. We have festivals all summer long: ethnic, food, music, all kinds." Other lakeside attractions include "the Great Lakes' tallest and oldest operating lighthouse"—Wind Point—and one of the last free zoos in America.

Leaving Racine, I am astounded to see a flag-flying castle amid fountain and gardens, but it turns out to be a water treatment plant. Below blocks of grassy banks, bright yellow lifeguard chairs preside over generous beaches polka-dotted with gulls. I visit the lighthouse but pass up the lakeside zoo. By six-twenty, shadows begin gathering in the lake. Colors deepen. After a serene spell on a bank-top bench, I press on: time to locate a campground—there are no lakeside state parks until halfway up Wisconsin. Time to find a PDQ.

"YOU CAN BUY an excellent kringle for about three-fifty in any PDQ," a neighboring diner at Whey Chai's downtown restaurant informed me earlier this evening, referring first to a Danish pastry (Racine has been called the most Danish city in America), and second to a chain of convenience stores. "You can't leave Racine without one."

I'm not too fond of goopy-middled Danishes, but when I see a PDQ at the edge of town, I stop. Inside, an affable lady is pleased that there's one kringle left. "I'll never eat this by myself," I protest as she slides a cherry-filled ring the size of a large pizza over the counter.

"Oh yes you will," says a second jovial clerk, who debates with the first whether I will actually chew it or simply inhale it. "We don't think you're going to share it with anybody," she says. "You're going to eat it all by yourself."

"But if you do feel as if you have to share it," Clerk One assures me, "you'll have no trouble finding somebody to share it with."

"Mmmmmmmmm," agrees county campground caretaker and college student Ben Lake thirty minutes later. We're seated at a picnic table on a manicured lawn in view of my van, three RVs, and two tents.

"The lady said chocolate is the best," I tell him. "What do you think?"

"Cherry," he says with his mouth full. "Cherry is best."

I think so, too, but she was right about the kringle's short life span. We restrain ourselves, leaving enough for my breakfast.

Before the sun sets, Lake and I walk about a half a mile to the shoreline, en route encountering monster ruts in the fragile prairie grass. The ruts were left by the caterpillar that rescued the tractor that got stuck pulling out the ORV that drove in here illegally last spring, Lake despairs. The resulting damage will require truckloads of dirt. At the shore, we look sadly down eroding ravines from the top of a ragged cliff.

We can't stand it. We head back and polish off the kringle.

JULY 12

OVER HALF OF Milwaukee's half-million people hold jobs at some twenty-four hundred factories. Already, as so often happens in the south end of Great Lakes cities, I notice a concentration of industry. However, following a sign for Grant Park, I come upon a delicate blue-green metal bridge arcing over the mouth of a gentle creek that empties into the lake. To my right, light streams from behind a mask-like cloud, spilling a pool of blinding white over the dark lake; to my left, under a tunnel of overhanging green, five raucous kingfishers dive-bomb a surface as flat and polished as a courthouse corridor. Along the banks, Queen Anne's lace frills, star-flowered purple nightshade twines. Ducklings leave streaks in shimmering rows of mirrored cattails, as if swimming through wet paint.

"Ke-ke-ke-ke!" warns a plunging blue kingfisher. "Ke-ke-ke-ke!" rattles another, disclosing its maple-high perch. Hurtling past my head, through a swarm of martins and swallows, the kingfishers seem big as ducks.

At first I assume I'm standing in the middle of the stingy sort of park one sometimes finds at the working end of a city, but this park goes on and on. Driving through it, I notice an inviting bike path snaking through woods, over rolling lawns, edging the lake, slipping back into trees. (Seventy-six miles long, it continues all the way around Milwaukee.) I pass a golf course, a picnic area in a little meadow, then another, tennis courts, a big playing field, more picnic areas. Footpaths vanish into more woods; a creek bubbles past. A white rabbit, the same size as the crow it feeds besides, suddenly chases the bird across the grass. The crow runs until the last possible moment before lifting off, like a plane.

At last, a stop sign. A red flashing light. But wait! Here's a new park: a senior center, nature trails, an exercise track along a shaven roadside, another golf course, wetlands, woods, meadows, beach, the Milwaukee skyline, lake views, wildflowers, prairie grass. Then another park, and another! Even downtown, Milwaukee is banded by parks. Blue-collar town indeed! The "machine shop of the world" is green-collared, if you ask me.

LOOKING DOWN from an overpass, I see seven ponies tied to an odd-looking railroad car. When I stop to investigate, none of the hands sitting around on hay bales will talk. But then I find Ted Piekutowski.

"I come to Milwaukee every year for the Great Circus Parade," the circus aficionado tells me. "It's a once-a-year, one-of-a-kind event. About seventy-five wagons come down from the Circus World Museum in Baraboo, Wisconsin, which was the original winter quarters for the Ringling Brothers' Circus. This is as close as the train can get to Veterans Park, where the circus is being set up. The train cars that you see here were used for this kind of transportation as far back as the 1900s. This morning six horses unloaded all the wagons, just like they used to."

"How did they get the animals up to the Veterans Park?" I ask.

"The only animals that come in on the train are the horses. All the other animals used in the circus parade are privately owned by game ranches and individuals who raise lions and tigers and things. The Sunday parade is a re-creation of an old-time circus parade, which used to advertise that the circus had come to town and could stretch out as long as a mile."

Piekutowski confesses he's spent his life studying the circus. "I'm a circus model builder and a circus fan. Probably a million and a half people will watch the parade on Sunday—people come here from all over the country and the world."

At Veterans Park, between a high, hard skyline and a wide blue lake, white-and-red, white-and-yellow, and white-and-green striped tents seem to spin like giant tops across a vast lawn. I ask if there's anything to eat there, and a skinny ticket-taker answers in a W. C. Fields whine: "There's all kinds of funny-lookin' things! Wait'll you see 'em, you won't wanna eat 'em! They got food from all over the world. They got stork's nests. They got everything."

Crowds are streaming into the grounds around tractors, horses, enormous semi trucks, muscular crews, fire trucks, and police cars still busy setting up the circus. Massive horses sway in tented stalls. Lions loll in animal-cracker cages. And scattered everywhere are unbelievably ornate antique circus wagons.

Even primed by Ted Piekutowski (who looked and sounded like John-Boy Walton), I'm not prepared for the gilt, mirrored, elaborately carved and painted grandeur of the restored circus wagons, some over a hundred years old. I especially like a magnificent baroque gold one perched by the lake, cranking out an ear-splitting calliope tune.

Inside a tent so red that light coming through it tints the white dogs and horses pink, I watch the first performance of the Royal Hanneford Circus from a ringside seat. A female ringmaster's deep, sexy voice resonates, announcing performing dogs, sequined trapeze artists, silly clowns, elegant steeds, and a horse that looks like a giant Dalmatian. The band tootles. Elephants clump close enough to touch. The best clown has a mouth so big he doesn't need makeup. He dances on the rump of a galloping horse, then slides off the tail end to the sound of cymbals. Drums. Screams. Laughter. Applause. Organ music.

After the show, Hugo Zachini, the Human Cannonball, sprinkles himself (fully clothed) with baby powder, climbs into a cannon bolted to the top of an old truck, and—*boom! poof!*—sails 160 feet along the shore.

NEXT DOOR, I drink in the tall, cool quiet of the Milwaukee Art Museum—but the respite is brief. In minutes, I'm jazzed again. Entire walls, glassed ceiling to floor, showcase the lake like a moving mural. I pass a painting of an oversized Pabst Blue Ribbon beer can, then a big red tomato, a big orange. I see myself in a crowd painted on a mirror, take in a special exhibit of offbeat Catholic/voodoo Haitian art, then am startled by a huge window framing the city. Exhausted, I sink into a chair facing two Warhols: a can of tomato soup, a box of Brillo pads.

Move over, MOMA (New York's Museum of Modern Art)—you have a rival for my heart. I love this startling art, marvelous lighting, columns of Plexiglas, rainbow colors, strange objects hanging off the walls. Even the windows are art: blue seascapes, skylines, a circus-delirious park.

My eyes feel glazed. Time to climb into the van and look for a nook to nap in. On my way out of town, I am startled by four life-sized human silhouettes, black on white before blue lake and sky, staked along the waterline at the lakeside Milwaukee Gun Club. Suddenly: *bam! bam! bam! bam! bam!* A row of policemen shoots them full of holes.

I'M FINDING Wisconsin park-precocious. Not only do lakeside towns often provide unusually inviting, beautifully kept Great Lake access, but twenty-three of the state of Wisconsin's seventy-seven parks and forests employ full-time naturalists. In addition there are private, "self-supporting" organizations like the Schlitz Audubon Center in Bayside, which at the moment is buzzing with a well-trained staff, children, and wild bees in a glassed-in hive.

"This is where Schlitz used to keep the draft horses that pulled the beer wagons through the streets of Milwaukee," a harried receptionist tells me. "After automobiles replaced them, the Schlitz Foundation eventually gave the property to the National Audubon Society."

"Our priority is teachers," director Bob Nichols explains from behind a piled-high desk. "We have a small staff, so we want to multiply the impact on the million people that live in this area. We offer eleven university courses through the University of Wisconsin

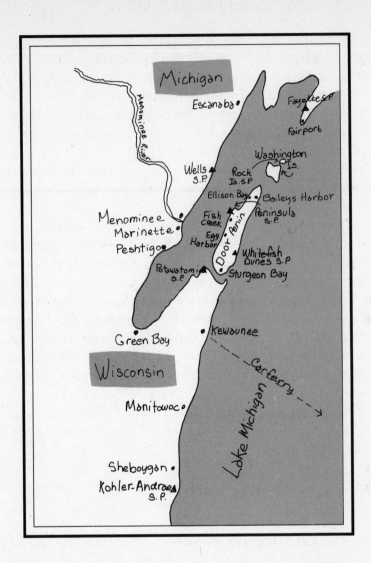

Western Lake Michigan

and distribute curriculums called 'Living Lightly in the City' and 'Living Lightly on the Planet' all over the United States."

The center sits amid trail-webbed acres where, Nichols claims, 251 of Wisconsin's 300 known bird species have been sighted. "Birds are a good barometer to the environment," he adds. "If you have a good diversity and population of bird life, it follows suit that other things are in balance."

I don't find many birds when I walk it, but I do see half a dozen deer. One stands just yards away for a long time, moving only to lick her nose.

Back on the road, I take a supper break in the quaint, New England–like town of Port Washington, then drive through exquisite, dusk-gilded farmland to the extraordinary Kohler-Andrae State Park, a delicious combination of wetland and forest just south of Sheboygan. Here I pay $28 for my Wisconsin annual state park sticker (as opposed to Michigan's $15) plus an additional $10 to camp for the night, a startling total of $38. Wisconsin state parks currently charge the highest nonresident fee of any state in the country, the next-highest for residents. But I count myself lucky. My site, which I obtain only because the legitimate occupants had a sudden family emergency, is beautiful and private, surrounded with high, dense trees. A woman I meet in the shower room can't believe I got in—she'd made her reservation last January.

JULY 13

I'M ACQUIRING a taste for brats and beer, and "the best of the wurst," claims a local resident, is right here in the "roaring metropolis" (her words) of Sheboygan (not to be confused with Michigan's Cheboygan). I smile. I find Sheboygan an unassuming working town with a downtown beach and some recently renovated waterfront charm, but she was right about the food. At Randall's, despite being a woman alone, I am offered the best table, where I enjoy a view of the water, a tasty meal, and a modest tab.

On the riverside, among a row of boutiqued fishing shanties, I find a couple of Native American fishermen unloading boxes of chubs from a black-and-white wooden fish tug docked before the one shanty serving its original purpose. Inside, two more men roll a two- or three-foot-wide, possibly mile-long net from a large wooden spool, checking it for holes, passing up one big enough to crawl through. If they mended all the holes, one man tells me, they'd be there forever. Back outside, I stick my head in one of the fish tugs and find it empty and clean. I thought it'd smell, but it doesn't.

NORTH OF SHEBOYGAN, the road swings dramatically close to the lake. It's rocky here, not a swimming beach, but absorbingly lovely: bluff-top panoramas, farmland cultivated almost to the surf, blue seascape filtered through manila rows of wheat. Driving through this fussed-over farmland feels deeply restful, as if I'm being fussed over, too. Some fields are solid yellow with mustard, sandwiched between slices of green before map-blue water.

Approaching the middle-size town of Manitowoc, I'm puzzled by a group of shallow silver domes at the end of a small peninsula, but what looks like a UFO parking lot turns out to be a water treatment plant. The downtown seems oddly vertical for its small size: steeples, grain elevators, a candy-cane-striped smokestack, a concrete smokestack. I wander down a narrow street through a villagelike assemblage of mammoth kilns and perhaps fifty huge silos, entering the Manitowoc Malt House near a grain elevator labeled "Budweiser."

"We make malt for beer," begins a pleasant woman who wonders what I'm doing here. At the word "writer," she freezes and looks at me as if I were holding a gun.

"Better let Jim handle this," snaps a man emerging from a cubicle.

While I wait, I wander into the office of the head engineer, who can't help describing how barley is steeped and rinsed for malt. He is happily striding into the third step when the receptionist races in and tells him he isn't supposed to be talking to me and that Jim can't be found.

No luck, either, at the Manitowoc Maritime Museum ("the largest marine museum on the Great Lakes," claims a museum brochure): the director is in a meeting until closing. This season's main display presents a wide selection of new and old "knucklebusters" and "speed machines," which includes a 70-pound Spinaway two-horsepower motor, a 382-pound V-6 Mercury that appears powerful enough to propel the building, Evinrudes, Johnson Seahorses, and some antiques as quaint as eggbeaters, one sporting a sexy red script "Elto" on a black-shadowed yellow ellipse.

IN KEWAUNEE, across from the Michigan-Wisconsin Ferry Service, known to most people as the Carferry, a "trout boil" is in progress. Boiled fish sounds awful to me, but the aroma is tantalizing. I buy a six-dollar ticket from William Peterson, president of the Union State Bank. "We use Lake Superior lake trout, onions, carrots, potatoes, and herbs," proclaims the aproned Peterson from behind a church-supper table. Then he brags, "Kewaunee's is the best natural harbor on the Great Lakes."

I counter that I've heard that Beaver Island's harbor is the biggest natural harbor on the Lakes.

"Maybe so, but it probably freezes," counters Peterson. "Ours never fills up with ice. Carferries run all year. Fish tugs run all year."

From one of the picnic tables set up along the river, I watch the chef, another bank president (retired), hover over a steaming barrel on a smoky fire until the basket of trout steaks is raised to shouts of approval. I devour a meal so good I doubt I'll recover for days. Bracing myself for a display of chefly temperament, I inquire after the recipe.

"No problem," says Adrian O'Konski. "You use Bascom's Louisiana Style Shrimp and Crab Boil. Then you put in about one box a bay leaves—five, six leaves. And be sure you put in some lemon extract and a good chunk a celery. That's basically about it. The potatoes you boil for thirty minutes; carrots and onions eighteen, twenty minutes; and the fish for fifteen minutes."

"Maybe you don't want me to use this, my being a writer?" I ask.

"Oh no, you can use it. Go right ahead. Oh, I forgot to tell you, you also put in dill seed and fresh dill, in season."

JULY 14

AT ONE O'CLOCK in the morning, somebody bangs on the van door. I whip awake, adrenaline pumping, but I'm not being cited for vagrancy. I'm just asleep in one of a long line of parked cars that a kid is rapping on, waking all the people who, like me, are waiting for the Carferry, my smug solution to my lodging problem. Last night the parks were full and available motels too expensive, so I bought a forty-dollar round trip ticket (six hours each way) on the Carferry to Ludington. And here it comes, the S.S. *Badger*, last of its kind, bright lights blurred in a black, breezeless murk. The old ferry lumbers up the channel, creaks, stops, and, rumbling like an elephant, churns backward, railroad tracks at the rear connecting with the set on the dock.

The ship is unloaded; passengers clump off. I board and claim one of the shabby sofas in the large, tiled lounge that opens onto the stern. Even before departure, the furniture sags with snoozers huddled under blankets and coats. Leaving my quilt to mark my territory, I move to the massive bow as the boat hums out of the harbor. Someone shouts "Bon voyage!" from the shore. A full moon emerges, performs briefly, then vanishes behind a curtain of clouds. We pass the pier; shore lights recede; finally, the only person I see is the pilot, pale and remote behind a high band of glass.

Finding not one employee anywhere to interview, I join the sprawl for six hours until the Ludington lighthouse sweeps by, foghorn honking like a car. Pandemonium ensues: vehicles are unloaded; passengers disembark; a long line of cars and bicycles waiting to board jerks forward.

I spend the layover at the end of the Ludington pier.

The return trip is bedlam. After three long warning blasts, twenty minutes later, at 10:10 A.M., we're under way. I push past swarms of adults, pets, and kids—there doesn't seem to be seating for everyone—still unable to find an employee of any kind. At last, a small booth opens and the purser, a youngish man named Tom Budreau, invites me in. Between inquiries and T-shirt sales, he talks informedly. "The *Badger* measures 410 feet by 60 and weighs 4,244 tons," he says. "In the late forties and fifties, seven boats ran to Milwaukee, Manitowoc, and Kewaunee, with two waiting in the wings. The *Badger*, the only usable ferry left, has a fifty- to sixty-member crew, most of whom have no direct contact with the passengers. It's the largest coal-fueled train-carrying passenger ferry in the United States."

That explains the smudgy horizon! I'd wondered about the trail of smoke that hung behind the ship as far as I could see.

"The 'S.S.' before '*Badger*' stands for steamship," Budreau confirms. "We burn eighty tons of coal per day." He speaks with authority: although he's in his first year aboard, his father and uncles all worked for the railroad that owned the Carferry, as did his grandfather. "I've been riding the ferry for twenty-nine years, and I'm twenty-nine," Budreau says as we climb to the upper deck.

High in the pilot house, I peer out at the gloomy day through cinematic windows while third mate Bob Mason tells me that we're carrying 107 autos and maintaining about eighteen knots an hour. "It's about fifty-six miles across." He shows me a bank of weather equipment. Twice a day, a satellite polls the ship for a weather report, a valuable source for early storm warnings.

On a lower deck, a crew member who has been working on the ferry for twenty years tells me his dad had worked on the ferry, too. "Ya wanna know the difference between a sea story and a fairy tale?" he adds, voice raised against the screaming engine. "Fairy tale starts out, 'Once upon a time.' Sea story starts out, 'No bull.' "

Note: After struggling to stay afloat financially for many years, the year-round Michigan-Wisconsin Transportation Company closed down for a summer, then was opened by new owners as the Lake Michigan Carferry. A renovated *Badger* presently runs between Ludington and Manitowoc from May 1 to October 11.

THE DOOR PENINSULA is actually a series of islands laid out beyond a mainland promontory like fingerbones, accessed by a bridge to Sturgeon Bay and to the far islands by a couple of ferries. Across the bridge, a short distance up the eastern shore, I watch a red fox leisurely lunch on a rat at the side of the road while mosquitoes bump at the windows. Then I wind through an umbrella forest on a two-track road to Whitefish Dunes State Park. Here, Patrick Warner, assistant park manager, informs me, under the site now occupied by a new interpretation center, archaeologists discovered evidence of several Native American cultures. "Before the state can build anywhere, they have to make sure that the area is clear of any artifacts," explains Warner.

Warner describes Whitefish Dunes as the biggest dunes in Wisconsin. (The tallest, reaching 93 feet, is called Mount Baldy.) "Basically, the park is here to protect and preserve them," he says. "There are miles of trails to hike here and a mile and a half of sandy beach, but we do have a problem with riptides."

A sign I later find on the beach describes these:

Sometimes misnamed "undertows," rip currents may be strong enough to pull even an experienced swimmer from shore. Rip currents are formed when water moves shoreward in the surf zone and then rushes with intense energy back out to sea in a narrow path. This happens when longshore currents moving in opposite directions meet, usually in a bay, or if there is a break in an offshore sandbar, or if the longshore current is diverted by a jetty, groin or other obstruction. Rip currents are seldom wider than ten yards and rarely extend farther than 100 yards offshore. However they have been known to reach 30 yards and extend as far as 1,000 yards offshore. They can travel at speeds up to four feet per second.

Signs of rip currents are a change in water color from surrounding water; an agitated surface with whitecaps extending beyond the breaker zone; a gap in advancing breakers where the rip current is forcing its way seaward; a floating object moving steadily seaward.

If you get caught, don't panic. Don't try to swim against the current. Swim parallel to shore until you get out of the current since it will probably not be more than 30 feet wide. If you can't break out of the current, float calmly out of it until it subsides, usually just beyond the breakers, then swim diagonally to shore.*

ANOTHER SIGN, this one in the Ridges Sanctuary north of Baileys Harbor, declares all the plants protected here. I find Indian paintbrush, juniper, sunflowers, fat pink lady's-slippers, blue chicory,

---

* The information on this sign was adapted from publications of the Pacific Sea Grant College Program.

daisies, coreopsis. Rare red wood lilies grow singly here and there, about a foot high, like flung stars.

At the Ridges nature center, volunteer Steve Waller tells me that what started off as a Coast Guard gift of ten acres has grown to over a thousand. "The Ridges is a unique geological formation," he says. "There's nothing between the harbor opening to the south and Indiana, so the prevailing southern winds bring up sediment and deposit it here in a series of sandbars, which over the years fill in."

Outside his home next door, naturalist Paul Regnier, who is playing catch with his dog, tells me that nearly five hundred plant species (excluding lichens, mosses, and primitive plants) can be found in the sanctuary. "It's kind of a pocket here," says Regnier. "People come here—down, Peaches!—from the western side of Door Peninsula, which is the more touristy side, in shorts, T-shirts, and here we are in long pants and long sleeves. Driving here, the temperature can go down a degree a mile. The ridges were old lakeshores, and this created a special climate and a boreal forest more typical of Canada or Lake Superior areas—Peaches, stay down!—with plants such as cedars and firs."

JULY 15

I FIND the Door Peninsula a lot like California in that it lives up to considerable hype and everyone's welcome. From the laid-back eastern shore to chic little western towns like Fish Creek, Egg Harbor, and Ellison Bay with their B&Bs, glamorous shops, gourmet eateries, and famous fish boils, one can bliss out in private, camp comfortably in sprawling, voluptuous parks, or backpack tiny Rock Island State Park.

I myself am camping on the western shore of Green Bay at Peninsula State Park, a place so big I had a choice of three campgrounds and drove four miles from the computerized main office to get to my serene site. I was welcomed here by an American redstart singing under a canopy of maple leaves, a deer lounging by the picnic table, and smoke drifting from a recently abandoned campfire. It affords amazing privacy, considering there are four hundred sites in this park, seventeen miles of bike trails, and nine miles of hiking trails. Along one of the latter I see a hairy woodpecker, watch a phoebe drop bugs in a wide-open mouth in a small, round nest, and try to find the nest a baby cheeping under a bush must have fallen from.

On a pebbly beach, a young man flicks stones over a still, small bay. Does he practice?, I ask Brad Pelzek from Milwaukee. "Not really," he shrugs. But he knows that the world record is thirty-five skips, and before I leave, he scallops one so fast that we lose count. Nearby I notice boats, bikes, paddleboats, sailfish, and windsurfing things for rent.

Back at the campground, I introduce myself to Darcy Debelack, the second woman I've seen camping alone all summer, a naturalist at the Schlitz Audubon Center that I recently visited. "I could have stopped at Point Beach or Potawatomi, both really nice state parks, but I wanted to hike and the trails here are the longest," Debelack responds when I rave about the diversity here. "Every time I've come here it's been a different experience: I notice something different, or it's a different time of day, or I have a different feeling about myself as I drive up here. I've never camped in this part of the park before. Last time I camped at Tempison Bay, which was noisy and crowded —a lot of kids and families. So this time I asked for something quiet and the ranger sent me here."

It really is quiet, too, until a midnight storm rains on the van roof like stones on a bucket. In the morning, right by the road, a baby bird clings precariously to a low, skinny branch; every few minutes, Mama gets on the branch with it and stuffs bugs in its mouth. When I return from the shower room, however, the birdlet's on a higher, safer perch, and I can't imagine how it got there.

JULY 16

ROGER ANGELETTI, a volunteer at the Peninsula State Park White Cedar Nature Center, explains the scarcity of mosquitoes. "We have a lot of little brown bats," he says, leading me around the building to show me one napping upside down in the roof peak. "A bat eats three times its weight in mosquitoes every night. This little guy'll come out during the day once in a while and grab a few mosquitoes. Bats aren't supposed to do that. Maybe he doesn't know he's a bat."

Angeletti, who has retired here and is also a volunteer fireman, loves animals. He tells me about raccoons: "Last year two women were camping out here in a tent and they went into Fish Creek and bought two bags of groceries—milk, cheese, butter—and they put them in the tent. That night they were sitting by their fire and they happened to see a raccoon, so they put the food in the trunk of their car, but they left the keys in the lock. The next morning the trunk was open, milk was all over, and everything else was gone. Raccoons can get into anything. That cooler with the two latches? You don't put a sixty-pound rock on the top, they're gonna get in it."

About bear: "We have bear in Door County, but visitors rarely see them. They say a bear will never bother you unless you bother it or unless she has a cub or it's injured or starving to death." (A bear-phobe, I count *four* attack scenarios here!) "Bear certainly don't starve in Door County. They've got all the corn, apples, and cherries they could ever want."

About porcupines: "Porcupines love to chew on wood. They climb anything. It's funny to watch 'em. A raccoon will come down head first, but a porcupine always shimmies down backward."

FISH CREEK, the small bayside town just north of Peninsula State Park, reminds me of Saugatuck. "This is an artists' town," confirms "Smilin' Bob" MacDonald of the Bayside Tavern, a year-round, family-owned restaurant and bar. "Used to see artists all over town with their easels. Now they have studios so you don't see them as much." I order "Cincinnati-style chili," invented by Smilin' Bob himself, and am soon toasting the chef. "Say that again!" MacDonald commands, grinning.

"I don't care how many pictures you take up here, you can't capture the beauty," a patron two seats down chimes in. "When I was a kid, I used to sit on the shore and look out at Nicolet Bay and say, 'Boy. Wish I had a boat.' Now I sit in my boat in the bay and look at the shore and I think, 'If I didn't hafta get my feet wet, I could go lay on the beach.'"

Of the many old photographs posted about the establishment, my favorite features the Central Hotel, now called the Whistling Swan, a four-story building that years ago horses pulled across the ice from Michigan, a bit of history as spicy as the chili, which is just hot enough to make me sweat along my upper lip and ask for another beer.

WE'RE REALLY ROCKING and rolling on the pretty little car-and-people ferry to Washington Island, but it's a short ride, and in no time my van is tearing through forest and farmland on roads trafficked with cars, bikes, horses, mopeds, and pedestrians. At the popular Nature Center, I complain to naturalist Jim Kopitzke that because the main road goes up the middle, I have to take all these finger roads to the shore and it's driving me nuts.

"The island is densely wooded around the edges," agrees Kopitzke, "but that makes for a nice natural community. We have many habitats, including a small wetlands and several distinct forest types. There's a real good combination of beech and northern hardwoods, swamp forest, good boreal forest, and some hardwoods without any conifers that make habitat for different warblers. We do two bird walks a week and one plant walk."

Kopitzke shows me on a map how the same rock escarpment that forms Niagara Falls runs through both Upper and Lower Michigan to Door County. "This whole line is an ancient coral reef," he explains. "The fossils you see here have been collected all over the island. This is pipe coral here. Here's a piece with five or six different fossils on it—chain coral, pipe coral, honeycomb, some cup corals, some brachiopods." A beehive-shaped fossil I pick up he calls honeycomb coral.

I get back on the ferry just as a storm breaks loose. About halfway back to the mainland, as the ferry bucks through driving rain and spitting lightning, a commuter informs me that I am at Death's Door. Amused by my startled expression, she explains that the straits we are crossing are called "Death's Door" (officially called Porte des Morts) because so many ships have sunk here. "They say that so many ships went down here—sometimes as many as two a week—because this is where the currents of the lake and Green Bay come together." Suddenly, a ray of sun escapes and throws against the charcoal sky a shimmering, vibrant rainbow.

JULY 17

AN EMPLOYEE at Sturgeon Bay's Palmer Johnson Company, which builds dreamy yachts for people like the king of Spain, tells me that "a tremendous number of the guys workin' out in the yard are Belgian, and a tremendous number are father-son teams—we've had up to three generations workin' there at once. Belgians over here are real good at shipbuilding. Real craftsmen. There're other ship-builders in town, too. Bay Shipbuilding builds lakers—up to thousand-footers. On the other side of us, Peterson Builders are building a buncha mine sweepers, but they also build ferries and fire boats for major cities, that typa thing. We're the toy factory in the middle."

Receiving no invitation to tour the company, I wander over to Peterson's rows of Quonset huts rattling with metal parts, hard hats, machines; but nobody will tour me here, either. At Bay Shipbuilding, however, I'm greeted as if I were Charles Kuralt and ushered into an office.

"It's no secret that Great Lakes shipping is at a low ebb, and there's not a large demand right now for new vessels," says Ken Caves. "Our focus right now is on the repair, retrofitting, and recommissioning of the existing fleet, which is primarily done in winter, the shipping off-season. During the other periods, when all the boats are busy carrying grain and coal and iron and salt and cement and everything else—the large bulk cargoes—we take on subsidiary jobs. Right now we're working on a group of lock and dam gates for the Mississippi River. We also have an asbestos removal company."

"Asbestos is used in the ships?"

"Oh yes. Tremendous amount of it. Most Great Lakes ships were built before 1980, before 'asbestos' was a naughty word. Asbestos was used heavily, especially in the boilers and as insulation for the steam pipes. When the environmental hazards of asbestos were recognized, the shipping industry was one of the first to begin replacing it with fiberglass or other safe material. We developed a technology for doing it in a very safe, efficient, clean manner, which keeps our crews working while we are waiting for ships to come in. Right now we're removing asbestos from the smokestack of the *Maricosa*, a Coast Guard buoy tender."

Startled by a crack of thunder, I glance out the window, which frames a huge yellow crane shaped like a squared-off, upside-down U spanning a concrete pit. "That's a two-hundred-foot gantry crane," explains Caves. "And the pit is a dry dock, called a graving dock because it looks like something you'd lower a casket into. When we want to bring a ship in, we pump the dock full of water, lower the end, bring the ship in, position the keel blocks, and then start lowering the water level until the ship settles very gently onto the keel blocks. Then we pump the rest of the water out and there the ship sits, high 'n' dry. We also have a floating dry dock. Operates in a different manner—kind of like the hoist in a garage that raises your car in the air."

Caves takes me to vice-president Bob Fischer, who tells me that of the three places a freighter can be serviced on the Great Lakes, right now this is the only dry dock big enough to accommodate the thousand-footers. But there aren't a lot of ships out there. "I think we're down to about sixty-nine U.S. flag vessels on the Great Lakes," Fischer says sadly. "Foreign ships go home to get service, usually, unless they run aground. Not that many years ago, there were five hundred ships out here."

"What happened?"

"They started building thousand-footers in the early seventies, and every thousand-footer replaced three, four smaller vessels. Today there are about thirteen, fourteen thousand-footers. We built the last three commercial vessels made in the United States. Delivered the last one in 1987."

Safety director Terry Knight drives me through pouring rain on a spontaneously narrated tour, holding an umbrella over my head to keep my camera dry when we peer into the abyss of the huge dry docks. We check out the Coast Guard vessel and a big pulp barge called the *Lillian*. By the time Knight drives me to the van, it's raining so hard that in the one-second dash between vehicles, I'm soaked to the skin.

SOMEWHERE NORTH of Green Bay, I'm gaping at a stunning panorama of misty, overlapping hills, when a birdsong I don't recognize sails out of a tree to my left, answered by the same song to my right. The sensuous love song orbits my head like a silk-tailed comet while I return to the van to fetch my binoculars. They're indigo buntings. What else could be so intensely, Persianly blue? The pair sings on for fifteen minutes, one from a paper birch, the other from the top of a power pole, probably a cedar from Door County, while goldfinches burst excitedly upon the scene, landing in pairs on the looping power line.

Back in the van, I continue toward the city of Green Bay. Wet deer, darkened by the rain, emerge from dripping woods, cross the road in front of me. Little ponds and meadows bloom. I pass another deer. Cattail-filled wetlands. I think about a new bird to look for— I'd been looking for indigo buntings all summer—and decide on a pileated woodpecker. I wander farmland, lose the shore, backtrack, circle, pass field after farmer's field, a pasture graced with blond palominos, another grazed by two deer. Finally I stop at a small restaurant, sit down at the lunch counter, and ask directions.

The patrons find my confusion hilarious. David Rettler, sitting next to me, could use a laugh, he says: he's here because his boat sunk. "I had three of 'em sink," he admits morosely. "My big boat sunk on Lake Winnebago. Then I got this brand new nineteen-foot Conquest with a 150 Evinrude on it. I love to sit out on the water, anchored, but the waves got so high that the anchors got taut and the boat wouldn't roll with the waves. If I'd left it loose a little bit, it'd have been all right. But it went down. That was a week ago. Then I got an aluminum boat with a twenty-horse motor so I could go fishing, and damned if I didn't sink that, too."

Another luncher thinks I ought to stop at the Green Bay Packers Hall of Fame. "I hear somebody has to die before you can get a ticket to a Green Bay Packers game," I say, repeating a statement I just overheard.

"Yeah. I'm number 12,070 on the waiting list to get a season ticket."

"You mean, 12,069 people have to die first?"

"Something like that."

All the men at the bar rib me for being lost. They think it's the most ludicrous thing they ever heard of.

"Where ya going?" asks one when I pay up and head out.

I say I am following the Great Lakes.

"Oh boy, I'm glad I got here before they started moving!"

As I head the van out, I glance in the rearview mirror: there they all are, peering at me out the window, laughing their heads off. Well, heck, if that poor man who sunk all the boats hadn't looked so sad, I'd be laughing my head off, too.

I COME OVER a hill on Highway 57 and there's Green Bay— smokestacks, smog or fog, storage tanks, power plants, and an over-whelming smell. Looking down from a huge bridge, I see industry crowding the river and notice that, at least here, Green Bay isn't green; it's brown. Storage tanks crowd a small island like layer cakes. I am trying to figure out what exit to take to the lake when I realize I've bypassed Green Bay altogether. Guiltily, I keep going. I don't feel like dealing with a city today.

At the Sensibo Wildlife Area near Suamico, I happily encounter acres of gorgeous wetlands, ponds, lilies along the road. I pass a dead fawn, brake for a chicken crossing the road, brake again to snatch a big, battered, black snapping turtle from the path of an oncoming car. Holding it away from me by its dinosaur tail, I sling it into the marsh.

I don't stop again until Peshtigo.

"It's pronounced *Pesh*-tigo," corrects a white-haired volunteer at the Peshtigo Fire Museum. She tells me that on October 8, 1871, the famous Peshtigo fire, called by a museum postcard "America's Most Disastrous Forest Fire," destroyed one million acres and was carried by tornado winds eighteen miles across Green Bay into Door County. A graphic mural of the fire stretches across the back wall of the museum in three sections—before, during, and after. "Eight hundred people died here," the woman comments. "Almost half the popula-tion. We lost everything, wiped out. Still, people were rebuilding two weeks after. Musta liked it here."

YOU'D THINK THINGS would get greener going north, but in-stead I'm encountering some pretty heavy industry. As I leave Pesh-tigo, I try to identify a bad smell, wondering if it's the paper mill I'm passing or if I need a bath, having endured a recent shortage of shower facilities. But when I get to the big plastic Holstein, I realize I'm inhaling the aura of a full-blown livestock market.

Farther north, I'm welcomed to Marinette by mown grass and trees, boats in the water, wetlands. Tiny houses line the lake along narrow city streets. Black fishing nets dry in a backyard; fish tugs bob in the river. But soon I pass a factory, a foundry, a power plant, a depressed-looking business area crying for paint, and more bars than I've ever seen in one town—did I really count two per block? Leaving Wisconsin, I cross the Menominee River to Marinette's twin city, Menominee (now I'm in Michigan), where I find some riverside galleries, restaurants, and like attractions.

Hungry for the feel of "north country," I head toward Escanaba along a road that hugs the shore. Aahhh! At last I can smell the wind coming off the water. In J. W. Wells State Park, fragrant with firs and cedars, a ranger describes Menominee, his hometown, while evening fireflies flicker in the tall grass.

"All I know of the place is what a fourteen-year-old would know," John Hoornstra tells me. " 'Menominee' is the name of an Indian tribe. It was principally a lumber town. As that industry died, other industries, like chemical industries, moved in. People began to use Menominee as a place to live and Marinette as a place to work. So the economic vitality of Menominee is quite modest and Marinette's is fairly respectable for a town of eleven thousand people.

"Around here the culture of the young person growing up—I can't speak for the women—is sports. The schools stop taking attendance when deer and duck seasons open. During the winter you'll see a lot of ice fishing along here. And iceboats. Every year somebody gets in his snowmobile, cautiously checks out the ice, and marks off the safe areas. I've iceboated right along Menominee's main pier and harbor and along that whole section down to the city and back, just for the thrill of it."

JULY 18

ESCANABA is commercial enough to feel like a small city or a big town, but it's pretty too, built right to the soggy shore, cattails lining and willows sweeping lakeside front yards. The Coast Guard cutter

Escanaba is docked along a grassy park, festive flags snapping bright as a board game above a wide green lawn. Despite its name, however, the *Escanaba*'s not stationed in Escanaba; it's not even assigned to the Great Lakes. "The only Coast Guard cutters on the Great Lakes are buoy tenders and an icebreaker," an officer tells me as I join a crowd of tourists. "This is an oceangoing law-enforcement vessel, touring the Lakes to celebrate the Coast Guard's two hundredth anniversary."

Escanaba, like many northern Great Lakes towns, seems a study in contrasts: shiny in one part, a little shabby in another. The recently restored Escanaba (Sand Point) Lighthouse, where once the first woman lighthouse keeper was employed, is scheduled for dedication tomorrow, but up at the harbor a number of the buildings look burned out or vacant. Big piles of coal and gravel dominate the far side. Many of the downtown buildings are flat brick fronts.

Not far out of town, however, I find ranger Stan Benes in his Hiawatha National Forest District Office. "The Hiawatha National Forest includes somewhere around 880,000 acres, 440 inland lakes, seventy miles of Lake Michigan shoreline, many varieties of trees and plants, and a lot of campgrounds," claims Benes. "There're kind of a shortage of campgrounds along Lake Michigan, so we've put in a new one on the Garden Peninsula. Most of your campgrounds, you might as well be in the suburbs"—I nod in despair—"but these sites each have a view of the lake."

He waves at a map upon which the Hiawatha National Forest stretches impressively across the UP to Lake Superior. "The agency also now owns Grand Island in Lake Superior," says Benes. "We've got a barge that goes across three times a day."

"Is it true that one can camp anywhere in a national forest?"

"You aren't limited to a campground," confirms Benes. "But there is a limit of fourteen days, and there are some other regulations."

Is Lyme disease a problem?

"We're aware of it, but not every tick is a threat: Before we send a case to the clinic, it has to be a bite by an infected deer tick that's been embedded for twenty-four hours. In May and early June, our foresters and tree markers sometimes come back with counts up to twenty-five ticks.

"The tick problem is probably connected to the prevalence of deer here. It's often warmer here in winter than it is farther north, and we've got a lot of cedars here: often you can see them trimmed off in a straight line at the level deer can reach. We also have eagles and some black bear. We've transplanted the fisher, which is the natural enemy of the porcupine: when the fisher was trapped out of this country, the porcupine population increased to the point that it was damaging the timber.

"And a couple of years ago, we had a twelve-hundred-acre forest fire, which rejuvenated some things. We've got jack pines coming back by the thousands, and lots of blueberries. You might want to go pick some."

The stark remains of the forest fire are easy to spot from the road, and the ranger was right: wild blueberries grow everywhere. They're tiny, not much bigger than capers, but there're forty to a hundred on each delicate, knee-high plant. I find a patch mixed with juniper and harebells near the only other picker, a middle-aged man, who nods amiably. It's very pleasant work. You just kind of hunker down out there where the black stubs of trees are defined by a blue sky flat as a wall and plink fruit like gravel into a pot.

BIG BAY DE NOC is formed by the Garden Peninsula as it reaches for the Door Peninsula, some small islands plunked into the gap between the two. Although the Garden Peninsula feels wild and remote, a good road leads along its length to cottages, small streets, woods, the beautiful new U.S. Forest Service campground Benes described, a ghost town, and, at the tip, a fishing village. The forty to fifty deer per square mile have trimmed the cedar boughs in straight lines at nibble level, giving the place a peculiar, illustrated air. At Fayette State Park, I wander a lovely trail through woods fluting with birdsong around a pond-sized harbor. From a near-vertical cliff on the far side, through a gauzy screen spun by hundreds of spiders dangling from spruce branches over the abyss, I watch the sun set behind the Gothic-looking, picture-perfect ghost town.

I camp here, next to Pat and Paul Evens from Detroit, who claim that their old pop-up camper has been known to accommodate themselves, their seven children (now grown), plus a couple of friends. "We love it here," Paul says, nudging our starry-night campfire. "You can't buy anything, you can't go anyplace. When your grown kids come

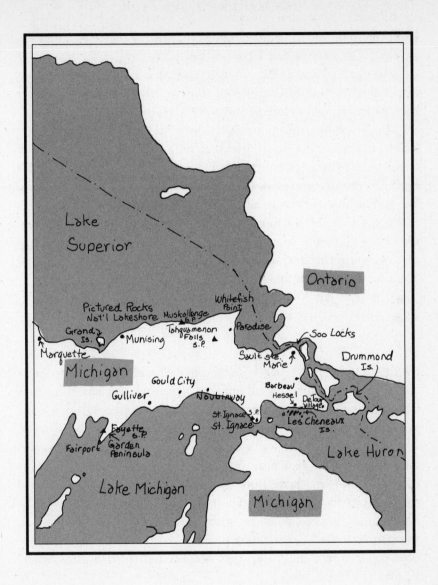

Eastern Upper Peninsula and
Eastern Lake Superior

back, that tells you something. They think that if they haven't gotten up here, they haven't had a good summer."

The next morning, Pat's cousin Earl Mercier, who lives around here, comes in with his big pickup truck to haul the pop-top camper back to his garage. Before he leaves, he tells me a bear story:

"I've lived here all my life and I have only met a bear here once. The bear was coming down toward us on a path, so we made a lot of noise, but he just kept on coming and pretty soon he raises up on his hind feet. He's not even as tall as me, but he scares us all to death. We yell at him and throw cans at him and he keeps on coming. This is a black bear. He's curious. The more you yell and clank to keep him away, the more he comes to see what the noise is. Finally I clap my hands together real loud, which sounds like a rifle shot. BANG! The bear drops to all fours and skedaddles."

JULY 19

FAYETTE STATE PARK smells of cedar and fir and lies so quiet on the harbor, I can hear a sail luff, but once it was so clang-bangorous here that the church, the school, and many of the homes were built at miles' remove. I join a group guided by college student Neil James, who is saying: "Fayette was a charcoal iron center. . . . Iron ore was brought by rail to Escanaba, shipped by tug-pulled scows from there to Fayette, smelted here. Instead of using the usual coal, hardwood charcoal was made in kilns." The pig iron—thus called because the molds lining either side of the main channel where the molten iron was poured looked like suckling piglets—was formed into large hundred-pound bricks and loaded on schooners and sailed to steel centers all over the Great Lakes.

The stark, restored village, oddly immaculate, lies below tree-topped cliffs that rise from the far side of the harbor. A massive stone building with rectangular towers and arched windows that resembles an ancient cathedral was once a smelting furnace. Scattered round, charcoal kilns look like big brick beehives. The remaining buildings are weathered wood, stark and rectangular, including a severe, gray-planked hotel that looks haunted.

"Before the town site was acquired by the state of Michigan, the company office had been used as an auto repair garage," James tells us. He shows us the blacksmith shop, where nails, among other items, were made. A machine shop. Saltbox homes. An opera house that probably saw more dancing dogs than divas.

Neil James grew up on the Garden Peninsula, which may be where he learned to kill mosquitoes by snatching them out of the air instead of smacking himself on the head like I do. His great-grandmother died a a few years ago at the age of 105. She knew Fayette when it was still booming, James says. "She said the trains were running all day, men were blasting the cliffs for limestone, the steam equipment and whistles were noisy, and along with the other commotion, Fayette was an appalling place to be."

FAIRPORT, a fishing village at the tip of the Garden Peninsula, looks microscopic on the map, but the locals boast there's more active commercial fishing licenses here than anywhere else on the Lakes. George Peterson and his son are packing whitefish into iced, wax-covered cartons—110 pounds of fish in each—when I enter the Fairport Fishery. It's slow this time of year, says Peterson senior. "Best time is the spring and late fall."

"What do you do the rest of the year?"

"We fish. We fish all year, except for the month of November."

"Isn't the ice a problem?"

"We break our way out to open water."

Peterson pulls a lamprey about a foot long off the side of a large whitefish, leaving a bleeding circle where the sucker mouth was. He tags the eel-like creature, drops it into a jar of formaldehyde, writes down where he caught it, and says he'll send it to the DNR. "There's enough of 'em come in to let 'em know they've gotta keep treatin' the rivers, otherwise the lampreys'll get outa hand again," Peterson explains. "DNR's got some kind of chemical that they spray. These lampreys'll lay dormant for about seven years in the rivers before they come out of the mud, then they raise hell. Within a year, they can be a yard long."

Peterson finds a second lamprey and sticks the mouth on his thumb, demonstrating that he can pull it right off. "Now put it on yours," he says, handing it to me. I gulp, and in the name of research put the cushion of my thumb against the terrible mouth and, *ffft*, it gloms on. It feels soft, as if I'd put my thumb in the mouth of a nursing baby. I yank it off.

"Looks like a submarine, don't it!" laughs Peterson.

Out on the dock, Kenneth Peterson, George's brother, tells me there's been a hundred years of fishing in the family. "Lotta people made a livin' down here for a lotta years," he says. "And the fishing's still good. My dad fished here before me and his dad before him. And now my son, he's fishin'. It's a clean life. Healthy life. You get so many years and that's it anyway."

I notice the boats here are more open than fish tugs I've been seeing.

"Them are trap-net boats," he says. "Gill-net boats are covered. Gill-net boats are Indian boats. Only Native Americans can commercial-fish with gill nets now, though; non-Indians have to use trap nets. They gotta stay on the lake and we gotta stay in the bay. That's the way they do it now."

"Are there hard feelings about that?"

"Not really. We get along okay. What can you do about it? Indians didn't decide it. Somebody else did. Somebody that don't know too much about the fishing game, that's for sure."

IT'S A COFFEE-DRINKING, hot-soup, do-the-laundry day. In industrial Manistique (not to be confused with Manistee, just east of the Garden Peninsula), I start my clothes washing at a Laundromat, then escape the rain in the tiny Imogene Herbert Museum, where docent Helen Schnurer insists that the "Siphon Bridge" just a block away lies four feet *below* the canal's water level. "The water is forced under by atmospheric pressure," she claims. "It's in *Ripley's Believe It or Not.*"

"How do they keep the canal from flowing over?"

"It does flow over—from time to time," says Schnurer, who has lived here for fifty-eight years and ought to know. "But they say the water helps support the bridge. In the winter and spring, people sit out there with a pail under 'em and they fish."

Ignoring the rain, I walk over to see for myself. Sure enough: the water, pouring as if from a spout toward the concrete bridge, is sucked under, continuing toward the Manistique Pulp and Paper Company. A big sign confirms Schnurer's story; and back at the museum, she waits with more delights: a lampshade that closes like an umbrella, an 1883 quilt made completely of neckties, and a piano that got played so hard for so long that the ivories wore through to the wood. "It's called the Gorsche Piano," explains my kind docent, quoting, " 'When the Gorsches thumped / Manistique did jump.' "

AT A KNOTTY-PINE BAR in Gulliver, Marilyn Fischer pours me a cold one. She's the owner of the Old Deerfield Inn, this rustic log lodge with stone chimneys, and professes a passion for loons and lighthouses. "I'm president of our Gulliver Historical Society, which got a twenty-three-thousand-dollar Michigan State Equity Grant last year to refurbish the Seul Choix Lighthouse and make the foghorn building into a museum," she tells me. "It's located on Seul Choix Point—'Seul Choix' means 'Only Choice.' The lighthouse is fully operational. It has a computer system and a weather station in it. But it hasn't been painted yet; the Coast Guard only paints its lighthouses every twenty to twenty-five years.

"I'm also a 'Fish and Loony,' " continues Fischer from behind the bar. "A member of the National Loon Society. I'm the designated loon ranger for McDonald Lake and Gulliver Lake. I watch where the loons are in the spring, where they nest, see if they have babies, count how many fledged and how many survived. We close public access when the loons are nesting, because they'll abandon their nests if they're disturbed."

The room has been filling with locals, who join or listen in on our conversation. A forester (who does not like to be called a logger) asks if I get my information in bars. When I say, "Of course," he tells me about a DNR-controlled fire meant to create habitat for short-tailed grouse, which somehow leads to a discussion of an upcoming pig roast.

"We put a spit through 'im," says one expert. "Get a generator turner and baste 'im. Or we take a whole deer and stuff the inside full of apples and onions and cabbage and let 'er rotate."

"You do this over an open fire?"

"Oh no," says another. "You put it in a big drum. You just wrap chicken wire around to keep all the insides inside. Pretty soon, when they finish the roof on my cabin, I gotta do it. It's to celebrate somethin'. Just invite all your friends over when you're done with your work. Barrel a beer and you roast somethin'."

"So what's this week's pig roast for?"

"He finished his camp. That's a place where he likes to hunt. Mine is a fishing camp. Camp's a place to get away from the routine life, away from houses. Just live a little bit more rustic. Me, I don't have running water, no electricity."

Everybody's kidding everybody else. One man teases another about his new dentures. "You don't sound too damn incoherent to me!"

"I *feel* incoherent."

"Did you tell Leif off today with your teeth in or your teeth out?"

"I had 'em in."

"Did he understand you?"

"I'll know in the morning."

Someone mentions that when they ("they" in the UP often means the DNR) took the commercial fishing rights away from non-Indians, some families starved. "This place here is like Appalachia in the late fifties. We're running eighteen, twenty percent unemployment. Then the quarry, which supplied most of the employment locally, went out of business last fall and put a couple hundred men out of work. So it's been a hard winter."

JULY 20

I WAS SURE that once in the UP, I'd see some serious wildlife— elk, moose, or bear—but the UP seems to be more about the hundreds of wood nymphs and cabbage butterflies basking on the warm road, fluffing up before the van like feathers. I poke along the dirt road through woods to Seul Choix Point. Iris are blooming. I slow for a deer and two fawns, stop to name a hawk, pass the defunct quarry, where conical piles of crushed stone lie in unnatural silence. Wildflowers bloom: coreopsis, daisies, Indian paintbrush, field thistle, black-eyed Susans, yarrow.

At the lighthouse, I wander out to the point over rocks like huge flagstones. Suddenly I hear a gull crying, incessantly, on a treetop at the wood's edge. I raise my binoculars but see nothing. The sharp wailing continues for ten minutes without stopping. I've never heard a gull go on like that, so I investigate, moving in closer. I am almost under the tree before I see, high in the branches, the large, dark shape. Irrationally, I think it's a monkey; then I get it: it's a bear cub—and where there's a small bear, there's a big bear.

I never knew I could move so fast.

I "BEARLY" RECOVER before spotting a gleaming gray shark on a serene sandy beach south of Gould City. It's plastic, of course, about as fierce as anything I'm likely to find here. It must belong to one of the children who ask me why I'm standing ankle-deep in warm wetland water among turquoise damselflies, talking to my tape recorder. This unmarked public beach was recommended by a Gould City restaurant owner on Route 2 who bakes a scrumptious coconut cream pie. The lake water here laps in shallow and clear over brightly colored stones. Gulls sit on larger stones not far out. I find a black feather, heavy and oily, maybe a cormorant's. Huge, domino-winged dragonflies dart like biplanes. Maybe the Caribbean feels like this.

Blissed out by warm pie and beach, I crunch back up the long green finger road, van windows down, belting out "Southern Nights" along with the radio, creeping around the S curves. I pick up Route 2, then follow another potholey road, this one six miles of jarring, dash-chinkling washboard, to the wildish Big Thumb State Park campground, which despite its rustic nature and remote location is already full. The bagful of shiny wintergreen leaves I gather there, however, fills the van with fragrance all the way to Naubinway, a wide place on the highway close to the water.

I find Carl and Mary Ann Belongia cleaning their boat. They've finished the day's fishing and are getting ready for tomorrow morning. They fish for Menominees, also called round whitefish, which look like whitefish but are a little smaller, they tell me, as I squat on the dock. "They're better eatin', I think," adds Mrs. Belongia, a pleasant, solid-looking woman with a low-pitched voice.

I like being with these two people. Carl Belongia has a kind face, amused but not superior eyes, and a voice so soft I have trouble hearing it. He and Mary Ann have been married for twenty-seven years, he tells me. After the first nine, they figured it was clear sailing, and they've been fishing together for the last eight. I begin feeling oddly at home with them.

Note: On a later visit, Carl and Mary Ann Belongia take me out on their new big fish tug. I watch them lay at least a mile of gill net off the loveliest bay I've ever seen, feeding the narrow net off the back of the boat with the enthusiastic help of their thirteen-year-old son, who, when we come back in, scrambles onto the bow to watch for rocks.

JULY 21

HIGHWAY 2 between Naubinway and St. Ignace hugs miles and miles of sandy beaches and spectacular lake views and showcases the dramatic Cut River Bridge, where I stand looking 147 feet down. The ravine below is so steep that places on the bottom are piled with trees that lost their rooting and tumbled down the sides. A romantic nature trail goes under the bridge and along the rushing river through magical woods, across a little wooden bridge, and back up the other side under the peculiar, repetitive wailing of tires across the metal grid high above.

After a wild meal of smoked Menominee, huckleberries, and wintergreen tea, I photograph the Mackinac Bridge from a lookout at the Straits State Park, a place I find uncomfortably crowded for camping but great for bridge ogling. The best view, though, has to be the one from Jack Barnhill's seaplane, which is presently soaring over the bridge's middle span. Barnhill's plane feels like a Mack truck compared with the amphibious model I flew in on Beaver Island. These pontoons are heavy but reliable, says Barnhill. "I've been flying fifty years, thirty of them here and ten in this plane. Sometimes I fly fishermen into Canada, but I don't do huntin' anymore. Too much blood 'n' guts. Takes two trips just to get the damn moose out. They chop the meat up in pieces. Then the guy wants the rack and the head, which weigh six hundred pounds, unless you clean the head out real good, which they never do. You can't even get it in the aircraft. You gotta tie it on the outside."

At one time, Barnhill owned a Mackinac ferry line and a tourist business in St. Ignace, but now he's content to paint pictures and fly tourists over the longest suspension bridge in the world, the cream-and-green five-mile-long "Mighty Mac." Before it opened in 1957, people waited for hours, sometimes in ten-mile lines, for the ferries, which could transport only 462 cars per day. Six thousand cars a day can make the trip now, each in about ten minutes.

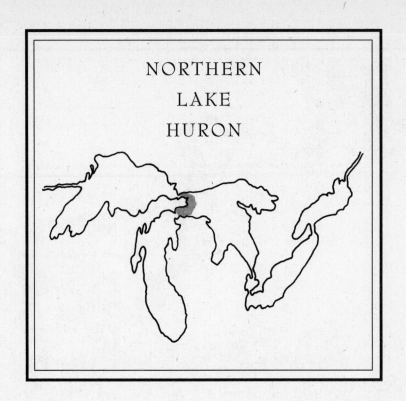

NORTHERN

LAKE

HURON

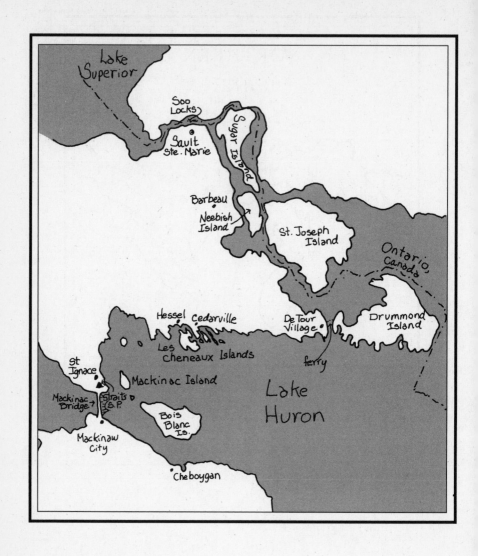

Northern Lake Huron

SEATED NEXT TO ME on a garden bench beneath a treeful of gossipy waxwings, director Carol Hosler tells me that the Marquette Mission Park and Museum of Ojibwa Culture celebrates St. Ignace's brief, three-hundred-year-old boom as a world fur-trade center, the explorations of Father Marquette, and the area's native cultures. The museum has erected an Ojibwa wigwam in front and, on the site of a 1671 Huron village, is reconstructing a Huron longhouse.

"The Huron were agricultural, not fishermen and hunters like the Ojibwa," says Hosler, who is not herself Native American. "They established villages and were matrilocal as opposed to the patrilocal Ojibwa: when a Huron daughter married, the husband moved in with her family; if the house was too small, it was lengthened. Some longhouses got up to a hundred feet long, with campfires going down the middle and smoke going out the top. After about thirty years, the Hurons followed the fur trade to Cadillac and Detroit. I've never met a Huron locally; native people here now are mostly Ojibwa, with some Ottawa and Potawatomi.

"The Huron came originally from lower Ontario, where they'd been allied with the French in the fur trade, while the nearby Iroquois were allied with the English. The competition between the English and the French encouraged the enmity that already existed between the two tribes. When the Iroquois won, the Huron were greatly massacred. Smallpox and such from white contact further decimated the population. Some fled east, some west. Here they established a village with the help of Father Marquette."

It's fascinating how differently the Puritans and the Jesuits related to native people, claims Hosler, a student of theology. "The Puritans believed that everything the Indians believed was wrong. The Jesuits, however, believed in the doctrine of natural religion, which says that any persons who live under this beautiful sky and on this beautiful earth and appreciate it are going to know God the Creator; it's just a question of their coming to understand God the Son and God the Holy Spirit. Of course, there was a lot of messy stuff, like how far can you go with the business of all living things having souls, or which dances were all right and which were not, and so on. But compared to what the Puritans were doing, the Jesuits came out smelling like roses. And of course, the French Catholics intermarried and lived with the Indian, while the English established separate communities."

I ask Hosler whether the term "Native American" or "Indian" is preferred, having heard both used by native and nonnative persons. "We use the words interchangeably," she answers.

"I've also been told to use 'nation' instead of 'tribe.'"

"It depends on who you are," Hosler says. "Like this is the Sault Ste. Marie tribe of Chippewa Indians. That's what they themselves say. I've heard 'nation' used with others, but not here." ("Chippewa," I'm told later by a politically active native person, is the French pronunciation, while "Ojibwa" is the English.)

Hosler seems a good person to ask about the contempt I've heard expressed by some well-heeled UP business owners for year-round residents who work in the summer and live off welfare during winter. I haven't noticed any of these "lazy" persons living in splendor and can't imagine what work would be available to them off-season.

"People say that generations here have not wanted to work," Hosler says. "And maybe in fact some wouldn't take a year-round job if it were offered to them. But to say that they're all lazy is overlooking the complexity of the situation. People up here live in a way that's comfortable to them. Of all our many motels and restaurants, only about three motels stay open in the winter and about two restaurants. Where are all those people who help run those places going to find jobs in winter when the owners close down and go south? Maybe when you've lived for generations with that kind of a cycle, it's important to your well-being to be in it. There's no Joneses to keep up with here."

JULY 26

ALTHOUGH A MICHIGANDER, I seem to have grown up with the unconscious belief that there's nothing on the Upper Peninsula east of the Mackinac Bridge, but this is far from the truth. I am amazed at the geographical amplitude, not to mention the intense beauty and the number of interesting residents, that I find there.

For instance, I'd never heard of the Les Cheneaux (pronounced "Lay Shen-O") Islands, where, in the tiny town of Hessel, I find Bonnie Stewart Mickelson in a small building amid stacks of her award-winning cookbook *Hollyhocks & Radishes*. ("A unique look at a little known corner of America . . . where the simple values of life . . . family, friends, the good earth and the good food it produces . . . still abide," the cookbook proclaims itself.)

"My husband and I put our families together, his seven kids and my six, then had two of our own, and they were all at home eating," explains Mickelson, pausing from her packing. Her self-published books, she says, have sold over seven hundred thousand copies. "I didn't have time to write the Great American Novel, so I wrote this." Mickelson has spent most of the summers of her life at the family "camp," established a hundred years ago on the largest of the thirty-five Les Cheneaux Islands.

Across the road, from behind a counter at E. J. Mertaugh's Boat Works, owner Jack Mertaugh credits his dad, Eugene, with opening the store in 1926, the first Chris Craft dealer in the world. Eugene was a man of enthusiasm, says Mertaugh, and stories are still told about him, including one in which he wrestles a bear that for some reason climbed into his boat. Chris Craft doesn't make boats anymore, so today Mertaugh's Boat Works restores old ones, many of which occupy the boathouses perched over local docks.

However, it isn't until I wander through the boathouse, a cavernous affair full of swallows and glowing wooden pleasure boats, that I understand what's special about a Chris Craft: the boats look like perfectly preserved antique furniture. Five gleaming mahogany bullet shapes are lined up on one side, three more at one end, one on the other. Parked in a middle U are even more. It's a watery Chris Craft museum.

Outside, I approach a couple of men taking stock of a battered-looking Chris Craft dropped off for a restoration job.

"It's all sheltered waters here," I'm informed by Francis "Geet" McCloud, a large, grizzled-looking man. "No matter what the weather, you can find someplace to water-ski here. Sailing's good, too."

The two men seat themselves on an overturned aluminum dinghy. I settle on the ground facing them, tape recorder between us. The sun shines down hot.

When I say the area seems awfully quiet, Matthews says condominiums are coming in. He shrugs. "That's progress. Not much you can do about it. Boy, our taxes'll just skyrocket. Lotta the people here, they're not that wealthy, and they're hungry for something like this. But a lotta people have been bounced off the shore for the rich guy."

Matthews and McCloud discuss between themselves which stories I might like to hear. Matthews begins: "We used to chase coyotes with the Mertaugh boys from here way out to Mackinac Island, over to St. Ignace, and way around the shore. On the ice. We had these propeller-driven machines, you see—an airplane engine on skis. The coyotes would go out to the islands to hunt for food and we would hunt them for money. There was a bounty on them in those days. It was very cruel."

"It sounds dangerous."

"That's what's exciting about it. No brakes. Sometimes it's glare ice. We'd hafta aim between islands, 'cause we couldn't stop."

"Missy," says McCloud, sounding like John Wayne, "I put mine through the ice twice."

"The biggest antique boat show in the world will be right here in Hessel in a couple of weeks," says Matthews. "Did you see the movie *On Golden Pond?* That could be this area, you know. Them old solid mahogany boats, there's hundreds of them here."

Matthews, who's been working at the nearby quarry, claims exhaustion and heads for home, so McCloud and I proceed up the block, settle on a couple of bar stools, and regale each other with bear stories that never in a hundred years could I admit to telling or believing.

I'M ALMOST ASLEEP when I hear singing. I dress and slip away from my camp site at Cedarville's Les Cheneaux Landing, finding my way by torchlight past log resort cabins to the beach, where the shadowy members of several large families are gathered around a reunion-size fire. The singer pauses. Stars wink on the water like fireflies. Kids talk softly. Birch logs snap. I ask permission to tape the singer. He says fine, blows on a harmonica, strums a guitar, and begins "Stormy Weather." He has a clear voice, irresistible timing, and a campy, funny-bone style. I begin feeling unreasonably content.

"Hey, Adrian, she's taping it!" Bare feet squeak in the sand; happy bodies surround me. Small hands light on my shoulders like birds.

"Why are you taping it?"

"I'm writing a book about the lakeshore."

Kids begin shouting that I'm writing a book. One asks my name and, when I tell it, wonders if I'm famous.

"Have you heard of me?"

"No."

"Then I guess I'm not famous."

There's more excitement as every kid there says his or her name into my tape recorder, begging to be named in the book. Then after a night of singing, and following a long period of begging—"Do 'Smelly Feet!' . . . *Please?*" singer and improviser Tom Savage blasts on the harmonica and shouts:

> *I know a girl who's name is Sarah*
> *And she's got a rotten pair a*
> *Nasty smelly feet.*
> *Smelly feet, smelly feet, smelly feet, ooooooooh,*
> *Smelly feet, smelly feet, smelly feet, ooooooooh,*
> *Smell them feet across the street.*
>
> *Well, we all know a boy whose name is Steve,*
> *You smell his feet, you're gonna heave,*
> *He's got rotten smelly feet.*
> *Smelly feet, smelly feet, smelly feet, ooooooooh,*
> *Smelly feet, smelly feet, smelly feet, ooooooooh,*
> *Smell them feet across the street.*

There are many, many verses, each trailing screams of laughter: one for Kate, Emily, Steven, Kathy, Pete, Jess, Larry, Nancy, Mona, Jill, Kim, Deb, Joany, and after a long pause for the difficult rhymes, Adrian and Loretta.

"Yodel-lay-hee, yodel-lay-hee, yodel-loo."

JULY 27

"THE VOYAGEURS USED to stop over in the Les Cheneaux Islands, especially when the weather was rough." Mark Engle, a short, frank-faced man who reminds me of Dick Cavett, is standing behind the counter filling out a bait order next to an ornate antique cash register. The room is hung with a few stuffed fish and birds, some maps and fishing gear. Soft piles of T-shirts and sweatshirts fill a wall with ice-cream colors: peach, pistachio, raspberry, lemon. Mark owns the Les Cheneaux Landing resort with his brother-in-law, Larry Penrose, who off-season is a college history teacher. Mark and Larry, whom I can't bring myself to call by last names, banter congenially.

"Before the bridge went in, the only way you could get here was by water or through Wisconsin," Mark says in his Dick Cavett voice, handing the order to the larger Larry. "Used to be a lot of posh hotels along here, two of 'em right in our front yard. Time was, people'd get off the ferry with all their stuff, stay in these hotels for weeks, and go out fishing in swallowtail suits and top hats. Give kids a nickel for a frog. Mostly, though, this stretch between the bridge and Drummond Island has been overlooked. You can't really see much from the road, and there's not much development, no power plants and no big industry. Except for one flashing light, there's not one traffic signal east of the bridge, not even in St. Ignace."

Larry (pointing to a big wall map): "This area is geologically unique—scoured right out. You can actually see the movement of the glaciers." I look: the thirty-five islands appear stretched like chewing gum away from the coast in a southeasterly direction: long, thin, oddly parallel formations. "You're looking at thousands of miles of protected anchorage and water," continues Larry. "And there's nowhere in the channel you can't explore in a fourteen-foot boat."

Mark: "You've picked up your Yooper tapes yet?"

Me: "Excuse me?"

Larry: "Never heard of the Yoopers? Go to any hardware store—
we don't have many music stores up here—and buy the tapes. They
live in Marquette—that's the capital of the UP—and they got the
UP culture down pat. They write songs about the people who pay
our bills—ten people from Ohio on a pontoon boat, stuff like that."

Mark: "Like 'The Rusty Chevrolet,' 'Second Week in Deer Camp,'
'She's Three Weeks Late,' or a song about a giant pig sung entirely
in Finn. You may not want 'em when you find 'em, but you stay up
here, you'll find 'em."

Larry: "Hey, Mark, what was the figure somebody came up with
for a per-day expenditure of the average tourist? Was it eighty bucks?"

Me: "Not for me!"

Mark: "Well, we can charge you more!" (Laughter).

He doesn't, though. Instead Mark takes me and his young son on
an all-day tour in his open whaler. What impresses me most about
the Les Cheneaux Islands is the ubiquitous two-story boathouses in
which, cosseted like pets, an amazing number of glowing Chris Crafts
appear. Over the roar of the outboard motor, Mark tells me who lives
in what house, mansion, or shack on each, often tiny, island. Julie
Andrews had an island here, but she sold it, he claims, because she
didn't like the bats. Lots of brown bats around; keep the bugs down.

Just before lunch, we pull up to a substantial-looking dock under
construction by a group of noisily working men. A chicken-wire crib
under the dock is filled with rocks to hold it against next winter's ice.

"Damn thing's crooked, George," Mark says to the man who
greets us as we tie up. "I think you better tear it out." Mark introduces me as a representative of the Christian Counseling Service.
George Collins promptly instructs a man hammering nearby to put a
nail through Mark's foot.

After my real mission is revealed, however, George quits kidding
and gets down to brass tacks. "Back in the early days, the only type
boats that were in here were rowboats—no outboard motors. These
rowboats were very beautiful flat-bottom boats made by a fellow over
in St. Ignace. He made 'em all by hand, and we've kept a few just to
show what existed. As modernization came, they put more horsepower
on the motors, and these flat-bottom boats began to seep and leak,

and that's why we went to aluminum-type boats. But people kicked about those because they figured sound carried with aluminum boats, which it does. Used to be, with a flat-bottom boat, they could walk on it and they wouldn't make no sound, and so they could fish better on it. So a lotta history is in these islands. You'd never find all of it out. . . . Anybody lives in these islands don't get rich. I mean, you can make a living, you can get along beautiful and all, but the only people's gotten rich the last five years have sold property."

We shove off. We're quiet for a while, watching George melt into the tree line. Then Mark says: "This place is changing fast. My recommendation is, turn it into a federal reserve and stop everything. Now, George is a hard guy, but he'd go over in a corner and cry if he knew this place was going to go down the tubes in his lifetime."

HAND-LETTERED SIGNS lead me to Paradise Point Resort, a small motel and a couple of campsites just north of De Tour Village, the town at the easternmost tip of the Upper Peninsula. From the back of the van, I watch a pair of osprey cruise and hover over the quiet St. Mary's River, edged with lush wetlands. They are fishing. The big "fish eagles" plummet feet-first and miss, plunge and miss, until after half an hour one emerges with a large fish in sure talons and flies over the tree line. Wandering the gravelly edge of the marsh, I find the dry, shed skin of a northern water snake and drape it around the van's rearview mirror. I settle at the picnic table, sip sherry, munch mixed nuts, breathe in soft evening air. Two big freighters pass each other right in front of me, one black-and-white, the other red. The sun descends; terns hover high, drop like stones in pink water. A herring gull lands on a nearby piling and sits there, still as wood. The remaining osprey comes up empty, flies so close I can see, without binoculars, the black mask, the hooked beak, the perfectly round, black-pupiled yellow eye. A chickadee scolds. The gull's still glued to the post. Tall green weeds part at water level and out pops a brown duck, followed by six ducklings. *Plop!* a muskrat swims away in a V. Its languorous wake, upon reaching the shore, sounds like a cat lapping.

JULY 28

THE FERRY RIDE FROM De Tour Village to the island just offshore is so short that all I learn from the captain is that Drummond Island is unusually large (twenty-four miles by twelve); that he, his mother, and his mother's mother and father were born there; and that the village is twelve miles from the dock.

Debarking and heading toward town, I encounter an unsettling number of vehicles driving toward me down the middle of the road. I turn off, exploring byways; watch a deer excavate a stand of skinny cedars; enjoy the ferns, black-eyed Susans, mullein, and fragrant milkweed edging bay after island-bejeweled bay. The few people I drive by wave. Although there are signs for resorts, I see little development. When I inquire about a museum at a general store, I am sent up the street to talk to Kathryne Lowe, whose front door is open. I knock on the screen. "Come in!" orders a voice from the kitchen. I glimpse an older woman in a white cotton nightgown.

"You don't know me," I warn.

"No matter." Kathryne Lowe comes to the door, opens it before I can explain who I am, leads me to a large kitchen table, pours me a cup of coffee, and joins me. In a few minutes, her daughter, Kasey, a red-haired reporter and cameraperson for CBS in Sault Ste. Marie, comes in, also wearing a white cotton nightgown. She reminds me of Shirley MacLaine. When she sits down, a red-haired cat climbs onto her lap.

"I was born here seventy-five years ago," Kathryne is telling me, "so I guess I know a little bit of the history. I'm the caretaker of the museum, which doesn't mean that I mow the grass. But the roof has caved in. There's no museum anymore. Last winter it happened. We saved the artifacts, but the building is gone. We're trying to get it rebuilt."

I settle back in my chair and Kathryne continues: "Seems to me we've changed a lot over the years, but summer people have remarked that we're about twenty years behind the rest of the country. We didn't get electricity here until 1954. Some people had generators when I was a girl, but we didn't."

"Well," I begin, "someone in the Les Cheneaux Islands told me that Tom Monaghan, Domino's 'pizza king,' 'owns Drummond Island.' I've never heard of Tom Monaghan before. I understand there's been some kind of controversy."

Both women bristle.

"Some people think he's just wonderful and no one's as good for the island as he is, and some people think he's terrible, that he's threatening our island way of life," begins Kasey. "He's put a lot of money here—bought a lot of property, built motels, a golf course, bowling alley, all sorts of stuff. He doesn't seem to have much of a plan, so he keeps things kinda roiled up. Like he traded twenty-eight hundred acres of land off the island for fourteen hundred acres of state-owned land on the island, which riled some people."

"It was kind of a colonial thing," says Kathryne. "Sometimes UP people feel the DNR treats us as though we're a bunch of savages. But others do, too. People used to come here for the summertime and say, 'What in the world do you ever do in the wintertime?' As though you dropped dead until spring. But we have a full life of our own here. People seemed to think that we stayed here because we didn't know any better. But now we've got people in the telephone book that I don't know who they are."

The two women carry on, one picking up the other's thoughts.

"When I'm in Sault Ste. Marie, I think of home as this little piece of property that I have. But when I'm on the island, home is the whole thing."

"You're sort of insulated from other people here."

"There's a different attitude living on an island."

"It's kind of an extended family."

"You feel detached from the world. That you have some control, that what you do and say means something. Township is the grass-roots government of our country as far as I'm concerned."

"It's interesting how Drummond Island became part of the United States," Kathryne says. "This state—rather, I mean, island—is part of an archipelago that goes east into Lake Huron for over a hundred miles. On the map, the international boundary line takes an odd turn north, cutting Drummond Island off from the other islands that now belong to Canada. Well, the story goes that when the Lakes were surveyed, the Americans got the British guy drunk and made this big detour—now called the False Detour Passage and the De Tour Passage. If they'd stayed on a fairly straight course, the logical course, Drummond Island would now be Canadian."

Kasey: "Some say that's just a story, that the U.S. took the island as part of the spoils of the War of 1812."

"Anyway, this is a special place. And we're afraid of losing that. We've got all kinds of bear here, you know."

"One's named after me. Our camera crew went down to the bear dens to cover the DNR going in, anesthetizing the mother, taking the cubs out and weighing them and checking the vital signs. The cubs when we found them were probably six weeks old and weighed about two pounds each. Well, when they collared them—they put on radio collars that rot off in eighteen months so the cubs aren't strangled—they called the female cub Kasey. I held those baby bears inside my jacket to keep them warm, but they wailed loudly the whole time they were away from their mother."

"Used to be, island people sometimes went away, to Detroit or someplace, to work in a factory, and they'd come back because they couldn't stand the life. People were used to having something to do when they got home from work. You could go fishing or hunting. And everybody takes off for deer season."

"You didn't dare have a baby during deer season!"

Kathryne's son, Jack, comes in. I realize I'd met him on the ferry. I joke with him about the way people drive here, down the middle of the road.

"They're trying to avoid hitting deer," explains Jack. "It gives you more time to swerve."

Later, waiting in the ferry line, it occurs to me that living on an island must be like riding a raft: any sudden move is felt by everyone.

Note: Since my visit, Monaghan has sold his holdings on Drummond Island and left, and the museum has reopened.

JULY 29

AFTER SOME IMPRESSIVE ship-watching on a misty St. Mary's River—the Lake Huron / Lake Superior connection—and an extravagant beer-drinking and tall-tale session with a bunch of "the boys" in Barbeau, I end up at the Antlers, a big, square stone restaurant at the edge of Sault (pronounced "Soo") Ste. ("Saint") Marie. My God. If, as some claim, taxidermy earns UP restaurants their stars, the Antlers rates Orion. Nowhere have I ever seen more reconstituted wildlife: every undinable wall, nook, cranny, beam, and niche is occupied.

I spot a window seat under a deer antler, a sheep horn, and a moose rack, cross the swelling old wood floor, and sit at a small, beat-up wooden table. An impressive python drapes coils from an overhead beam. A bear head, a whole duck, several geese, a pheasant, a fox, a wolverine, a timber wolf, another fox, a coyote, a skull, something small, and some squirrels are displayed in the small area in front of me. On my right there's a pheasant. Over my head fly three ducks, for whom the cheeseburger on my plate to come will provide a perfect target. Behind me hangs a buffalo head, a deer head, a pair of ducks, a ram's head, a boar, and a mallard. Skins hang here and there. Lampshades are poised above deer hooves. And that's just my corner. There are five more sections, and I haven't even mentioned the leopard, the entire zebra, the vertical, full-sized polar bear, or the pack of African lions.

The menu, heavy on beef, includes a five-pound, thirty-two-dollar Paul Bunyan Burger—reasonably priced considering the ambiance. From my place mat, I learn, among many other things, that "the Antlers Bar was first known as the Bucket of Blood Saloon and Ice Cream Parlor. . . . It was closed down when Internal Revenue agents discovered [during Prohibition days] that it sold only one quart of ice cream a month and yet took in a profit of $900."

JULY 30

AFTER A NIGHT in the Parkway Motel, the manager beckons me into the office, exclaiming, "You're a Voyageur, aren't you! Sit down and tell me about it!" I do for an hour, and how good it feels, to be recognized and appreciated like that. Usually I am the one asking the questions, but now and then someone with the heart of an adventurer but stuck in a routine wants to know how I dare do this thing.

Afterward, I walk the short distance from the motel to the Soo Locks. From massive bleachers and observation decks I look down on four long, narrow tubs, eight hundred to thirteen hundred feet long. In the longest one, a brick-red thousand-footer is visibly descending. Traffic passing through the Soo is raised or lowered twenty-one feet, at approximately two feet and a million gallons of water per minute. Huge ships, sailboats, yachts, and tour boats—thirteen thousand vessels per year—line up for a turn in this giant fluid elevator, known as "the Great Lakes bottleneck." I move on to the town, a carnival of diaphanous delights: flowery parks, a musical glow-in-the-dark fountain, lots of drop-your-money-in-here shops, and a real ship turned museum. Sault Ste. Marie feels to me an odd combination of denim and chiffon.

By late morning, I come upon a grassy knoll where, behind a plastic orange fence, some college students dig in and around some oddly spaced, precisely square pits. A signboard in hand-painted script reads, FORT REPENTIGNY ARCHEOLOGICAL PROJECT, SPONSORED BY LAKE SUPERIOR U., MICHIGAN STATE U. AND THE DEPARTMENT OF STATE.

Chris Stephenson, the tall, assured field supervisor and doctoral student from Michigan State, extends her hand, her crinkly sandy hair lifted by the wind. "The fort was built in 1751," begins Stephenson, speaking rapidly in a low, well-modulated voice. "It was occupied by the French for about twelve years, until the British took over at the close of the French and Indian War. In 1762, the fort burned to the ground. The only house left standing belonged to a French trader who had helped run the fort for the French. Makes you wonder.

"Excavations here began in the late 1960s. There also were excavations in '76 and '77 by a student who was looking at Fort Brady, an American fort built in 1822 which later expanded to this area on top of the French fort. The early excavations picked up the western and southern palisade lines. We're looking for the southwestern palisade lines."

"What else have you found here?"

"Just last week we found a coin that dates back to 1782 and was minted in New Spain. It was first minted in 1772 and served as legal tender in the United States all the way up to 1857. A couple days ago we found a corked, three-piece molded bottle that is still half-full of some kind of an oily-looking liquid. We've been finding artillery buttons and some Native American artifacts, too—lots of little flint chips, some colorful glass 1700s trade beads, and what are called 'tin-kling cones,' made from recycled European kettle brass and worn on their clothing."

"But why these scattered square holes?"

"They're two-meter pits. We lay out a grid unit using a transit so everything is very exact. When we dig down, we dig in ten-centimeter levels, so we can keep artifacts separated from each other. As we go down, we expect to find older and older artifacts. Within each level we can discern different soil colorations. Those all get labeled. Everything has what we call 'provenience unit' to keep the context intact, so we know exactly where artifacts, which all get washed and labeled, are coming from. The tripods—the teepeelike frames above each pit—are set up for screening, the dirt is shaken through the screen, and the artifacts are picked out. It's very careful work. Archaeology is a destructive process—once it's gone, it's gone —so we take lots of notes, make maps, take photographs. Later, in the analysis phase, we put it all back together."

Stephenson confirms what I'd heard elsewhere, that archaeological work is often required at federal and state government building sites. "Road construction, a building, a sewer trench, whatever, an environ-mental review process is required, and that includes what we call archaeological mitigation, which might mean having an archaeologist present while the backhoe is there to halt construction and call in a team of archaeologists if artifacts appear."

"So we don't just send archaeologists off to distant lands any-more?"

"Oh no. People don't realize what's in their own backyards! This area, for example, is very rich. Long before the locks were built, the falls were a great gathering place for Native Americans, all the way back to prehistoric times. It's always been a major waterway, linking Lake Superior to Lake Huron. When Europeans came in, they stopped in the same places that the Indians did, because that's who they were trading with. During World War II, it was highly guarded."

("We had to stop the lock tours during World War II," Captain Richard Brawley later elaborates when I take his Soo Boat Tour. "Freighters carried steel or tachonite through here to the factories to build tanks. The government was afraid of airplanes coming over trying to bomb the locks. Searchlights and military personnel were everywhere.")

"And here we are today, digging it all up," concludes Stephenson, who, given her voice and looks, could anchor network news. Instead, she's poised at the rim of a four-cornered pit, meticulously unearthing time.

LAKE
SUPERIOR

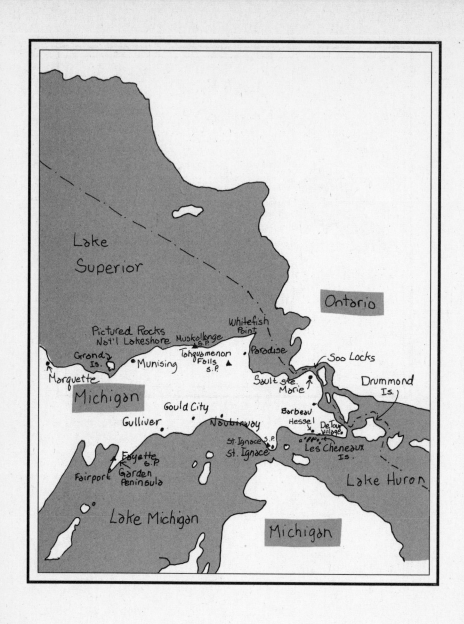

Eastern Lake Superior

JULY 31

AT LAST I've reached Lake Superior, and I'm not one bit disappointed: it really is clear as a jewel, the largest freshwater lake in the world (31,700 square miles), glass-green, wide as Iowa, big as Maine. Variously framed between columns of white birch, a thousand aspects of it flash past my right as I head from the Soo to Whitefish Point. Then, just past Paradise, I lock onto a string of cars longer than a Wyoming freight train. Chug, brake, chug, brake, we crawl for miles behind a wheezing locomotive-size RV. Traffic jams don't fit my Northwoods fancy, and I arrive at the busy Whitefish Point parking lot peevish as a badger in a mall.

The first thing I notice is that none of the fifteen soaring raptor silhouettes painted on the side of the Whitefish Point Bird Observatory—a well-known place from which to watch hawks fly over in "kettles" in the spring and fall—is labeled. I've been finding it so difficult to identify big birds from below, and here is this no-help help. Generally open from April through October, today the place is closed. If there is a brochure, I don't get one.

Reminding myself that I often become cranky at this time of day and not to take it out on this lovely place, I calm myself in the murky interior of the Great Lakes Shipwreck Historical Museum, located here to commemorate the more than three hundred ships that have sunk along the eighty miles of coastline between Whitefish Point and Munising to the west. In a dimness calculated to simulate fatal depths,

I learn that the *Invincible* was the first recorded loss, in 1816. The most recent was the *Edmund Fitzgerald*.

The *Edmund Fitzgerald* went down off Whitefish Point in November 1975; all twenty-nine crew members drowned. Little survived beyond two empty lifeboats, one of which I saw yesterday displayed on the museum ship *Valley Camp* in Sault Ste. Marie. A curator there explained: "Raging northwesterly winds that build over the two-hundred-mile sweep of open water here, along with poor visibility, heavy traffic, and converging shipping lanes, have contributed to our great loss of ships. But this accident was odd, because another freighter right behind it came through the storm without a scratch. There are many theories as to why the *Edmund Fitzgerald* sank. I've even heard theories of UFOs. But I don't think we'll ever know."

The Whitefish Point museum offers generous information on Great Lakes shipwrecks and disasters, and my ticket is good for a movie on the subject as well. I skip that and sprawl on the warm, sandy beach, not wanting to imagine anything more treacherous before me than this casually rumpled, softly sunlit sea.

Note: Informed by telephone later that the raptor silhouettes at the Whitefish Point Bird Observatory remain unlabeled, I suggest that somebody run out there *right this minute* with a permanent marker and write in all the names. Promising to do so, volunteer Faye Smith laughs and remarks, "Others have expressed similar frustration, but you're the first person who's said she wanted to break down the door."

I'M ON A BEAT-UP old road looking for Muskallonge Lake State Park. I can't seem to find it. I lost the traffic and tailgaters way back at Tahquamenon Falls (a worthwhile inland side trip). Then suddenly here it is. The sign seems small for a state park, but I turn in. Two outhouses and six campsites dot one side of a small round lake, which I take for Muskallonge, but no one is here. Flies buzz in the sun; wind drifts through the high tops of trees. It's around four o'clock. I'm usually nervous about camping alone, but I decide to stay.

Having a lake and woods to myself feels unexpectedly safe and sweet. I sip at the late afternoon: wander through ferns, gather wintergreen and blueberries, lie under a towering pine. Finally, draping my clothes on a lakeside bush, I wade into bath-warm water, swim to the middle of the lake, play like an otter, float in the late sun, summon, unsuccessfully, a moose or a bear from the woods. My hair is still wet and I'm eating supper when a man and his son drive in and set up a tent at the other end of the campground. This isn't the state park campground at all, they tell me on their way to the outhouse, but one of the many state *forest* campgrounds; these two are here because the state park is jammed, completely full, a zoo.

I smile at my luck. As evening deepens and the edges of things blur, the four fluting notes of a wood thrush echo like a duet over the lake. The song—and song—go on and on. Two ducks appear; a heron. Landscape and water blacken. The thrush stills. Lily pads under a choir of mosquitoes are joined by a free-for-all of stars, and I sink into sleep like a moon.

AUGUST 1

CAPTAIN CHUCK COOK, who is piloting our tour boat along the Pictured Rocks National Lakeshore, disagrees with me about why this water is so green. I think it's because Lake Superior's deepest measurement—1,333 feet—was taken near here. The captain maintains that the color results from a sandbar and reflected trees.

Leaving Munising, we're soon roaring along Grand Island past tiny cottages, little A-frames. "See that white house over there?" Cook shouts over the motor. "That's the site of the original trading center. Guy built that house in 1840 and made everything himself. Even made his own nails. Lived there year-round. Basically that's the same structure, improved a couple times, so apparently he built it pretty good."

Soon vertical, rusty, tree-topped cliffs rise from the flat emerald lake along the mainland. I pull out my camera. "Save your film," says the captain. "It gets better." Stunning, knockout views glide by unfilmed: orange-and-white bluffs, limestone caves, primordial arches, water so green it looks dyed. Occasionally, trees grow right out of the rock face, as if they'd slipped and barely saved themselves, clinging by the roots for dear life.

The cliffs, here 140 to 160 feet high, in some places reach 200. As we get closer, I notice horizontal stripes. "The green is from copper," Cook says. "The white is limestone, and the reds are iron ore." He smiles as if about to give me a gift he knows will please. It does: Miners Castle soars majestically above tiny bathers waving from the beach. The camera clicks at last, then at a peregrine falcon nest, Lovers Leap, Rainbow Cave, Indian Head Rock. Because it's calm, our captain risks entering an intimate, cavelike pool, turning the boat not ten feet from rock walls.

On the way back, I learn from a teenager selling refreshments that one can hike the entire forty-mile stretch of Pictured Rocks National Lakeshore and that the average snowfall here is over 200 inches. "One year we had 450 inches," claims Andy Anderson. "Some nights it's so cold you can walk in the snow in your socks and they'll be dry when you go back inside."

Heading back into the wide Munising bay, we tear up Wonder bread and throw it to the gulls from the back of the boat, squeezing whole slices into lumps, the better to hurl them. Gulls scream. Kids scream. I photograph wings, beaks, mouths, and flying bread balls over a frothing wake.

AUGUST 2

THE SEVENTY-FIVE-FOOT-HIGH ore dock in Marquette juts twelve hundred feet into Lake Superior about halfway between the world's largest wooden sports dome—Northern Michigan University's new retractable turf indoor football field, nicknamed "the Yooperdome"—and a peninsula showcasing Marquette's Presque Isle City Park. A miners' strike began today, so no freight cars are rolling around up there, no ore clatters down big chutes into ship holds. Everything is unusually quiet.

I huff and puff up a nearly vertical staircase, watched by the workers at a maintenance barn across the street. Are they betting on whether I'll make it—whether I'll be kicked off? I reach the top, panting, feeling a little giddy, and catch my breath before knocking on an office door by the stairs. Lloyd Young, the man in charge, looks startled to see me, but he's soon informing me that over nine million tons of ore per day slide off this "gravity dock" into one to three self-unloaders and that the average boat takes seven or eight hours to load.

He even agrees to let me walk the dock if I'll sign an insurance release.

I walk to the end, carefully, avoiding a number of large holes that make my knees go weak. The block-long dock reminds me of a dream I had once, sky-high, dangerous, silent and unreal. The dock is covered with iron pellets that look exactly like deer droppings. It's like walking on marbles up here. At the end, as I exult in the views from this rare height, a man saunters toward me. He's Sid Koski, who's worked here a long time.

"Guys go over the side here and they open trapdoors down there," Koski tells me, leaning confidently over the side to point out a catwalk high over the water. Imagining someone perched there makes me queasy. "See those little ladders down here?" continues Koski. "Guys go down those and—see those round handles? Those open the pocket doors. It takes at least two people to operate a chute."

According to Koski, railroad cars (three hundred per average ore boat) roll onto the ore dock and funnel their cargo into one of a hundred "pockets" along the dock. A tonguelike chute, hinged in the middle of each pocket and stored folded up, is lowered, the door to the pocket opened, and the contents hurtle into one of the twenty to thirty ship's hatches below. "When one pocket empties out, the boat moves to the next one," Koski concludes.

I descend back into the real world covered in fine red dust.

THE TWO-MILE paved road around Presque Isle, Marquette's peninsula city park, is closed for a couple of hours to accommodate joggers, so I'm spared engine noise and exhaust. Along a narrow, woodsy path that meanders through the woods below the road, I find stunning lake views from high bluffs. This is all so unexpected, such beauty so close to a city. I suppose it wouldn't be quiet here if the ore dock was operating; within sight, it must be within easy hearing, too. But today, I pick my way through junipers, harebells, orange hawkweed, and thimbleberries, recognize the scaly lace of northern white cedars, smooth white birch bark, white pine; canopies of oak. I walk on three-lobed oak leaves bigger than my shoe and sidestep fungi shaped like champagne glasses. I encounter almost no one.

Leaning against a sun-warm bluff-side tree, I stare out at yet another stunning view, then down at bright stones beneath clear water.

Cliffs and rocks twist and rise like statuary. Intimate coves protect scooped out, gravelly beaches. In one, a father skips stones for his two children. In another, gulls screech en masse offshore from a messy oblong rock. I climb down to the water, sit on a beach of coin-sized stones. My shoes fill with gravel. Suddenly two ospreys land, talons extended, on a nearby rock near the now frantic gulls.

Back on the road, a little girl lags behind her family, trying not to spill the stones she carries in cupped hands. Suddenly, we come upon a red-mouthed plastic lion, which signals a small zoo: a group of cages displaying large animals, including a live coyote, cougar, and bear. A herd of deer stand listlessly inside a fenced yard.

I feel cheated, to be so soon saddened.

Note: According to the Marquette Chamber of Commerce, the zoo has since been disbanded. New homes have been found for the caged animals, and the deer now run free in the park.

AUGUST 3

THE ROAD IS so rocky and rutted halfway up the long, thin Abbaye Peninsula that I'm down to first gear and looking for a place to turn around, when a raven appears and flies in front of me, as if leading me into a fairy tale. I am alone out here, grinding through the sort of woods I get jumpy in on foot; I haven't seen a car for half an hour. The road is so narrow that the trees lock above it, forming a winding tunnel through which the raven glides like a stingray. After two and a half minutes, it perches on a low branch and waits for me to catch up before resuming its eerie flight.

Convinced I must be headed for a magical place, I continue doggedly on, bumping along the S curves even after the raven disappears. It's awful, this road. I just hate it. Finally, at long last, it ends at a welcome outhouse and a sign for Abbaye Point that describes a short nature trail. I'm raring to go, in more ways than one, and I leap from the van in my shorts. Before a scream can travel the full length of my throat, twenty blackflies bite into each leg, while more crawl over the rest of me. Another swarm invades the van with the fervor of fans who've been waiting all night to get in. I jump up and down and slap myself, careful to keep my mouth shut, while I try to take a

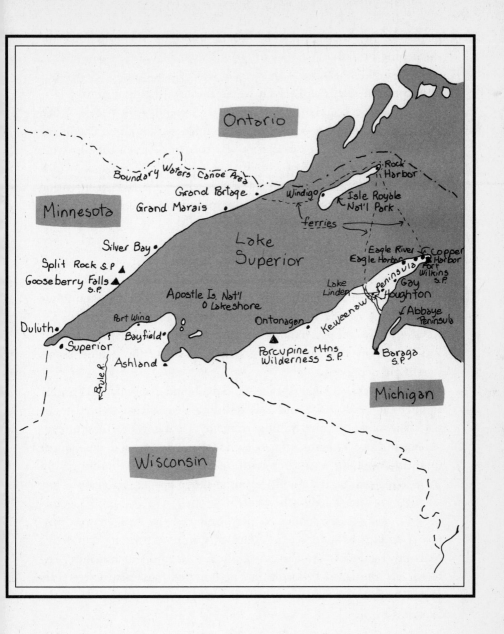

Western Lake Superior

picture of my transport, which could use a tail to switch off the thickening hordes.

Forget the outhouse. I head back, turn on the radio. A baroque flute concerto swells as I pass a whole muffler leaning against a tree. I brake, dodge boulders, roar over ruts. I could walk faster. When another raven escort appears, I'm not so impressed; nothing cranks me up worse than a busted expectation. By the time I reach the blacktop, half my day is gone. Fortunately, I've adopted UP time, in which deadlines really are dead and schedules wither for lack of attention and one is left with the present: this unimproved lake view, for instance, and that fuchsia patch of vetch.

ALTHOUGH THE KEWEENAW PENINSULA oddly resembles the Door Peninsula in size, shape, bisecting channel, and angle of reach, the feeling here is not the same at all. For one thing, the Keweenaw is lumpy, mountainous, cinched by the famous, scenic Brockway Drive; for another, the area northeast of the channel seems startlingly depressed.

Outside the village of Lake Linden, I find out why. "The only thing I can really say about this building here is that it used to be the main office for the mining company," curator Pearl Cote (pronounced "Coty") begins, graciously escorting me around the Copper Country Museum, a square, red-brick, twenty-room building. "In 1968 there was a strike and the mine never opened up again. Now all the mines are filled with water."

The strike ended serious copper mining in the Keweenaw, a peninsula famous as a source for unusually pure copper for hundreds, probably thousands of years. According to a museum brochure, the Hecla & Calumet Mill during its one hundred most productive years mined half the estimated ten billion tons of copper shipped from the Keweenaw.

"How deep are the mines?" I ask.

"I think one of 'em mighta been close to two miles," guesses Cote. "There's only one or two mines that went straight down. They usually went at a slant. My husband used to be a miner. He'd come home with his clothes full of grease and wet from the machines. It was interesting! There were jobs down in the mines besides the drillers—

the trammers operated the railroad cars. They brought the blasted rock up to the shaft and put it on other cars to bring it to the surface."

"How long did your husband do that?"

"A good twenty-five years, if not longer. A lot of 'em'd start when they were kids. Oh yeah. Back in the 1800s, before child labor laws, some of 'em were ten years old when they started. Ninety-nine percent of the people up here made their living at the mines. After all the mines up here closed, my husband went looking for a job. Lotta people moved away."

The museum is honeycombed with carefully crowded rooms. An upstairs room displays mining remains, another a collection of logging tools and a full-body bearhide rug, yet another antique clocks. My favorite is crammed with lacy fans, six shelves of shoes, and mannequins (some headless, some not) in exquisitely embroidered turn-of-the-century bridal gowns labeled with the names and wedding dates of the women who were married in them. A groom is present, too, in top hat and tails.

Back at the office, we find an antique bread maker that somebody just dropped off. It looks like an ice-cream machine. Pearl Cote strokes it as she might a lost child.

EX–COPPER-MINING COUNTRY—the east side of the Keweenaw north of the channel—seems partly agricultural, partly depressed. I reach Lake Superior in a town called Gay at a desolate beach that looks like an endless cindered parking lot. Following the only signs of life, I enter the nearby Gay Bar in a large old Victorian. The screen door squeaks and slams. Senior citizens surround a big wood oval bar. A fast-moving, tanklike woman bellows, "What can I getcha?"

I order a beer and ask if I might run my tape. A quick, full-bar consensus is taken: Sure. Conversation resumes. It's a hot, humid day, so various drinkers guess how much hotter and more humid it must be "down below," meaning the Lower Peninsula. The man at my elbow informs me that the stamp mill tailings that I saw on the beach were once used to fill roads. The bartender vanishes briefly and reappears with some beautiful black-and-white photographs taken of Gay in 1931. "This was a booming town, then," she says, booming herself.

"Only thirty-five live here now. Most of 'em are in their eighties. And about ten of those can still navigate." I look around. I'd swear they're all at the bar.

AUGUST 4

THERE'S A LOT to like at Copper Harbor, a laid-back little tourist mecca at the tip of the Keweenaw: the delicious cheese soup at the Harbor House, or Fort Wilkins State Park, which, although crowded, is woodsier than last night's lawnlike Baraga State Park. I'm disappointed that many of Michigan's coastal parks often don't seem to me to reflect the wild environment. I'd prefer the cheaper, more rustic state and national forest campgrounds, but I rarely find those on the Great Lake shores. Still, Michigan's state park rangers tell me that most campers prefer their clean-shaven, open parks, not to mention their electricity, flush toilets, and hot showers. Fort Wilkins State Park, however, is woodsier than most, and located between two lakes: Fanny Hooe and Superior. And this weekend most campers are authentically garbed in replicated Civil War wear.

At the fort, inside an unbleached canvas tent, uniformed commanding officer Jim Newkirk motions me to a camp stool. "We come up here the first weekend in August every year and do an encampment," he tells me. "The original battle was not here, but in exchange for being allowed to camp within the fort in the surroundings of a National Historic Military Site, we do small arms and artillery demonstrations."

I wave at the nearby cannon. "Did you fire that thing today already?"

"Several times." Newkirk laughs. "It's not a thunderstorm coming in! It's us and our big-boy toys! My character is Captain Josiah Church, who commanded Battery D for much of the war. Before that he was a schoolteacher, and that's what I do, too, in real life."

"Where do you get these uniforms?"

"Most of our uniforms come from the Quartermaster Shop in Port Huron or from a store in Corinth, Mississippi. Purveyors of military goods—called sutlers—manufacture reproductions.

"There are different units around the state," Newkirk continues, "including infantry, cavalry, and eight or ten artillery units. We're Battery D: First Michigan Light Artillery. Originally a battery was six guns and 120 men, but although we're only 28 members and two guns, we're one of the biggest artillery units in the state."

"By 'guns' you mean——"

"Cannons. We have two of 'em. I brought this one up five hundred miles on a trailer; the other one's settin' at home in my garage. It's a weekend hobby. The membership is responsible for its own uniforms, accoutrements, sidearms, rifle or pistols or what have you. Everything you see is authentic. If you start rooting through my boxes, however, you're going to find a dandy can of WD-40 in there to keep the guns from rusting, and some spray paint so I can touch up the guns tonight if I want to, and a can of bug repellent so I can fight the Upper Peninsula monsters. But visitors will get a good picture of what it was like in Civil War times."

JIM ROOKS, a huge man with a megaphone voice, leads me to an office in back of the Laughing Loon, his wife's handicrafts shop. "I do what you do," he booms, nodding at a loaded desk. "I write."

He also might have said, "I fight." Naturalist Jim Rooks is trying to keep Highway 41's fabulous "tunnel of trees" from being widened. He's fighting to reduce the toxic chemicals released by paper mills into the Great Lakes. And he's spent years trying to protect the virgin trees in and around an acreage called the Estivant Pines, home of the "leaning pine," the biggest white pine in the United States. Which is what I'm looking for.

I'm too late, Rooks informs me. The famous pine fell last year and I can't see it. He's not showing it to anyone. However, he will show me the other Estivant pines. Soon I'm bouncing along in his huge, road-weary Suburban, along with two other ten-dollar "Bear Track Tour" takers.

Rooks entertains us with UP jokes, crediting an old Finn he knows: "We have six months of winter and six months poor sledding" and "We spend twenty-five thousand dollars on a foghorn and we still got fog."

As the route worsens, Rooks considers the yen of some Yoopers to secede: "So I ask them, 'Why be a separate state? Why not be part of Wisconsin?' And they say, 'Hey, Wisconsin doesn't know we're up here any more than Detroit does.' Well, Wisconsin knows a little more. The *Milwaukee Journal* even has an Upper Peninsula section. If an atomic bomb exploded in Mackinaw City, it would not be reported in this section. It would go under national news. That's right. That's really beautiful. Had the UP developed west to east instead of east to west, it'd be part of Wisconsin."

We pass a dump, scheduled to be closed soon, where tourists go to watch bears. "Used to see thirty bears at a time there," laments Rooks. "But the place is toxic, what with all the paint and chemicals people have pitched over the years." He points out numerous bear trails and some mangled wild plum trees downed for the fruit. We enter woods, pass an old copper mine, and then a "borrow pit."

"You're driving along the highway and you see these little lakes which are drying up now, and these are called borrow pits," says Rooks. "A borrow pit is as much a part of a town as a drinking establishment. You gotta have one. You gotta have a borrow pit. You use it for fill."

We come to another pond, this one made by beavers. The woods are getting wild. The road to Estivant Pines is awful, but I suggest that the Point Abbaye Road is even worse. Rooks nods knowingly.

We park at last near a pile of giant logs. "The loggers made a mistake and cut these thirty-six trees out of the preserve," says Rooks. He looks very upset. I'm beginning to sense that trees are individuals to him, that he finds the sight of these Old Ones, hacked up and stacked like this, unspeakable, bodies minus limbs.

"Everybody agrees that the copper-mining methods were destructive and something had to change," Rooks says as we start up a crooked trail on foot. "Well, the same thing applies to logging. Enough is enough."

He waves at a group of stumps. "What you see here is a phantom forest. This is the stump of a white pine. This is summer-cut stuff. Here's a winter-cut stump. Here's another. There were eighty along here. We call this the Phantom Cathedral because these trees were cut to build a cathedral. But the cathedral was here. Should have been left here."

We clamber deeper into the woods, off the path, to a decaying log. "This is what is left of a nurse tree," instructs Rooks. "Big white pine. Just huge white pine. Part of the carcass is still right here in this rise. And all these trees have grown right out of it. . . . Oh, wow. I almost stepped on a plantain orchid. Walk around here: this is a really precious orchid."

We proceed deeper into the woods, off the trail. Rooks's voice trumpets through the trees: "I don't bring a lot of people back here, but I want you to see this granddaddy. See this cat's-eye here? Well, one winter many years ago, a logger was gonna spend the next fifteen minutes cutting this tree down. That's all it would take to cut down five hundred years. But before he got very far, the foreman came by and said, 'It's too big, leave it. I think it's got some hollow stuff in it.' Today this tree'd be lying on the forest floor before anyone figured that out.

"Now we're going to take this trail through the Memorial Grove. . . . A bear has been here—bear scat! . . . Look: this tree is thirteen feet around, but our champion trees are sixteen and eighteen feet around. . . . Now look down: can you see where the forest fire still blackens the earth? I'm talking three, four hundred years ago. . . . There's over four thousand pines here, three thousand of which are over twenty-two inches in diameter. There's another thousand trees that are younger barely making it. But there's a third, maybe a fourth generation of white pine coming up. Maybe they'll make it and maybe they won't."

Now and then a vireo sings, but except for Rooks's voice the woods seem strangely still. "Now we're coming into some of the most spectacular parts of the forest. This is kind of the heart of it. This spot here has 282 trees. Fourth-graders from a school in Marquette went out, collected cans, raised over four thousand dollars and bought four thousand dollars' worth of trees in here. For this they got a national EPA award, presented to them by President Bush."

Suddenly the woods open up like a park. Rooks stops, then stabs a finger at the trail. "This is worse than anything," he cries. "People don't know what they're doin' when they do this. Even if they put that cigarette out, do you see what that is? That's charcoal. They put it out on charcoal. This forest burnt once and they're going to try to do it again."

AUGUST 5

ALTHOUGH MY VAN valiantly negotiates the hairpin turns of the Keweenaw Peninsula's famous Brockway Drive, the morning fog curtains off view after would-be dramatic view. But like a diminutive California, it's not far from the top (730 feet above Lake Superior) to the western shore, where I run my hands through rounded stones as cool and deep as water. I don't know how to recognize an agate, which is what the half-dozen people here are hunched over looking for. When the fog burns off, I head south on Highway 26 along a coastline studded with large offshore rocks, another reminder of California. I've never seen a Great Lake shore quite like this one. On my left, the occasional tasteful gift shop appears, often with some sort of bear name.

During a second beach break north of Eagle Harbor, a diver emerges from a blue bay holding a rock as big as a human heart. It's an agate, he claims, a stone best found under water, the shore having been picked over by rock hounds.

Not all the beaches are rocky; some are sandy, narrow and curved, like a pale wedge of melon. But Agate Beach, south of Eagle River, is pebbled. The sun has finally debuted; the stones have warmed. The blackflies aren't bad, either. I try my luck once more. For an hour, I handle ancient stones that click like beads and feel smooth and dry as a prayer: gray, green, pink, yellow, red.

AUGUST 6

PORCUPINE MOUNTAIN STATE PARK bulges into Lake Superior at the western base of the Keweenaw Peninsula: 58,335 acres containing the world's largest virgin pine / hemlock forest, a dozen 600-foot cliffs, eighty-five miles of hiking trails, and the wild Presque Isle River. I drove twenty-five miles yesterday from the entrance to the most remote campground I've stayed in all summer to find . . . yet another lawn.

Aware of nothing more than another stony beach and, later, the sound of snuffling bears (which the ranger said "probably won't bother you"), I retired early. This morning, however, I crunch past the agatehunchers to the mouth of a narrow river, turn sharply in from the beach, and find myself at the foot of a crashing, roaring, rock-sculpted, wild-wooded waterfall. I am absolutely amazed. How could I not have heard it?

Choosing the trail on the far side, I haven't walked upriver more than a few minutes before another waterfall appears, then another. The trail narrows, climbs through huge old pines, hemlocks, maples, and oaks, reaching alarming heights over frothing water hell-bent for Lake Superior. The riverbed is sculptured, scooped, solid rock full of bowls and deep holes, stone banks deeply scalloped. A ranger—one of the few people I meet—explains that these dramatic curves are ground by rocks as big as bowling balls kept turning in place for years by the force of the water. Farther upriver, through cedars too thick to permit much undergrowth, my steps thump oddly on cushion-deep needles. I even climb the river itself, where terraced rocks provide a giant staircase up the middle, water swirling around me. By the fifth waterfall, I'm hopelessly giddy. It's wild out here, rugged and intimate. My spirits ride high on the rush of the river and the clean, loamy smell of old woods.

On Maslowski Beach outside Ashland, Wisconsin, rock music thumps and blares from elevated black rectangles as big as doors. "It's the great WIMI Bay Area Beach Party Belly Flop Contest, people!" a man bellows into a mike. "Winner gets a hundred dollars! Getcherself out here!"

I scream over gut-quivering guitars to an official-looking helper. "Will you talk on my tape?"

"I'm a sales manager—I don't get paid for talkin'!" Scott Jaeger yells back. We move away from the speakers, and Jaeger talks anyway: "We're a radio station out of Ironwood, Michigan, and this is our fourth annual beach party. We invite everybody. We've got a sixteen-team volleyball tournament, a belly-flop contest, a tug-of-war, a hula-hoop contest, a pizza-eating contest. . . ."

"Who decides on the belly-flop winner?"

"It's gonna be audience appeal! But we get the final say."

A man with a bullhorn stands on the beach and eggs participants into the water. Men, women, and kids wade out to a lifeguard tower maybe fifty feet out. Kids dive first, then women, then men. Not everyone dives from the top. People boo or cheer, depending. Big cheers. Big boos. Little cheers. There are some big bellies out there and some pretty big flops, too.

Okay, here they come back. The announcer pumps the crowd for a favorite. Faint cheers for several. Bigger cheers. Medium cheer for the guy in the lime-green T-shirt, shorts, and red suspenders. At last, *ta-da!*—the winners: two huge men who look like bikers. In Japan, they would be sumo wrestlers. I doubt that Ashland wants to be known for a belly-flop contest, but, hey, it happens. I liked your museum, too.

AUGUST 7

DAVE STRZOK'S RUDDY, frank face breaks into frequent isn't-life-amazing? smiles as, facing me across a Bayfield coffee shop table, he skillfully slings me a line of surprises. Strzok owns and operates the Apostle Islands Cruise Service, lives here year-round, and writes books. His first book, *Guide to the Apostle Islands*, is doing well. "And I'm also writing a guide to the area in its historical perspective," says Strzok, "because for years I've been listening to people tell chopped-up stories that couldn't be true, so I decided to find out for myself.

"It's hard to get a real picture. People sometimes want to make the last three hundred years happen in the last thirty, talking about the various European settlers as if they all just kinda clumped up here and the only difference between then and now is the number of people. Well, that's not the way it is. Furthermore, it wasn't unknown for the Native Americans to get a big kick out of sending the biggest joker in the tribe to talk to the white guy coming in asking questions. They thought it was as amusing as heck. Then there were the missionaries, who had a tendency to weed out what they didn't want to tell people about, and on top of that, I think there was just a huge amount of hucksterism going on.

"Take my own family. My grandfather started in Le Havre, France. Two boats are there, it costs thirty-two dollars to come across, one boat's going to America, the other's going to the Boer War, take your choice. He's a mercenary soldier and he doesn't want to fight anymore, so he comes to America. Yeah. He gets here, goes to Pennsylvania, meets my grandmother, and then somebody tells him that the place to go is out to Colorado. So they pass through all this beautiful country—Ohio, Illinois, Wisconsin, Minnesota—to Colorado, and nine years later it's dried out and blown away, so he comes back to Minnesota and Wisconsin.

"What probably happened was, guys along the way are tellin' em, 'You better keep movin' west, there's nothing more available here.' Well, they just don't want the competition. Then there were the depots that hired guys to tell people that 'Yah, you gotta move out there, you can get land for nothin', live real cheap there, live off the land.' Of course, you had to pass through these depots to get supplied and the guy got paid for making that remark a thousand times a day. It was nonsense. It was a great game of hucksterism that got the settlers moving west."

Strzok stops long enough to sip some coffee, puts his cup down, and continues. "Then there's the question of why certain ethnic groups came across. I know for a fact that certain of the Finns were draft dodgers, my grandfather having been a mercenary soldier. At times the only job you could get over there was as a mercenary. Men got sick and tired of playing war games for some kaiser or baron who's decided to hire five thousand men to go attack somebody. So they'd come over here and they'd get someplace and they'd say, hey, this looks just like Norway here, or this place looks almost like someplace else, so they started clumping up. Imagine the letters going back saying, 'Ya, it's good here and there's plenty of work and we need more people and send women.'"

Leaping to the present, Strzok nods at the large table next to us. "This whole table of people here, you can find out everything you'd ever want to know about everybody in town. That table's full from five o'clock in the morning until evening time. The local people sit there.

"In this area perhaps twenty, thirty percent of the people are on unemployment. We also get a lot of educated people who don't want the rat race anymore and they'll end up waitressing and working hard for four months and taking it easy the rest of the year. Any way they can do it, they'll do it.

"It isn't a job around here, it's a lifestyle. And you can tell who's going to make it and who's not going to make it, just on the basis of experience. Usually it takes about three years for somebody to come up here with a brand-new idea for a business before they fold. They run out of money, they run out of patience. It takes some ingenuity. In the summer, out of a hundred days, forty-five of them are money-making days. I do well because a large number of people who come here take the boat ride. The time to come through, though, is in the late fall, winter, when we're right down to the grain. It's a very different place when the tourists aren't here."

AUGUST 8

OH MY GOD, what's that? I sit up in a flash, erect as a marionette. I look at my clock: 12:30 A.M. *Thunk!* there it is again! something on the van roof! *Snap! Crunch!* Step sounds fill my campsite. I aim a shaking torch beam out the windows, but see nothing. The night is matte black. The moonlight, which earlier kept me awake, pouring in between the hanging shirts, is gone.

Thunk! What *is* that? It's too loud for bats, although there sure were a lot of them darting through last night's path-of-gold sunset. It must be a bear. I'm in a city campground on the outskirts of Bayfield, but it's wooded here. Could be a bear. Sounds to me like a herd of bears. The crackling and snapping are amplified by the excellent acoustics of the cavelike spaces under the trees. Maybe I should wake up Val, the amiable guy tenting next to me—tenting, for Pete's sake! He's doomed! However, whatever concern I might feel for Val's safety isn't enough to persuade me to open the door. After a couple of hours, the noises stop. My hair lies back down on my head. My body lies back on my bed. At last I sleep.

When I stumble out of the van in the morning, Val Buckley is already up. "Val," I croak in my morning voice, "did you hear that ruckus last night?"

"Pretty noisy, weren't they?" says Val.

" 'They'?"

"The flying squirrels," says Val. "What'd you think they were?"

Thankfully, Val is too busy packing "wetsacks" (okay if the contents get wet) and "drysacks" (contents to stay dry) to push the matter.

I am spared. He's preparing to take a couple of friends kayaking among the Apostle Islands. Of the twenty-two islands, all but the largest (inhabited Madeline Island) are part of the Apostle Islands National Lakeshore, a northern paradise for kayaks and sailboats. Val has been here often. On top of his Subaru are strapped three kayaks.

"Basically you have the extremes of sea kayaks here," Val explained to me yesterday. "You have the real narrow one that's fast but kinda tippy. Paddling that's like sitting on a telephone pole—calls for some expertise. This other one I call a training boat, because it's real stable but it's a little slower and a little heavier. The third boat there, that's a plastic boat. It's kinda in-between. We call 'em Tupperware boats. Those you don't have to be so careful of as fiberglass boats. You put 'em on the rocks and sit in 'em and just boom-boom-boom-boom, down into the water. They're not made by Tupperware company, of course. We just call 'em that."

"I heard that canoes are kinda dangerous out in this area."

"Yeah, well, they fill up with water, basically. These here at least are covered."

"How long have you been doing this?"

"Too long." Val laughs with easy enthusiasm. "Twenty years. I mighta had one of the first sea kayaks in Wisconsin. Back when they used to have river racing with these long kayaks they use in Olympics now, I started using one of them for camping. I lost that one up on James Bay on the Hudson." He mentions many other far-flung places.

I'm impressed. "You're a really serious kayaker."

"That's true. I break ice to get my boat in in the spring. This kayak here"—the fast, thin one—"is from England. The Brits are ahead of us as far as canoes go—I mean kayaks. They call kayaks canoes. It's kinda weird."

"Can you take these anywhere, like rivers?"

"Not rivers. These are actually deep-water kayaks."

"Sea kayaks."

"Well, that's just a term. If I was to name them, I'd name them heavy-water kayaks. They're not whitewater kayaks. They're not made for turning, they're made for not turning."

I'd beg a demo ride, but Val's company has arrived. Instead, I take Dave Strzok's three-hour cruise that loops, at its far point, around Devils Island, where the sandstone cliffs are scooped and gnarled into the devil's-mouth caves that slosh and froth, though the island's inhabitants are mainly rabbits.

PAST THE LITTLE TOWN of Cornucopia, and then Port Wing, where I watch the bright sails of the International Regatta blow by like confetti, I come to a finger road, hesitate, and keep on going. I get tired of these corrugated back roads that jangle the van like a canful of change, jolt my bones, and coat us both with grit. But for some reason, even though it's late and I'm exhausted and I don't know where I'll stay tonight, still I brake, turn back, and take the long gravel road to the mouth of the Brule River.

The road ends at a rich river marsh and a sandy Lake Superior beach where, next to a scarlet kayak, a young woman in a lime-colored helmet, red shorts, canvas shoes, and sleeveless T-shirt identifies what she is eating from an aluminum pouch as reconstituted military-ration peaches. Her name is Kim Davis, and she is kayaking around Lake Superior, alone.

"I started in the Sault, traveled around the Canadian side, and I'll end up in the Sault again," says Davis. She consults a small notebook, densely scribbled in, which she removes from a plastic bag. "This is my forty-eighth day, I think. Takes about thirty-five to go all the way around if you go hard, but I'm just playing."

"Are you writing about it?"

"No, I just live. Basically I don't have an address. I kind of expedition full-time with the boat here. Sometimes I teach in environmental programs to make enough money to keep going. Kids call me Yak Lady. It's for the kayak, but also I yak a lot." Her "yak" is fast and intense. I can feel she hungers for compatible company, as do I. Although my trip is tame compared with hers, we're both women who crave adventure.

She lives on five dollars a day, Davis is saying.

"Where do you stay?"

"I tent. It's not too hard in Canada, but down here I'm kind of afraid to stop. People think that the Minnesota shoreline is desolate and rugged, but the loon population just plummeted as soon as I hit all those cottages. You can see all the wildlife go right down after the U.S./Canadian border. This place right here, it's kind of a fragile habitat. Lot of terns here and gulls. But the loons are farther north. I miss watching the loons. . . ."

A damselfly clings to her hair like a blue feather. "May I take your picture?" I ask her.

"As long as it doesn't come out before I get home." She shows me a small waterproof camera. Once in a while she does slide presentations to make money, she says. "Flora and fauna of the area, et cetera.

"I'm twenty-four and I've been doing this for about eight years," Davis says. "The whole East Coast; down to Florida and Texas. When I started, kayaking wasn't really a big thing. I didn't know what a sea kayak was. I walked into a place looking for a canoe you could put a cover over, because I didn't think a regular canoe would take the kind of trip I was looking at, and here were all these sea kayaks, very capable-looking crafts, and this boat here: nineteen inches wide and almost eight and a half feet long. It's perfect. It has all kinds of stability, but there's no width to it. Someday I'm going to take it overseas, but right now I'm doing all the big lakes, heading out to nowherelands."

"Don't you ever get scared?"

"No, but I credit that to a German dairy farmer I worked for once. I can't really put into words what it is I learned from him; I suppose that's why I'm not a writer—my vocabulary isn't too good. I tell stories, though, and memorize ballads by Robert Service and all those. Anyway, after a while you learn, people aren't going to hurtcha. Everybody thinks I'm going around the shoreline looking for a *man,* you know, because that's the mentality of most folks, and I get in some of these places and I scare away those guys. Obviously I can take care of myself, and that's not how a man thinks of a woman. He wants her to need him. But you're just not going to have any problem with people. They'd have to be really vicious and bad, and vicious and bad people don't expect a woman to be on her own."

Kim refers to Lake Superior as the Foxhead, or the Head of the Wolf, the eye being Isle Royale. Then, despite her self-deprecation, Kim articulates something I've begun to feel myself: "You sort of get addicted to wilderness," she says. "But you can get kinda crazy from being out there, too. You get kinda mad, actually. A lot of mood swings. Not depression. It's funny, people think it's depression, but actually it's a hell of a life when you get out there. When you're back in the city or civilization, you thirst for it. I hope someday I can figure out the words to say what it means to be alone and on a long adventure. When you are out there and responsible and independent, and what happens to religion and what happens to reality, not knowing what day it is—it's a hell of a story."

Note: Since this conversation, Kim Davis has completed several more ambitious solo kayak expeditions and become a welder to finance building a boat "so I can sail around the world."

AUGUST 9

WHATEVER I EXPECTED the Wisconsin / Minnesota twin cities of Superior / Duluth to look like, it wasn't this gleaming spread of industry, storage towers, superhighways, bridges, ports, ships, trucks, and trains. I suppose I should have known: the Duluth harbor, shared by both cities, is the largest on the Great Lakes and the second busiest in the United States.

Still, Duluth does seem a little off the beaten path to be this jammed. Last night I almost camped on a curb. I must have searched two hours for a hotel / motel / any kind of room before I brandished my writer's status at a Holiday Inn clerk and was granted what I was assured was the last room in town: a never-yet-slept-in executive suite in a not-quite-finished wing.

This morning, I hike to the lighthouse at the end of the long concrete pier that extends from Duluth's Canal Park into Lake Superior. A parallel jetty reaches from the Wisconsin side. Together, they reach out like arms to incoming yachts and sailboats, salties and lakers. There's a lighthouse at the end, with two rings of mud-jug cliff swallow nests wedged under the walkway that rings the room at the top. Standing way out here is almost like being afloat: sharp light, fresh breeze, water on three sides, and a shoreline panorama six separate camera shots wide, the buildings of Duluth spilling along the bottom of a high hill, practically into the lake.

At the land end of the pier, at the Duluth Canal Park Visitor Center and Historical Museum, I take in lovely ship models, a twenty-foot-tall engine, and a display of ship flags and stack designs. A replica of a freighter's pilot house looks out on the channel and posts the arrival and departure times of ships.

It's an easy stroll from the museum to the nearby Duluth Harbor's Aerial Lift Bridge, the longest aerial lift bridge in the world, which, shaped like a squashed letter A, is close to ninety years old. Traffic growling across the metal grate high over my head reminds me of the time I once lowered my naked ear into an open hive of fifty thousand bees. Suddenly, urgent clanging: traffic stops and the bridge, instead of opening like jaws, rises straight up, as if under a magician's wand, but attached to the towers at each end (full height is 138 feet). A cruise boat putts through. A cormorant, black and big as a goose, shoots through the gap like a jet. Two herons flap over the top. On a grassy bank, kids throw bread to hysterical gulls.

Upon leaving the inviting waterfront park, I become lost, entangled in one-way streets atop the bluff behind Duluth. Finally, I backtrack, cross a bridge slung over land and river like a fly rod cast to Superior, where dozens of towering grain silos line up like troops on parade. At one huge granary loading dock, I hike past a long queue of fourteen-wheelers waiting to unload, then a freight train jerking slowly through a railroad-car-sized tunnel. My guide, too young to have encountered insurance willies, allows me aboard a looming Canadian bulk carrier now being loaded. I find the decks slick with granules, the air a fog of chaff. A supervisor watches aghast as I slide around the gaping holds into which grain is raining from a giant overhead spout. One false step could bury me in gold.

But I survive, climb back down, walk past the train, past the trucks, back to my van, impressed with the power of what goes on here: grain in, grain out, a bursting satisfaction. Finding it all oddly lovely, I photograph lavishly. My favorite frame: an old black-hulled, white-decked laker "shelved" like a dusty antique behind a yellow Dead End sign in a swath of Queen Anne's lace. Nearby, goldenrod blooms between resting truck trailers, beneath underpasses, and along convoluted port roads trafficked by haulers of products with destinations east.

"MINNESOTA'S U.S. 61 is the second busiest scenic highway in the country!" a Duluth resident tells me, describing the two-way road that hugs the Lake Superior shore from Duluth to the Canadian border. As I head north, my mind drifts to other scenic routes: Has there been a bad leg on this trip? One that sort of limped? I can't remember one. I slip back through the summer, reminiscing, looking for the day with no redeeming features, when *wham!*—a waterfall. I almost go off the road. Gooseberry Falls is so big, powerful, and close to the road, if I'd been in a canoe, I'd have capsized.

I pull into a convenient parking area, get out, and gander. According to a Gooseberry Falls State Park brochure, the water spills off the thirty-foot Upper Falls to the sixty-foot Lower Falls, roars under the Highway 61 bridge upon which I am standing, and crashes almost immediately into Lake Superior, which I see when I turn around. The park itself offers eighteen miles of trails, a campground (full), river and lake picnic areas, and an interpretative center. The place is majestic, the state money evident.

After a short hike inland along the river (the area reminds me of the Porcupine Mountains), I jump back into my van. In minutes I come to Split Rock Lighthouse State Park: another roadside waterfall, another glorious park, a state historic site, a lighthouse undergoing state-funded restoration, more trails, and convenient roadside parking. I check things out for a couple hours—more woods, waterfalls, wildflowers, trails, beauty—then keep going.

Although there are seven state parks in the approximately 180 miles between Duluth and Canada, not all have campgrounds, and the ones that do are full. Don't count on finding a place in August, Gooseberry Falls rangers warned me. These beautiful parks are paradise, booked tighter 'n a NASA shuttle. As I go north, I check anyway. The rangers are right: they're all beautiful and they're all full. The terrain becomes steeper. Cliffs line the lake. The roadside is pillared with the white trunks of birch. At Silver Bay, ore slides into a ship at an ore dock behind a chain-link fence. At last, I find a campsite in a bird-thick KOA, a small commercial campground. I gratefully shower, crawl into my quilts, and plunge like a river into sleep.

AUGUST 10

AS RIVER AFTER river crashes into Lake Superior over cliff after sharp, rocky cliff, I begin to see a pattern that reminds me of the rivers swelling predictably behind the bosomy Michigan dunes. Here, it's the drama that's predictable. A billion years ago, explain the state park brochures, a rift split what is now the Lake Superior lake bed. Lava pouring from volcanoes eventually formed all this bedrock, these western Lake Superior cliffs, which were themselves eroded and sculpted by glaciers and deep-cutting rivers to their present-day splendor.

Continuing north, I stop at nearly every one of the handy turnoffs to view yet another breathtaking waterfall, often padding up an inviting footpath and snacking on raspberries, blackberries, and thimbleberries. Trails, berries, white water, and dark woods: I'm entering an area where urban slickers venture during paid vacations to take on nature, brave bears, paddle their own canoes, where what's respected is muscle power. Here, an intricate network of trails supports quiet modes of transportation—canoes, bikes, or boots—from short loops near the highway to the wilderness Superior Trail that runs inland from Duluth to Grand Marais. There are trails for mountain bikes and horses.

There are "trails" for canoes. This tip of northern Minnesota's "Arrowhead" forms the gateway to the million-acre, lake-laced backwoods Boundary Waters Canoe Area Wilderness (also BWCAW, or just Boundary Waters) between here and Canada. Cars up here without canoes on top look odd. I count seven canoes atop the five cars at a Superior National Forest information center, where adventurers come for their Boundary Waters permits. A blackboard message chalked just inside the door suggests that if I camp in one of the areas listed, I should gather a pile of rocks to throw at invading bears.

"That's negotiating time," comments a short, plaid-shirted man. "Once the bear's in there, you can't get him out. You going in canoe country?"

"No, I'm sticking to the lakeshore."

"Softie, huh?"

Whatever I reply, it is far more polite than what I am thinking.

GRAND MARAIS is an oddly sophisticated northwoods, artsy tourist town of comfortable proportions, where, in the local museum, one can look upon the fishhook crown worn by the Miss North Shore Queens of 1957, 1958, and 1959, or, at the Grand Marais Trading Post, charge to one's credit card expensive northwoods gear. None of these, however, tops Sven and Ole's hand-tossed Scandinavian Pizza. Entering the restaurant, I pass a fast-food counter on one side and walk through a casual sit-down section on the other to a bar at the back, where I order a beer and a "Vild Vun."

"Good choice," comments a man two stools down. "Definitely a new taste experience." Bart Austin, I soon discover, has sailed here from Bayfield with his wife, Karen, who sits between us. The bartender, whose name I never quite get, works as well at a local sawmill, one of the biggest employers in the area, and is also a wilderness guide.

"It's always wise to hire a guide," he tells us. Two of the bar's five other occupants nod. "You get people from Chicago who don't know north from south. There have been some big screw-ups with people who go into the Boundary Waters on their own and can't even get a fire going. I see it all the time."

I tell him that I was called a softie because I wasn't going there. He responds, "I find that rather humorous. Some people think they know a lot about the wilderness, but they've never had a crisis."

"Have you had a crisis?"

"Oh," he laughs in a pleasant, assured voice, exactly the kind of voice I'd welcome in a crisis, "quite a few. Broken ankles, broken collarbone. About twelve miles back in, a guy was holding on to a log with one hand and the ax in the other and I said, 'You shouldn't do it like that,' but he did it anyway and split his hand right down to here. End of trip."

Bart's also a guide. When not in Bayfield, he and Karen live in Colorado. To be a guide in the Rockies, Bart says, you have to go through a recognized guide school. To guide in Alaska, you have to serve a seven-year apprenticeship. But in Minnesota, anybody can be a guide.

"I could be a bear guide?" I ask, unbelieving.

"You betcha. You just fill out the forms, send them in, you're mailed a license, and there you go."

"I'd have to replace the 'y' in 'Mary' with a 'k.'"

"Listen, I know some lady bear guides."

"If I wanted to explore the Boundary Waters, I should take a guide?"

"Well, you could take lessons," suggests Bart. "And the Boundary Waters is usually very well marked. It really is. All you need is a good compass and a good set of maps."

"Even if you get lost, if you're fairly self-sufficient, you'll run into somebody eventually," says the bartender.

Talking to Karen Austin, I discover she is an amateur mycologist, a subject that starts the so-far quiet woman running. "We have some of the most excellent edibles in the country outside of the Pacific Northwest," Karen begins enthusiastically. "Oh, definitely. And only one mushroom that'll kill you, and that's very easily identified: the death angel, with the bulb on the bottom of it and the veil. We have twenty to thirty types of mushrooms that are easily identifiable and foolproof. The book to start with is called *Thirty Easily Identifiable Mushrooms.*"

"We have the usual boletuses, chanterelles," adds Bart.

"Oh, yeah," says Karen. "There's a chanterelle that you can make wine out of. Chanterelle wine. We can pick enough mushrooms in people's lawns around here to make a casserole."

My wild-rice pizza arrives. As I dig into this taste sensation, I confess that I've never eaten a wild mushroom.

Karen is aghast. "Oh, you're kidding! My word! Well, they're all subtly different. And the trick to cooking wild mushrooms is to cook them over very low heat, because otherwise you destroy the taste. You wash them real good and sauté them in butter and onion and garlic and cook them very, very slow until their natural moisture kind of boils off.

"We also have oyster mushrooms, a spring oyster and a fall oyster," continues Karen, "and we always find it on downed popple [aspen] trees, although occasionally we'll find it on birch. It layers down in veils and it looks and tastes like an oyster. It's a real slurpy, sloppy mushroom. You cook it and put a little oyster sauce in the butter and garlic. And, oh yes, we have your sulfur shelf, which is your highest-rated mushroom up here. When people find one they usually keep it quiet. It's called chicken of the woods. It's a bunch of layers sometimes as big as two feet across which can be harvested for two or three weeks.

You can use it just like chicken. And it freezes well. Another of my favorites is the lobster mushroom. This one you have to dig out—the best part is underground. It has the texture of meat.

"I have certain places that I go at certain times of the year. I'm a painting contractor and my husband is a carpenter, but we'll put off work to go mushroom hunting. We've found a lot of mushrooms on the Apostle Islands, because there's dead stand on the islands and even virgin timber and record birch in there. But with the sailboat, it's hard to bring them back. I've considered bringing my pressure cooker and canning on the boat."

Note: The author remains leery of wild mushrooms and takes no responsibility for the well-being and health of any reader who eats one.

AUGUST 11

CR — ACK!!! A man in period costume snaps a sinuous bullwhip in the middle of the backyardlike Grand Portage National Monument stockade, a large grassy area enclosed by gray, pointed, weathered posts. A woman tries it: nothing. There appears to be a trick to it. She tries again.

Many members of the mellow crowd milling around these two are dressed as eighteenth-century fur trappers, traders, or their close relations. A man in a kilt blows hard into a shrieking set of bagpipes. A target twangs with thrown knives. A knot of boys thunks tomahawks into a slice of log mounted on some boards. In the middle, teacher and student continue to crack whips.

This last mainland stop of my trip coincides with the annual Grand Portage Rendezvous and Powwow on the Grand Portage Reservation, a piece of good news I got yesterday when I visited superintendent Steve Einwalter at the Grand Portage National Monument headquarters in Grand Marais. "Grand Portage was the Voyageurs' fur-trade route and the Indian headquarters for the Northwest Company in the 1700s," Einwalter almost whispers. "Eventually the fur trade routes extended all the way from Montreal to the West Coast. The Grand Portage—an eight-and-a-half-mile trail between the Pigeon River and the Grand Portage stockade—connected the whole transportation system. Between 1760 and 1802, thousands of furs passed through Grand Portage, the first European settlement in what was to become the state of Minnesota."

"Can a person still hike the Grand Portage?"

"You can hike it. The trail is maintained to some extent, but we've tried to save both the historical and environmental authenticity of it, so there's lots of mud puddles, mosquitoes, flies, and things that the original users had to put up with. Hikers who start at this end come out at Canada's Old Fort William. There's a campground up there."

"So this weekend is celebrating the Voyageurs?"

"Well, the fur trade was a combined Native American and corporate activity in which the Voyageurs played a major role. In the summertime all the participants would meet at this end of the Grand Portage to exchange goods and get supplies. Two hundred years ago, there might have been two thousand people at a Grand Portage rendezvous. Today, the National Park Service and the Grand Portage band of the Minnesota Chippewa tribe sort of do it together. Native Americans hold the powwow, and several Voyageur companies interested in reenacting the fur-trading days and activities do the Rendezvous."

One of these reenactors is sorting furs in a room under a corner lookout tower. "Persons reenacting the Voyageur times come here from all over the Midwest and Canada," Walt Duvveld tells me. He points to some displayed knives and beads ("most of the steel items were from England; beads were from Italy"), which were traded with Indian people all over North America for the furs.

I stroke pelts of skunk, otter, beaver, raccoon, bobcat, muskrat, and coyote stacked in plush piles. "This is what a Voyageur camp looked like," says Duvveld, gesturing at the scene out the glassless window. "The Voyageurs came over the Grand Portage and ended up here. Tomorrow there'll be canoe races and we'll be doing some carving of canoe paddles and things like that. My family and I do this about every other weekend someplace all summer. Rendezvous happen all over the country."

I notice that the tents—white canvas wedges pegged in rows on the bright green grass—resemble those I saw at the Civil War reenactment at Copper Harbor. Duvveld tells me they're ridge tents, "a predominantly military tent used since the American Revolution. Just canvas and three poles—a ridge and two uprights. They're practical, easy to transport."

The whip cracks have grown loud as gunshots, hurting my ears. Duvveld explains that the noise results from the tip of the whip breaking the sound barrier. Soon the reports are replaced by laughter: the two whips have become entangled. I smile as the embarrassed pair picks at the knots.

ACROSS THE STREET, the powwow is setting up behind a dark brown general store and post office. There doesn't seem to be much organization, but it's not chaos, either. It's Friday evening—tourists aren't due until tomorrow. I have never been to a powwow before, and I feel nervous. I have no place to camp, and although the cars and pickups are pouring in, everyone looks native and seems to belong. I feel like an intruder.

From one of the small food stands setting up behind the store, I buy a "fry bread"—a bunlike cross between a doughnut and a tortilla, handed to me by a man in his late forties with black hair tied back and a red bandanna headband. Lucky I chose this stand, he says with a smile; his wife is famous for her fry bread. When he hears that I am a writer, Jim Northrup, author of a column called "Fond du Lac Follies," syndicated in Native American newspapers, seats me in his "office," a nearby picnic table.

I shove my tape recorder between us. "May I?"

"No problem." He waves at the shallow birch-bark baskets hanging from the roof the fry-bread stand. They are "fanning baskets," he says, for removing the chaff from wild rice, but he calls them "treaty baskets" because he gathered the bark in a state park, which he can do and I can't.

"So you have the right to hunt, gather, and . . ."

"Fish. Spearfish. Which has been getting so much publicity. We sold all that land, but we retained the right to hunt, fish, and gather. In Minnesota, some tribes are leasing their treaty rights to the state; they say they will follow the state law in exchange for 1.6 million dollars annually. At Fond du Lac they did this, but since then they voted it down, so now we're out of it."

"So now you can gather legally."

"We could before, but we were always getting arrested by the state game wardens for doing it. It was just a way of life. Go out and gather wild rice or shoot deer or duck, anything from the woods, you took a chance of being arrested. Having your gear, guns, car, everything, confiscated. All along we've been saying it's wrong, it's illegal, but just in the last couple of years the Indians are saying, 'Wait a minute, those old people saved our rights for a reason, and this is the reason.' So we exercise them."

"I've noticed that some people brag about having Indian blood."

"Yeah. Or spend hours at a tanning salon." Northrup's humor and low, aggressive, resonant voice carry an unpredictable spin. "That was the subject of one of my short stories," he continues. "I grew up listening to people telling stories, so I had to tell a pretty good story to be heard. There's a character named Luke Warmwater and another named Ben Lookingback. It fits right in with storytelling." (See Note.)

Recognizing the volley of a pro, I ask, "You do storytelling too?"

"Oh sure. I'm doing it right now."

In the middle of a nearby arena, drummers are warming up. Northrup invites me to camp with his family. I park the van among a sprawl of vehicles. Children play around and under a nearby tree, giggling.

"Better lock your car; these Indians'll steal you blind," and "Never trust an Indian," Northrup warns, startling me. Being caricatured for my skin color makes me feel invisible, distorted, projected on, teaches me a little bit about how that feels. But these tiny barbs, coming between gestures of warm hospitality, are perhaps a sort of ritual, a test, because something about this place is making me feel inexplicably at home, immeasurably safe.

Note: A collection of Jim Northrup's stories and poems have since been published as a book entitled *Walking the Rez Road* (Voyageur Press).

AUGUST 12

"A POWWOW'S SORT of a cross between a street dance and high mass," Northrup tells me when I see him the next morning. We're eating outdoors, a hearty breakfast of eggs, potatoes, sausage, and fry bread, scooped from cast-iron pans. "It's got religious, ceremonial, and social reasons for being."

"It's not a tourist event, then?"

"It's a lot more than that. I guess you have to go to the dance circle and feel the drumming against your chest before you realize what it is. All the socializing and meeting people, seeing friends you haven't seen for years, that's extra. The powwow satisfies a need for solidarity."

"Do you spend the summer traveling to different powwows?"

"No, I spend the summer making baskets. I spend the fall ricing. I spend the winter writing. I spend the spring making sugar and spearing fish. It's called living with the seasons, doing what you're supposed to be doing at that time of the year. My grandparents and great-grandparents and great-great-grandparents did the same."

We can hear drumming. I ask if today the dancers will wear—

"Not costumes," interrupts Northrup, although I wasn't going to say that. "Outfits or clothes or regalia, but not costumes. We don't like that word. It's stepping on people's cultural toes." Northrup carries a shard chipped off the Smithsonian Institution to remind him of the remains of thousands of Native Americans kept there as specimens, a practice I tell him I find appalling.

"There's talk about returning them to the people," says Northrup.

"That'd be nice."

"We thought so."

I ask about the wild rice I bought at a shop on Highway 61. Northrup calls it driveway rice: "If you get stuck, you put that stuff under your tires and you can drive right outa there." He says that the industry producing this "paddy rice" is badly hurting Native Americans like himself who collect, hand-process, and sell "true wild rice" for triple or more the price. Real wild rice, I learn, is collected in the wild as it has been for centuries—knocked into a canoe with "knocking sticks." If the rice is good and everything is right, Northrup claims, he can harvest three hundred pounds in three hours. "You just touch it and it drops into the boat. And different parts of the plant ripen at different times, so you go over it and over it and over it."

"And you really do use a canoe."

"Yes, we do." Paddy rice, however, Northrup says, has been genetically altered to produce uniform ripeness, uniform length, and shatter-resistant grains, so machines can be used to harvest and process it. "They got a recipe for cookin' that stuff: You get a rock about the size of a sweatlodge rock or a softball and put it in there with your water and start cookin' that at the same time you cook the paddy rice, and when that rock is soft, that rice is almost done.

"But our process uses no machines. You go out and harvest it, come home and spread it out and dry it in the sun, clean it—pick out all the stuff that ain't rice—and after it's dried for a couple hours, you put it in a cauldron over a trench fire about two pounds at a time and stir it with a canoe paddle until it starts to crack and pop and smell right. Then you put it in a rug lined with canvas or deerskin and my wife dances on it—sometimes to rock and roll. After she's ground the hulls off, she gives it to me and I fan it. The weight of the falling rice makes a little breeze, picks out the chaff if the wind isn't strong, and the good rice sits down in the basket. At that point you've got maybe eighty-five percent rice and fifteen percent rice with hulls on it. The next stage is taking off the remaining hulls, so that takes, well, until you're done. We do this all day every day for two or three weeks at a time."

"Then you have rice for the year?"

"Oh yeah, for weddings and funerals, gifts, supper, and everything. That's the way my grandfather did it. I've heard of the way they did it before the coming of the iron kettles, but we've had iron kettles for two, three hundred years now. I cook mine over maple and birch and I think sometimes that smoke sneaks in that kettle, because the rice tastes different than anything you buy. It's got that hand touch all the way through."

I ABANDON MY TAPE RECORDER, which appears to be offending everyone except Northrup, stop "working," let go and enjoy just being here. I wander the open booths that have been set up along the road, admiring silver and turquoise jewelry, beadwork, leather work, drum and flute tapes, and dreamcatchers—spidery webs of feathers and beads woven inside willow hoops to prevent nightmares. But when I pick up an especially inviting, satiny pine box, a man behind the table cringes.

"Why did you do that?" I ask him. "Why did you make that face?"

He says, "There is something inside."

"I know," I say. "I can hear it."

The other man, the maker, smiles. "It's okay. I think you just needed to touch an eagle feather today." I sigh, apologize, move on. More and more I'm becoming aware of how little of this culture I know.

I go to the arena where the dancing is about to begin. Earlier I watched the drummers and singers set up, first circling the covered center of the arena carrying a large, apparently sacred drum in a quiet, mostly unobserved ceremony. The Four Directions were honored. The drum was set gently down in the center. At least one pipe was passed. My memory is undependable, but what stays with me is the way the rituals were performed: respectfully but without pomposity, with now and then a smile, amid a hubbub of children, a few sightseers and moms sitting on mostly empty bleachers sewing the last metal cone on a daughter's jingle dress, the last bead on a small pair of moccasins.

At one o'clock, the Grand Entry begins. By now, an audience fills the bleachers: powwow participants of all ages, tourists, visitors, some reenactors from the Rendezvous, and, finally, a busload of Afghani War veterans from the U.S.S.R., none of whom speak English. An emcee with a microphone smoothly directs the events from a high booth in both Chippewa and English.

The dancers enter the arena from the east in full, magnificent regalia, I'm guessing in order of seniority. Lacking my tape recorder, I can't relate details with any accuracy, but some things, like the men's headgear, are unforgettable. I hate to admit that until this summer, I never knew that the flowing, feathered headdress that I have associated since childhood with "American Indians" has never been worn by the nations of the Great Lakes. "A headdress like that," Paul Gromosiak explained to me way back in Niagara Falls, "would not be practical for a woodland people." Today's eagle feathers are worn sparingly, each one significant, each one, I'm told, sacred, and a dancer dropping one might be shunned; a ceremony, and probably a great deal more, would be required to replace it. Great care has gone into every piece of beadwork, every piece of clothing.

Another surprise: the dancing is a slow, two-step shuffle. The dancers double-step, often side by side, in a wide clockwise ring around the drummers and singers in the middle. Dances are performed to honor particular persons, often veterans, who are honored as warriors. Women dance in jingle dresses, fringed with hand-curled metal cones that clink musically with every movement, enhancing the dignity of the stately older women but sounding like laughter on young girls.

Once the dancing begins, it goes on and on and on, through the afternoon, into the night. Sometimes the drumbeat is close to the tomtom of my childhood games, but I've never heard anything like the singers, all men, wailing in high, intense unison. Walter Bresset, a well-known Native American activist from Bayfield, Wisconsin, who has a booth here, suggests I join the dance. Self-conscious, I decline. I didn't think I was permitted to dance, I say, but he insists there are some dances in which anyone may participate. "Around the arena are four directions and four poles," says Bresset, smiling. "On one of poles, there's a hook. That hook is for you to hang your ego on."

So I dance, the drumbeat entering my rib cage, my throat, my skull, as I step-step with my right foot, step-step with my left, around and around the arena. Children, an unusually happy lot no one seems to yell at, play around the dancers. They run in and out of even the most serious ceremonies and nobody seems to mind. Dogs romp joyously. The intimacy draws me to a symbolic door I can't quite enter as I dance around the circle, becoming the drum, longing to belong, knowing I never can.

The tourists go home, but the drum throbs on. I never dreamed a powwow would be like this. I thought the dances would be choreographed, a show for sightseers, but it isn't like that. Tourists are invited, tolerated, but mostly ignored. This powwow seems to me more like a family reunion, in which what is honored in life is recognized here in ritual. In the van, parked close by, I fall asleep to the drum beat-beating, beat-beating, beat-beating, like a heart.

AUGUST 13

BY SIX O'CLOCK the next evening, I have found, at a private Grand Portage resort, the campsite of my dreams, a bliss-out of trees, beach, long hot shower, and privacy. The powwow has dispersed and I am seated in splendid solitude next to Lake Superior, listening to the surf wallop the rocky shore . . . *whomp* . . . *whomp* . . . *whomp* . . . when all of a sudden, as if a switch is thrown, all hell starts howling from a house across the bay. I glare through my binoculars: dogs. Lots and lots of dogs. *Dogs?*

My hosts assure me that the animals only bark at certain times of day. "You get used to it," they say. I don't believe them.

By the time I've walked around the stony beach, the dogs have gone quiet, but the many huskies are reinspired by my emergence into their yard, each yowling passionately from a blue plastic barrel. They are in full chorus as I knock on the door of a modest house and am invited in by Jayne Gagnon, who is cooking supper for her three school-age children.

"We got into the dogs about four years ago," Gagnon begins. She and her husband, Curtis, who is off firefighting in California, train the dogs for the Seagram's Beargrease Dogsled Marathon, a five-day event than runs from Duluth to Grand Marais and back. It's the biggest dogsled race in the contiguous United States, drawing such luminaries as Alaskan Iditerod (the most famous United States dogsled race) champions Susan Butcher and J. J. Jonereau.

"The first time we entered, we only made it halfway," Gagnon sighs over sizzling onions. "The next year, though, we finished fourteenth."

"How many enter?"

"Anywhere from twenty-four to thirty-four teams."

The kids spread piles of color snapshots in front of me on the kitchen table. "It's a family sport," explains Gagnon. "As the kids get older, they help too. It takes commitment to raise and train your own dogs and have them responsive to you. We have thirty-seven dogs right now, and it's very hard for us. We've been out of it for two years because we couldn't afford it. Next year we plan to race again. The race, sponsored by Seagram's, will offer a purse of seventy-five thousand dollars, just twenty-five thousand under the Alaskan Iditerod."

"Why do you need so many dogs? How many are on a team?"

"Each dog is unique; every dog is a different age, matures at a different rate. Up to sixteen are allowed on a team, but not all will make it. Some will get injured and some won't want to do it."

"Why the name Beargrease?"

"John Beargrease was an Indian mail carrier in the 1800s, I think. He carried the mail from Two Harbors up to Grand Marais and Ely by dog team, sled, walking, or by horse."

The family is so friendly that I work up the courage to ask how they can stand living next to so many howling dogs. "The dogs need to howl," replies Gagnon, in a soft, singsong voice. "That's part of their group identity. It's the pack instinct. They're very much a group of dogs. They get to singing their songs together. When the bitches are in heat, you know, they sing different songs. When I come home from work, they sing a song, I don't know why. Seven o'clock in the morning, they like to sing. They'll sing a song later on tonight. It's music. Really."

The next morning, exactly at seven, I am awakened by a thirty-seven-voice chorus. I wouldn't go so far as to call it a cantata, but I do seem to detect a sort of wolfish harmony I hadn't noticed before.

AUGUST 14

I'M ABOUT TO WALTZ into the wildest, most remote national park in the continguous United States equipped with no more than a credit card, a quilt, and a toothbrush. Lacking both boat and hotel reservations, I hadn't expected to make it this far, but thanks to a no-show and a sympathetic captain, I am now aboard the leaping, silvery *Voyageur II* on my way to the largest island in Lake Superior, Michigan's roadless Isle Royale (commonly pronounced "Eye-la Roil"), where the forty-seven other passengers will no doubt head either for the trail-webbed interior bearing backpacks or to the Rock Harbor Lodge waving reservations.

After twenty-two miles, we arrive at Windigo at the south end of the island, but our destination—Rock Harbor, at the other end—is still forty-four miles away. At Windigo, we let off some hikers and take on some kayakers. Passengers mill between the serviceable cabin and the windy outdoor decks. The deep-green Lake Superior waters begin an impressive swelling. "Be grateful we're going with the wind—otherwise, the waves'd be breaking over the boat," drily comments Captain Frederick Funkey, our thin, harried pilot, whom I guess to be in his forties.

The captain doesn't seem to mind if I appear now and then to ask questions, but he's clearly got a lot on his mind. Funkey worries about the complex schedule for this trip, which includes more stops as we travel up the Isle Royale shore to let some folks off and others on. He has to keep track of their myriad belongings. Mail has to be delivered to the few persons summering here. If anything can go wrong, he expects it will, and sure enough, people who are supposed to be at one dock aren't, and come shouting out of the woods as we leave them behind. (He goes back.) A canoe has been abandoned and no one knows whose it is. At one stop, yachts block the dock, the owners elsewhere.

Meanwhile, passengers prime me with stories and information. I learn that although base-camping is not encouraged—only short stays are allowed at any one camping area—some shelters are available. "In Windigo, there are screened shelters that'll sleep eight," says one veteran hiker. "And most of the 166 miles of trails on the island are pretty well developed. Toward the center, there's a lot of steep climbing—the island is actually a series of fairly high ridges—but stairs have been built in. A lot of work's been done out here. How, I don't know. They musta used a helicopter."

A couple who've been coming here for years say they favor Chippewa Harbor, "and you won't never see anybody," swears the husband. I ask what they do there, and the wife confesses, "What we really do is sit around and read magazines."

A hiker who has just boarded after several days of backpacking complains that he didn't see any moose this time; last year he saw plenty. "Last year I saw a moose in Rock Harbor walk down the sidewalk and right out onto the pier," says the lady who reads magazines. A ten-year-old girl who's been hiking with her dad outmooses them all: they saw six moose this year, one a big bullmoose right in their path. "You can usually hear moose before you see them, though—they sound like elephants crashing along," she says, her eyes sparkling. She giggles. "I had a lot of fun scaring hikers by making crashing sounds in the woods."

The storyteller prize, however, goes to one of three men in their early thirties who say they get together every year to hike or go hunting. They've just boarded after backpacking almost a week and they're more than ready for a gourmet meal at the Rock Harbor Lodge dining room. Which reminds Gary Garn of a story he heard about a couple who, a hundred years ago or so, got caught in a fierce winter storm out on one of the more than two hundred smaller islands that orbit Isle Royale. "The man died and the wife munched on her husband but eventually she died too, and when they were found the next spring, they were like Jack Sprat and his wife."

Garn, whose energy appears undepleted by a week's hiking, relates story after heartbreaking story, including the one about how Sleeping Bear Dunes and the Manitou Islands got their names: Mama Bear's cubs drowned when the three swam from Wisconsin across Lake Michigan, but the Great Manitou spirit rescued the cubs and turned them into islands; Sleeping Bear Dunes is Mama. Another tells about a missionary whose heart was eaten by Ojibwa warriors because he'd died so bravely, and a third story is about a farmer's son who longed to sail the lakes: "So he went to school, got his maritime license, and got a job on a freighter, and the first time he went out, a storm hit, a really bad gale, the boat sank, and the boy's body washed ashore on his parents' lakeside property, his arms outstretched toward the farmhouse."

Soon after we arrive at Rock Harbor, the three men suggest that we celebrate the success of my Fourth Coast trip at the restaurant. We all order just-caught lake trout and vote it the best meal of the year. Later in the evening, the lodge being full and me being gearless, good Captain Funkey squeezes a cot along the narrow aisle on the *Voyageur II*, where I sleep, sort of, the no-frills boat rocking not at all like a cradle, clunking all night long against the dock.

AUGUST 15

THIS MORNING, Stuart Croll, chief of visitor services and resource protection, joins me on a bench with a pleasant view of Rock Harbor. "People go into such raptures about this place," I begin. "Is there really more variety of plant and bird life per Isle Royale square mile than anywhere on earth?"

"Possibly," answers the uniformed, pleasantly accommodating

ranger. "Isle Royale is the only national park that's ninety-nine percent wilderness. But the tree species are kind of sterile here. We're lucky here to have maybe twenty species: white spruce, balsam fir, northern white cedar, white pine, and jack pine are the prime evergreens. But there are lots of flowers. The orchids in the spring alone draw people. And it's kind of special to come to a place where wolves and moose interact."

"Is the number of wolves still dropping?"

"Last year the numbers went up to fifteen wolves. That's all that are left, but keep in mind we only have two hundred square miles here. In Alaska you wouldn't have fifteen wolves in an area that small. The big fish here also attract people. Isle Royale is probably one of the last lake trout spawning grounds."

When I ask how an unequipped person might get a feel for the island, Croll recommends the three-hour Stoll Trail, an easy stroll compared to most Isle Royale treks. I ask what I should do if I encounter a moose.

"Don't approach it," warns Croll. "The moose are rather active for this time of year. But they're not a problem yet."

"They're not belligerent?"

"Well, they're beginning to be. Their coats are beautiful. They have all the winter hair, and the racks still have the velvet on. During the next two weeks they'll be removing that. Last night I saw two of them sparring, which is two weeks early." Croll describes his family's annual fall moose-proofing, which includes putting the trash cans away and taking down the volleyball nets at night. "Moose use those as targets. They'll walk right into a net and toss their head back and tear it up." There are twelve hundred moose in the park, he says.

With all that food, I wonder why the wolves in the park are dying.

"The basic problem is that all the wolves stem from a single gene pool, which can be traced all the way back to a single female in 1948, when they came across from Canada on an ice bridge," explains Croll.

"Could you bring in wolves from a different stock?"

"Would you want to do something like that? It's an alternative, but we are probably going to watch for the next ten years or so. They may just die out. Then the question will be, should they be introduced again, or should we just let time go by and let them come back naturally like they did the last time?"

"Why don't deer come on the ice?"

"Deer were introduced here in the twenties, but they all died in a year of a parasite. Deer in this part of the country are pretty sparse. It's very cold. There were woodland caribou here, but they died out naturally. If wolves are here, caribou would never come back, so if the wolves leave, that might be an opportune time to reestablish caribou. But whenever you do anything like that you have to consider all the implications."

"I hear diving is a big draw."

"Right. Isle Royale has the greatest collection of freshwater shipwrecks anywhere in North America. Alpena definitely has some, but we have the biggest: ten major shipwrecks. The park boundaries go out a half a mile, so all these shipwrecks are within our jurisdiction. They are also on the Registry of Historic Places, the first time that that's ever been done."

Taking Croll's advice, I moose-hunt with my camera along the Stoll Trail, which starts near the Rock Harbor Lodge and traces the edge of a skinny peninsula. Although it resembles other woodsy trails I've been on, it doesn't feel the same. Trying to pin down what this is, I can only think it must be that I'm on an island. Islands just feel different from other places. The sun is shining and it's hot. The profusion of thimbleberries are, I note, disappointed, unripe. Resembling big raspberries but somehow both sweeter and tarter, thimbleberries have become my favorite fruit, easily gathered from thornless plants, where they dangle beneath huge leaves.

I dawdle among pearly everlasting, asters, daisies, harebells and bunchberries, roses, more thimbleberries, and bushy horsetails that contain a silicon I find handy for scrubbing pots. Curiously, the shaggy yellow birch bark is profusely hung with lichens thick as Georgia moss. A plaque explains this: "The lichens are breaking down both organic and inorganic materials to form soil. . . . Lichens are an alga and a fungus that live together in mutual support. While attached to a rock or a dead tree, they secrete a mild acid which slowly breaks down the support material, creating soil. The small amount of soil holds moisture, allowing true mosses to take hold. [These] create more soil, which in turn supports grasses, sedges and finally woody plants. The only thing that stays the same in the natural world is change itself."

Further on, another printed explanation identifies three shallow depressions in the rock as the remains of ancient Native American copper mines. "Copper deposits occured in limited areas around Lake Superior. Here, unlike most deposits around the world, copper is found in a pure state. American Indians began working deposits on Isle Royale and in the Keweenaw Peninsula about 2000 B.C. and continued for more than 1,500 years."

Sitting on a ridge, gazing over the spiky tops of evergreens to a green lake, greener islands, and a perfect sky as smooth and pale as the shell inside an egg, I'm painfully conscious that this is my last such excursion and stretch the easy three-hour hike to four.

AUGUST 17

AFTER A RELATIVELY smooth trip back on the *Voyageur II*, I sat up late near my campsite on a Grand Portage beach, watching half a corn-yellow moon play among fleecy clouds. By the time I turned in, the sky was streaked with starlight. Now, at dawn, a molten sun bumps an enormous pink cloud heavenward and a coral highway rolls toward me across the lake like a rug. It feels like an invitation to walk into a legend, tempting as a rope might be if I found one hanging from the moon.

It's early. Everyone here is still sleeping. The wind tears at my hair and small round rocks click under my new leather Trading Post boots as I walk out to Lake Superior, where waves spray fifteen feet above the rocks. I eat gooseberries and oatmeal close to the pounding surf.

And then I leave: pack everything up, slide the side door shut, glance over the snakeskins and feathers on the dash and, turning the key, crunch out over gravel. The highway follows the coastline south, then swerves inland. As I turn from the last glimpse of lake and sky, a hawk soars in front of the van, then melts into my rearview mirror: first white, then black, then blue.

FOURTH COAST
ITINERARY

Listed below are all the places I describe in this book, in the order in which I visit them. Directions seem unnecessary, given my it-has-to-be-within-sight-of-the-water rule and the spirit of adventure that goes with the territory. Get yourself a road map, stick to the route closest to the shore, and head for the appropriate towns, most of which are so small that if you can't find the place your heart is set on, probably any local businessperson will be able to direct you there. If you still can't find it, that's okay, too: you'll probably end up someplace just as interesting.

ST. LAWRENCE RIVER

NEW YORK

Eisenhower Lock, Massena
Coles Creek State Park
Chase Mills Inn, Chase Mills
Joe's Grub, Morristown
Uncle Sam's Boat Tours, Alexandria Bay
Kring Point State Park, Alexandria Bay
The Thousand Islands, Alexandria Bay
Wellesley Island State Park, Thousand Islands
Thousand Islands Bridge, Thousand Islands
Cape Vincent Fisheries Station Aquarium, Cape Vincent
Seaway pilot boat, Cape Vincent
Tibbetts Point Lighthouse, Cape Vincent
American Youth Hostel, Tibbetts Point, Cape Vincent

LAKE ONTARIO

NEW YORK

Snug Harbor Bar
Sunset Motel, Henderson Harbor
Pole and Winder Derby, Henderson Harbor
Verilli's, Henderson Harbor
Bill Saife Charters, Henderson Harbor
Scott's Mobil station, Henderson Harbor
Fort Ontario State Historic Site, Oswego
Fair Haven Marina, Fair Haven
Lancaster Helluva Good Cheese Stand, Sodus
Eastman Park, Rochester
Seabreeze Park, Rochester
Lakeside Beach State Park, Waterport
Breeze Inn, Waterport

NIAGARA RIVER

NEW YORK

Four Mile Creek State Park
Niagara Power Project, Niagara Falls
Niagara Falls
Maid of the Mist, Niagara Falls
Beaver Island State Park, Grand Island
Peace Bridge, Buffalo

LAKE ERIE

NEW YORK

Buffalo and Erie County Botanical Garden Society, Lackawanna
Seneca Hawk Cattaraugus Truck Stop Coffee Shop, Cattaraugus Indian Reservation
Sheridan Bay Park, Sheridan
U.S. Coast Guard Dunkirk (Point Gratiot) Lighthouse, Dunkirk

PENNSYLVANIA

United States Brig *Niagara,* Erie
Little Toot, Erie Public Docks
Presque Isle State Park

OHIO

Township Park, Conneaut
Kilpi Hall, Conneaut
Ashtabula Water Pollution Control Plant, Ashtabula
All People's Trail, Perry
Village Ice Cream Emporium, Fairport Harbor
Morton salt mines, Fairport Harbor
Mentor Marsh Nature Preserve, Fairport Harbor
Headlands Beach State Park, Fairport Harbor
Headlands Dunes State Nature Preserve, Fairport Harbor
Geneva State Park, Geneva
Sheraton Hotel, Cleveland
Port Authority, Cleveland
Cleveland-Cuyahoga County
Huntington Reservation Metropark, west of Cleveland
Wild Waves Motel, Huron
South Bass Island State Park
Put-in-Bay, South Bass Island
Wave pool, Sandusky
New Shoreline Fishery, Sandusky
Lakeside Pavilion and Pier, Lakeside
Crane Creek State Park, Ottawa National Wildlife Refuge, Magee Marsh Wildlife Area
Maumee State Park
Sonny's Bay Shore Supper Club, near Maumee State Park
Toledo Yacht Club, Bay View Yacht Club, Toledo

MICHIGAN (LOWER PENINSULA)

Sterling State Park
Pointe Mouillée State Game Area

THE DETROIT RIVER, LAKE ST. CLAIR, AND THE ST. CLAIR RIVER

MICHIGAN (LOWER PENINSULA)

Gibraltar
Grosse Ile
Ambassador Bridge to Canada
Summit Steak House, Renaissance Center, Detroit
Belle Isle Aquarium, Belle Isle
Whitcomb Garden Conservatory, Belle Isle
Belle Isle Zoo, Belle Isle

Metro Beach Metropark, Lake St. Clair north of St. Clair Shores
Selfridge Air National Guard Base, Lake St. Clair
St. Clair Flats, Algonac
The Boat (floating restaurant), Algonac
Algonac State Park
Harsens Island
Blue Water Bridge, Port Huron
Lakeport State Park

LAKE HURON

MICHIGAN (LOWER PENINSULA)

Tringali Orchard, Lexington
YWCA Camp Cavell, Lexington
James and Jane Grice House, Harbor Beach
Albert E. Sleeper State Park, north of Caseville
Bay Port Fish Company, Bay Port
Tobico Marsh State Game Area, Bay City
Gino's (smoked fish), Pinconning
Bear Track Inn, Au Gres
Tawas Point State Park
Sawyer Canoe Company, Au Sable
Oriental Market and Take-Out, Oscoda
Wurtsmith Air Force Base, Oscoda
Harrisville State Park
Thunder Bay Underwater Preserve
Thunder Bay Divers, Alpena
Roy's Camper Cove, Alpena
Jesse Besser Museum, Alpena
Presque Isle Old Lighthouse and Museum, Presque Isle
Rogers City Harbor
Nowickis Am See delicatessen, Rogers City
Gordon Turner Park, Cheboygan
Tugboat and barge, Derosher Dock & Dredge, Inc., Cheboygan
Cheboygan State Park, Cheboygan
Old Mill Creek State Park, Mackinaw City
Star Line Ferry to Mackinac Island
Jack's Livery Stables, Mackinac Island
Lake View Hotel, Mackinac Island
Fort Mackinac
Grand Hotel, Mackinac Island
The Mackinac Bridge

LAKE MICHIGAN

MICHIGAN (LOWER PENINSULA)

Wilderness State Park
Legs Inn, Cross Village
Route 119, drive from Cross Village to Harbor Springs
Harbor Point Club, Harbor Springs
Petoskey Marina, Petoskey
Stafford's Perry Hotel, Petoskey
Big Rock Point Nuclear Power Plant, Charlevoix
Top-O-Michigan Power Plant, Lake Charlevoix
DNR Great Lakes Fishing Station, Charlevoix
Fisherman's Island State Park
Beaver Island Boat Company
Shamrock Bar and Restaurant, Beaver Island
Erin Motel, Beaver Island
St. James Boat Shop, Beaver Island
The Beachcomber (now the Wild Rose), Beaver Island
St. James Boat Shop, Beaver Island
Beaver Island Toy Museum
Traverse City State Park
Traverse Bay Para-Sail, Traverse City
Great Lakes Maritime Academy, Traverse City
The tall ship *Madeline*, Traverse City
The tall ship *Malabar*, Traverse City
Tamarack Gallery, Omena, Leelanau Peninsula
Leelanau State Park
Traverse Bay Lighthouse, Leelanau State Park
Fishtown, Leland
Manitou Island ferry, Leland
South Manitou Lighthouse
Sleeping Bear Dunes National Lakeshore
Pierce Stocking Scenic Drive, Sleeping Bear Dunes
The *City of Milwaukee*, National Historic Vessel, Frankfort
JoAnn's Restaurant and Catering, Frankfort
Gliderport, Frankfort
Trinity Lutheran Church, Arcadia
Arcadia Harbor, Arcadia
Orchard Beach State Park, Manistee
The Manistee trolley tour
Lake Michigan Recreation Area, south of Manistee
Nordhouse Dunes
The Ludington pier, Ludington
Lake Michigan Carferry, Ludington

Ludington State Park

Anna Bach Company (candy), Ludington

White Pine Village, Ludington

Silver Lake State Park

Mac Wood's Dune Rides, Silver Lake

Duck Lake State Park

Muskegon State Park

Great Lumbertown Music Festival (Summer Celebration) and Three on Three Round Ball
   Classic

U.S.S. *Silversides* Maritime Museum, Muskegon

Gillette Nature Center, P. J. Hoffmaster State Park, Grand Haven

Tri-Cities Historical Museum, Grand Haven

Bil-Mar Restaurant, Grand Haven

Ottawa Beach State Park

Fun Incorporated, Ottawa Beach State Park

Power plant, City of Holland Board of Public Works

Point West restaurant, Lake Macatawa, Holland

Eldean Boat Sales, Ltd., Holland

The *Cisco*, U.S. Fish and Wildlife Service research boat, Saugatuck

Ox-Bow, the Art Institute of Chicago's summer school, Saugatuck

Golden Brown Bakery, South Haven

The *Idler* riverboat, a floating restaurant, South Haven

Great Lakes Maritime Museum, South Haven

St. Joseph waterfront

INDIANA

Indiana Dunes National Lakeshore

Indiana Dunes State Park

Paul H. Douglas Center for Environmental Education, Gary

ILLINOIS

Grant Park, Chicago

Adler Planetarium, Chicago

John G. Shedd Aquarium, Chicago

Field Museum of Natural History, Chicago

Grant Park Boat Tours, Chicago

Navy Pier, Chicago

Illinois Beach State Park

WISCONSIN

Kenosha County Historical Museum, Kenosha
Eichelman Park, Kenosha
Simmons Island Park, Kenosha
Festival Hall and downtown marina, Racine
Whey Chai restaurant, downtown Racine
PDQ, Racine convenience store
Grant Park, Milwaukee
Veterans Park (the circus), Milwaukee
Milwaukee Art Museum, Milwaukee
Schlitz Audubon Center, Bayside
Kohler-Andrae State Park
Randall's restaurant, Sheboygan
Downtown riverside renovations, Sheboygan
Manitowoc Malt House, Manitowoc
Manitowoc Maritime Museum, Manitowoc
Trout boil, Kewaunee
The S.S. *Badger*, Lake Michigan Carferry
Whitefish Dunes State Park, Door Peninsula
Ridges Sanctuary, Door Peninsula
Peninsula State Park, Door Peninsula
Bayside Tavern, Fish Creek, Door Peninsula
Washington Island Nature Center, Door Peninsula
Bay Shipbuilders, Sturgeon Bay, Door Peninsula
Sensibo Wildlife Area, Suamico

MICHIGAN (UPPER PENINSULA)

J. W. Wells State Park
The *Escanaba*, Coast Guard cutter, Escanaba
Hiawatha National Forest District Office, Escanaba
Fayette State Park (ghost town), Garden Peninsula
Fairport Fishery, Fairport, Garden Peninsula
Imogene Herbert Museum, Manistique
Siphon Bridge, Manistique
Old Deerfield Inn, Gulliver
Seul Choix Lighthouse, Seul Choix Point, Gulliver
Big Thumb State Park
Cut River Bridge, Naubinway

LAKE HURON

MICHIGAN (UPPER PENINSULA)

Mackinac Bridge
Barnhill's Seaplane tour, St. Ignace
Straits State Park
Marquette Mission Park and Museum of Ojibwa Culture, St. Ignace
E. J. Mertaugh's Boat Works, Hessel, Les Cheneaux Islands
Les Cheneaux Landing, Cedarville, Les Cheneaux Islands
Paradise Point Resort, just north of De Tour Village
Drummond Island Museum
Antlers restaurant, Sault Ste. Marie
Parkway Motel, Sault Ste. Marie
Soo Locks, Sault Ste. Marie
Fort Repentigny Archeological Project, Sault Ste. Marie
Valley Camp Museum Ship, Sault Ste. Marie

LAKE SUPERIOR

MICHIGAN (UPPER PENINSULA)

Whitefish Point Bird Observatory, Whitefish Point
Great Lakes Shipwreck Historical Museum, Whitefish Point
Boat tour, Pictured Rocks National Lakeshore, Munising
Ore Dock, Marquette
Presque Isle City Park, Marquette
Abbaye Peninsula Road
Baraga State Park
Copper Country Museum, Lake Linden, Keweenaw Peninsula
Gay Bar, Gay, Keweenaw Peninsula
Harbor House Restaurant, Copper Harbor, Keweenaw Peninsula
Fort Wilkins State Park, Copper Harbor, Keweenaw Peninsula
Bear Track Tours, Laughing Loon, Copper Harbor, Keweenaw Peninsula
Estivant Pines, Copper Harbor, Keweenaw Peninsula
Brockway Drive, Keweenaw Peninsula
Porcupine Mountain Wilderness State Park, Keweenaw Peninsula

WISCONSIN

Maslowski Beach, Ashland
Apostle Islands Cruise Service, Bayfield
Bayfield City Campground, Bayfield
Brule River outlet
Canal Park Visitor Center and Historical Museum, Duluth

Aerial Lift Bridge, Duluth Harbor
Grain loading dock, Superior
Gooseberry Falls State Park
Split Rock Lighthouse State Park
KOA, Silver Bay
Sven and Ole's Scandinavian Pizza, Grand Marais
Grand Marais Trading Post, Grand Marais
Grand Marais Museum, Grand Marais
Grand Portage National Monument
Grand Portage Rendezvous and Powwow, Grand Portage Reservation
Hollow Rock Resort, Grand Portage
Voyageur II, ferry from Grand Portage to Isle Royale

MICHIGAN

Isle Royale National Park
Rock Harbor Lodge, Rock Harbor, Isle Royale National Park

A GUIDE

TO GUIDES

Despite the recent official status of the Great Lakes Circle Tour, good current tourist information about the Fourth Coast remains remarkably elusive: neither I nor any of my well-informed bookstore owners, Great Lakes experts, or librarian friends have been able to unearth a comprehensive travel guide to our northern shores. Although I myself didn't need much tourist information on my trip—my only serious concern was that I complete the whole coast in a summer—most people, especially those traveling with children, might like to know where they're going to sleep for the night, not to mention what eateries, entertainment, recreation, and scenery might be worth the investment of their holiday.

Fortunately, informative guides do exist for much of Michigan, which covers at least half the Fourth Coast, and travel information can be found for Wisconsin and Minnesota. State Circle Tour and Seaway Trail telephone numbers and regional guides are available for other areas.

Listed below are the guides I've found useful, in the order in which I favor them. All are available in paperback.

GENERAL GUIDES

Hunts' Highlights of Michigan, by Mary and Don Hunt, 1991. Available from most Michigan bookstores (or order from Midwestern Guides, 506 Lindon, Albion, MI 49224), this 514-page guide is limited to Michigan. Nevertheless, it covers over half the Fourth Coast (Michigan's coastline includes shores on four Great Lakes: Erie, Huron, Michigan, and Superior) and stands without peer as the most comprehensive, useful, and reliable tourist guide I've found on the Fourth Coast. Restaurants, choice lodgings, scenic drives, interesting shops, great beaches, museums, good hikes, cruises, B&Bs, and much more are carefully selected, fairly objectively reviewed, and entertainingly described. Although this guide covers all of Michigan, it includes most coastal areas. There are even fun facts, some history, and an excellent index.

Around the Shores of Lake Michigan: A Guide to Historic Sights, by Margaret Beattie Bogue, 1985. Here's a remarkable piece of research that circles Lake Michigan, which includes Wisconsin shores. Bogue has done her homework, and although you won't find restaurants, motels, or B&Bs here, you will find excellent descriptions of anything remotely historical.

Lake Superior Travel Guide, updated annually. In this magazine-formatted guide you will find tourist information—reviewed, described, listed, and advertised—for all the shores of Lake Superior. There's a good color map, lots of handy charts, telephone numbers, and plenty of information for a careful reader. I found the many advertisements more distracting than helpful, but presumably they make this guide—the only one I could find to the Wisconsin and Minnesota coasts—available. Buy from bookstores and newsstands, or order from Lake Superior Magazine, P.O. Box 16417, Duluth, MN 55816-9960 (1-800-635-0544).

Great Lakes Circle Tour, including the Seaway Trail. It is now possible to explore Great Lakes shores by following Circle Tour or Seaway Trail signs. To learn about accommodations, sights, recreation, restaurants, and so on, along these routes or accessible from them, call the toll-free tourism office number for each state involved:

New York:	1-800-SEAWAYT
Pennsylvania:	1-800-VISITPA
Ohio:	1-800-BUCKEYE
Michigan:	1-800-543-2YES
Indiana:	1-800-289-6646
Illinois:	1-800-822-0292
Wisconsin:	1-800-432-TRIP
Minnesota:	1-800-657-3700

For nontravel, historical, and general information on the Great Lakes, write or call:

The Great Lakes Commission
400 Fourth Street
Ann Arbor, MI 48103
(313) 665-9135

Michigan State and National Parks: A Complete Guide, by Tom Powers, 1989. For those who like camping with water and electric hookups, this guide maps state parks, their campgrounds and trails. I like this book's positive attitude and enthusiasm, but I found it hard to determine the ambiance from the descriptions and whether or not a place was the kind of place I was looking for. Buy at your bookstore, or order from Friede Publications, 2339 Venezia Drive, Davison, MI 48423.

The Great Lakes Guidebooks, by George Cantor. The three titles in this series—*Lake Superior and Western Lake Michigan* (1980), *Lake Huron and Eastern Lake Michigan* (1985), and *Lakes Ontario and Erie* (1985)—offer historical comment on places along the Great Lakes and something of a guide to sights. I found these books frustrating to use because they're so oddly organized, but history buffs will enjoy the interesting backgrounds, especially for Lakes Ontario, Erie, and Superior (I found Hunt's historical perspectives more accessible for Michigan shores, and Bogue's for West Michigan and Wisconsin.) Purchase at your local bookstore.

SPECIAL INTEREST GUIDES

Many excellent, more narrowly focused books are available, as illustrated by this small selection from my favorites:

Plants of the Illinois Dunesland, by Elizabeth T. Lunn. The lovely color photographs in this 116-page guide apply to most of the Midwest dunes; I used it frequently after I'd bought it, and would probably have found it useful along the Michigan dunes as well. There's no purchasing address, so you'll probably find it in nature center gift shops along Lake Michigan dunes.

A Visitor's Guide to the Apostle Islands National Lakeshore, by Dave Strzok. This entertaining 136-page guide to and history of the Bayfield, Wisconsin, area is worth purchasing if you plan to go there. It includes maps, black-and-white photographs, and descriptions of every single Apostle Island! Order from Dave Strzok, P.O. Box 691, Bayfield, WI 54814.

Where the Wild Things Are: A Directory of Wisconsin Environmental, Education, and Nature Centers. Wisconsin takes its parks seriously, as becomes obvious when reading this full-color description of the state's facilities. Order from the Department of Natural Resources, Education and Youth Programs, P.O. Box 7921, Madison, WI 53707 (608-267-7529).

Know Your Ships, by Thomas Manse. If you're going to spend much time near Great Lakes shipping lanes, this book is a must. It will give you stats on all the vessels frequenting the Great Lakes, both salties (foreign) and lakers (American and Canadian). Includes, in color, U.S., Canadian, and major foreign stack markings, flags, and some photographs. Available at some regional bookstores, or order from Marine Publishing Company, P.O. Box 68, Sault Ste. Marie, MI 49783.

Angler's Guide to Michigan's Great Lakes. I'm not a fish-catcher, but I love this 80-page publication for its gorgeous color renderings of Great Lakes fish. It's full of maps purporting to locate fishing holes and includes rules and regs. I'd never go fishing without this. Order ISBN 0-941912-23-X from Michigan Department of Natural Resources, Box 30034, Lansing, MI 48909.

Great American Lighthouses, by F. Ross Holland, Jr. You won't find all the Great Lake's lighthouses here, but many of them are included, along with good descriptions and clear black-and-white photographs. Also find an excellent history of American lighthouses and descriptions of old lights and lenses. Find at your bookstore or order from The Preservation Press, National Trust for Historic Preservation, 1785 Massachusetts Avenue, N.W., Washington, DC 20036.

Living with the Lake Erie Shore, by Charles H. Carter et al. Sponsored by the National Audubon Society, this is the most accessible and complete description I have ever seen on Great Lakes erosion. Persons thus affected by Mother Nature and even more by those trying to control erosion might do well to educate themselves. Published by Duke University.

Seasons of the Leelanau, by Sandra Serra Bradshaw. This fond tribute to Michigan's Leelanau Peninsula includes history as well as rather complete shopping, eating, playing, and lodging information. Order from Northmont Publishing, 6346 Orchard Lake Road, #201, West Bloomfield, MI 48322.

BIBLIOGRAPHY

Begnoche, Steve. "Car Ferry Serves as Weather Service Eyes." *Ludington Daily News*, May 24, 1990.

Bishop, Joan. *Surfbeat*. Ann Arbor: Michigan Sea Grant Publication Office, 1979.

Bogue, Margaret Beattie. *Around the Shores of Lake Michigan*. Madison: University of Wisconsin Press, 1985.

Bradshaw, Sandra Serra. *Seasons of the Leelanau*. West Bloomfield, MI: Northmont Publishing, 1994.

Cantor, George. *The Great Lakes Guidebook: Lake Huron and Eastern Lake Michigan*. Ann Arbor: University of Michigan Press, 1984.

————. *The Great Lakes Guidebook: Lakes Ontario and Erie*. Ann Arbor: University of Michigan Press, 1985.

————. *The Great Lakes Guidebook: Lake Superior and Western Lake Michigan*. Ann Arbor: University of Michigan Press, 1980.

Cargo: The Game of the Great Lakes. Ogilvie, MI: V. & L. Heise Games, 1989.

Carter, Charles H., et al. *Living with the Lake Erie Shore*. Durham, NC, and London: Duke University Press, 1987.

Daniel, Glenda. *Dune Country: A Hiker's Guide to the Indiana Dunes*. Rev. ed. Athens, OH: Swallow Press, 1984.

Diede, Alan. *Best Choices Along the Great Lakes*. Vol. 1: *Lake Erie, Lake Ontario, U.S. Niagara, U.S. & Canada*. McKeesport, PA: Monongahela Publishing, 1990.

Eifert, Virginia S. *Journeys in Green Places: The Shores and Woods of Wisconsin's Door Peninsula*. New York: Dodd, Mead, 1963.

Fraser, Marian Botsford. *Walking the Line: Travels Along the Canadian/American Border*. San Francisco: Sierra Club Books, 1989.

Glenn, Barbara S., et al. "Lake Michigan Sport Fish: Should You Eat Your Catch?" Ann Arbor: National Wildlife Federation, Great Lakes Natural Resources Center, n.d.

Great Lakes Directory. Ann Arbor: Center for the Great Lakes, 1984.

Gromosiak, Paul. *Niagara Falls Q & A: Answers to the 100 Most Common Questions About Niagara Falls*. Buffalo, NY: Western New York Wares, Inc., 1989.

————. *Soaring Gulls and Bowing Trees: The History of the Islands Above Niagara Falls.* Buffalo, NY: Western New York Wares, Inc., 1989.

————. *Zany Niagara: Funny Things People Say About Niagara Falls.* Buffalo, NY: Western New York Wares, Inc., 1992.

Haltiner, Robert E. *The Town That Wouldn't Die: A Photographic History of Alpena, Michigan, from Its Beginnings through 1940.* Self-published, n.d.

Holland, F. Ross, Jr. *Great American Lighthouses.* A National Trust Guide. Washington, DC: The Preservation Press, National Trust for Historic Preservation, 1989.

Hunt, Mary, and Don Hunt. *Hunts' Guide to West Michigan.* Waterloo, MI: Midwestern Guides, 1990.

————. *Hunts' Highlights of Michigan.* Waterloo, MI: Midwestern Guides, 1991.

————. *Southeast Michigan.* Waterloo, MI: Midwestern Guides, 1990.

The Indiana Dunes—Legacy of Sand. Special Report 8, by John Hill. Bloomington: State of Indiana Department of Natural Resources Geological Survey, 1974.

Keefe, Bill. *The Five Sisters: 299 Things Every Great Lakes Buff Should Know.* Algonac, MI: Reference Publications, 1991.

Kelley, R. W., and W. R. Farrand. *The Glacial Lakes Around Michigan.* Rev. W. R. Farrand. Lansing: Michigan Department of Natural Resources, Geological Survey Division, 1987.

Komaiko, Jean R., et al. *Around Lake Michigan.* Boston: Houghton Mifflin, 1980.

Lake Superior Travel Guide. 6th ed. Duluth, MN: Lake Superior Magazine, 1993.

Lesstrang, Jacques. *Seaway: The Untold Story of North America's Fourth Seacoast.* Seattle: Salisbury Press, 1976.

Locks and Ships. Vol. 1: *November Shipwreck Edition.* Sault Ste. Marie, MI: Soo Locks Boat Tours, 1989.

Lunn, Elizabeth T. *Plants of the Illinois Dunesland.* The Illinois Dunesland Preservation Society, 1982.

McKee, Russell. *Great Lakes Country.* New York: Thomas Y. Crowell, 1966.

Mahan, John, and Ann Mahan. *Wild Lake Michigan.* Stillwater, MN: Voyageur Press, 1991.

Manse, Thomas. *Know Your Ships.* The Seaway Issue, 30th ed. Sault Ste. Marie, MI: Marine Publishing Company, 1989.

Michigan Atlas & Gazetteer. Freeport, ME: DeLorme Mapping Company, 1987.

Michigan History. Special Issue: Isle Royale (May/June 1990).

Pacific Sea Grant College Program. Seattle: Washington Sea Grant University.

Palmquist, John C., ed. *Wisconsin's Door Peninsula: A Natural History.* Apton, WI: Perin Press, n.d.

Penrose, Laurie, et al. *A Traveler's Guide to 116 Michigan Lighthouses.* Davison, MI: Friede Publications, 1992.

Pitcher, Emma Bickham. *Up and Down the Dunes.* The Shirley Heinze Environmental Fund, 1987.

Powers, Tom. *Michigan State and National Parks: A Complete Guide.* Davison, MI: Friede Publications, 1989.

Ross, Harry H. *Enchanting Isles of Erie.* Self-published, 1949.

Schaeffer, Norma, and Kay Franklin. *'Round and About the Dunes*. Beverly Shores, IN: Dune Enterprises, 1984.

Scharfenberg, Doris. *The Long Blue Edge of Summer: A Vacation Guide to the Shorelines of Michigan*. Grand Rapids, MI: Wm. B. Eerdmans, 1982.

Strzok, Dave. *A Visitor's Guide to the Apostle Islands National Lakeshore*. Bayfield, WI: Self-published, 1988.

Swatze, David D. *Shipwreck! A Comprehensive Directory of Over 3,700 Shipwrecks on the Great Lakes*. Boyne City, MI: Harbor House, 1992.

Where the Wild Things Are: A Directory of Wisconsin Environmental, Education, and Nature Centers. Madison: Department of Natural Resources, n.d.

INDEX